MULTIPLE MINI INTERVIEW (MMI)

WINNING STRATEGIES FROM ADMISSIONS FACULTY

SAMIR P. DESAI MD

FROM THE AUTHOR OF THE SUCCESSFUL MATCH

PUBLISHED BY
MD2B
HOUSTON, TEXAS

www.MD2B.net

Multiple Mini Interview (MMI): Winning Strategies From Admissions Faculty is published by MD2B, PO Box 300988, Houston, TX 77230-0988.

www.MD2B.net
www.TheSuccessfulMatch.com

NOTICE: The authors and publisher disclaim any personal liability, either directly or indirectly, for advice or information presented within. The authors and publishers have used care and diligence in the preparation of this book. Every effort has been made to ensure the accuracy and completeness of information contained within this book. The reader should understand, however, that most of the book's subject matter is not rooted in scientific observation. The recommendations made within this book have come from the author's personal experiences and interactions with faculty, residents, and students over many years. There is considerable variability in the admissions process from one medical school to another. Therefore, the recommendations are not universally applicable. No responsibility is assumed for errors, inaccuracies, omissions, or any false or misleading implication that may arise due to the text.

© 2016 by Samir P. Desai and Rajani Katta

All rights reserved

No part of this publication may be reproduced, stored in a retrieval system, or transmitted, in any form or by any means, electronic, mechanical, photocopying, recording, or otherwise, without the prior written permission of the publisher.

Printed in the United States of America

9781937978051

Dedication

To Ravi and Anna

For each book sold, two books will be donated to organizations supporting literacy.

How Else Can We Help You Get Into Medical School?

1) We are in the process of developing an online course to show you how to develop winning answers to traditional medical school interview questions. Visit TheSuccessfulMatch.com for course information.

2) If you will be visiting a school using the traditional medical school interview format, our book *Medical School Interview: Winning Strategies From Admissions Faculty* will provide you with the strategies needed to excel.

3) Read articles we have written about the medical school interview at TheSuccessfulMatch.com.

4) Mock interview services for the traditional medical school interview and the MMI are available with Dr. Samir Desai. During the 2014 – 2015 application cycle, 100% of our mock interview clients secured spots in medical school. For more information, visit TheSuccessfulMatch.com.

ABOUT THE AUTHOR

Samir P. Desai, M.D.

      Dr. Samir Desai serves on the faculty of the Baylor College of Medicine in the Department of Medicine. He has educated premedical students, medical students, residents, and international medical graduates, work for which he has received numerous teaching awards. As a member of the Clerkship Directors in Internal Medicine, he is deeply committed to medical student education. He has served on the medical school admissions and residency selection committees at the Baylor College of Medicine and Northwestern University.
      He is an author and editor, having written 18 books that together have sold over 250,000 copies worldwide. The inspiration for his books often comes from his experiences as a mentor, and he has a deep desire to help students and applicants overcome the challenges of the medical school admissions, residency selection, and fellowship selection processes.
      He is the co-author of *The Successful Match 2017*, a well-regarded and highly acclaimed book that has helped thousands of residency applicants match successfully. His commitment to helping medical students reach their professional goals led him to develop the website, TheSuccessfulMatch.com. The website's mission is to provide residency and fellowship applicants with a better understanding of the selection process. His book *Medical School Scholarships, Awards, and Grants* has been identified as a high-value resource by the AAMC Group on Student Affairs.
      Dr. Desai is deeply committed to enhancing the quality of patient care, reducing medical error, and decreasing health care costs. This desire led him to write the book *Clinician's Guide to Laboratory Medicine*, a resource widely used in the curriculum of medical, PA, and nurse practitioner schools, and listed as one of the "Best Medical Books of All Time" by The Medical Media Review. At Baylor, he is investigating ways in which technology can be used by residents and students to enhance patient care. One initiative currently underway is "Creating and Implementing a Patient Safety Checklist App for Residents and Students on Medicine Wards," a project that was awarded an Innovations Grant by the Alliance for Academic Internal Medicine. He is also a member of the Centers for Disease Control (CDC) Mobile Application Project Team.
      After completing his residency training in Internal Medicine at Northwestern University in Chicago, Dr. Desai had the opportunity of serving as chief medical resident. He received his M.D. degree from Wayne State University School of Medicine in Detroit, Michigan, graduating first in his class.
      He resides in Houston with his wife (and co-author) and their two children. He keeps fit by weight-lifting and biking with his children, and continues to follow his favorite team: the Detroit Tigers.

CONTENTS

Chapter 1:	Introduction	1
Chapter 2:	Importance of MMI	11
Chapter 3:	Qualities Assessed by MMI	21
Chapter 4:	MMI Format	32
Chapter 5:	MMI Interviewers	39
Chapter 6:	MMI Experiences of Prior Interviewees	44
Chapter 7:	Evaluating Your Performance	49
Chapter 8:	Basics of Preparation	61
Chapter 9:	Question/Discussion Station Preparation	75
Chapter 10:	Scenario/Acting Station Preparation	87
Chapter 11:	Task/Collaboration Station Preparation	95
Chapter 12:	MMI Scenarios	100
Chapter 13:	MMI and Your Future	187
Chapter 14:	Preclinical Years of Medical School	189
Chapter 15:	Medical School Scholarships & Awards	220

Chapter 1

Introduction

"Finally!" The patient, visibly frustrated, continued loudly with his complaint. "I'm in so much pain. That last nurse did nothing for me. I kept calling for her, and it took an eternity for her to come. That went on all night long. I couldn't sleep. I couldn't rest. It's like she was watching TV or something. I hope you can do better."

This is the type of exchange that could occur in any hospital. However, this particular encounter took place, not in a hospital, but during a medical school interview.

Playing the role of nurse was Sarah, a 25-year-old applicant who had desperately wanted to become a physician ever since childhood. Her chances of success hinged on her ability to interact effectively with an actor playing the role of an angry patient.

Early in college, Sarah had suffered from a variety of symptoms that left her weak and tired. Multiple visits to specialist after specialist failed to yield a diagnosis, and Sarah's grades suffered. One year later, with diagnosis finally in hand, she was appropriately treated and made a full recovery. By that time, however, the damage had been done and her GPA had plummeted.

Determined to reach her professional dreams, Sarah persisted and excelled in her remaining courses. Hopeful that medical schools would understand her situation, she applied as a college senior. She failed to receive even a single interview. After meeting with an advisor, it was clear that her biggest obstacle was a low GPA.

Following graduation, she enrolled in a two-year post-baccalaureate program. Several months into this new program, she applied again to medical school. Sadly, the outcome was the same. Although initially shaken, she persevered and maintained a 4.0 GPA.

In the fall of her second year as a post-baccalaureate student, she opened an email. "Thank you for applying to…After careful review of your application materials, our admissions committee would like to invite you for an interview…" It was her third attempt, and she was elated to see that her hard work and determination had finally paid dividends. Now all that remained between her and a seat in medical school was the admissions interview.

At this particular school, a relatively new and innovative interview technique, known as the multiple mini interview (MMI), was in place. To understand why, it helps to trace the origins of the MMI. In 2001, on the west end of Lake Ontario, in an area known as the Golden Horseshoe, a small group of medical school educators at the Michael G. DeGroote School of Medicine at McMaster University initiated an interesting pilot project. Eighteen graduate students were recruited to act as "medical school candidates." These students were asked to participate in a series of brief interviews. Each interview station was designed to measure a certain non-cognitive quality or skill deemed important in future doctors. Interviewees interacted with a different interviewer or rater at each station.

Promising results led to a larger, more robust study in 2002, this time with real medical school candidates. As the data was analyzed, it became clear that the educators were on to something big. The new interview technique showed high overall test reliability.[1] Subsequent research demonstrated that it was superior to the traditional interview as a predictor of medical school clinical performance.[2]

Just two years later, in 2004, McMaster University introduced the MMI to the world of medical school admissions. Since then, the MMI has been adopted by numerous medical schools. Its reach has expanded beyond medical schools to include veterinary, dentistry, and pharmacy schools. In 2008, the University of Cincinnati College of Medicine became the first medical school in the United States to adopt this new interview technique. Since then, interest in MMI has exploded among allopathic and osteopathic medical schools. At the time of this book's writing, over 30 U.S. medical schools utilized the MMI in the admissions process.

For medical school applicants, the MMI's arrival represented a major change in the medical school admissions process. Change, especially in the high stakes world of admissions, often causes great anxiety for students, parents, and advisors, and the MMI was no exception. For years, medical schools had utilized the traditional interview format, a one-on-one or panel-based interview experience where applicants answered questions, such as "Tell me about yourself" and "Why do you want to be a doctor?"

Many students spent months preparing for the traditional interview, and there was a plethora of books available to help guide preparation. There were also numerous advisors skilled in mock interviewing. With enough practice and the right guidance, students could feel confident in their interview skills.

INTRODUCTION

With the arrival of the MMI, everything changed. To maintain validity and objectivity, medical schools began requiring interviewees to sign forms preventing release of MMI information to others. On discussion forums, medical students who had taken part in MMIs were relegated to delivering generic advice such as "Be yourself and try to enjoy it."

Advisors and applicants turned to the Internet for more specific information. At the websites of those schools utilizing the MMI format, little could be found beyond basic information about its structure and the reasons why schools chose to adopt the new technique. "The strongest advice is to understand the basic structure, time limit, and number of stations," wrote one school in the South.[3] "It is not recommended that you try to prepare for specific MMI questions," wrote another school.[4]

Sarah faced these challenges when she prepared for the MMI. With a dearth of specific information to guide her preparation, she felt understandably nervous on her interview day.

How did Sarah handle the opening scenario?

Prior to entering the room with the actor playing the angry patient, Sarah was given the following information:

> During shift change, your nurse colleague informs you of a "problem patient" that you will be taking care of. She reports being "harassed" all night long by repeated requests for more pain medication. "I followed the doctor's orders, and there was no extra pain medication I could give." As the night progressed, their encounters became increasingly tense and hostile. "I gave him pain medication about an hour ago. He's not due for more for another two hours. Good luck with this one," she says. "You're going to really need it." Enter the room as the patient's new nurse.

MULTIPLE MINI INTERVIEW

Patient: Finally. I'm in so much pain. That last nurse did nothing for me. I kept calling for her, and it took an eternity for her to come. That went on all night long. I couldn't sleep. I couldn't rest. It's like she was watching TV or something. I hope you can do better.

Nurse Sarah: Well, I can promise you that she wasn't watching TV. What can I help you with?

Patient: Haven't you heard anything that I've said? I need some pain medication. How about getting me some? The other nurse told me to try some breathing exercises. Can you believe that? We're talking about real pain here. Eleven out of ten, do you hear me?

Nurse Sarah: I'm sure it's eleven out of ten. Now, we've already...

Patient: I don't like your condescending tone.

Nurse Sarah: I wasn't being condescending. What I was trying to say when you interrupted me was that you've already been given pain medication. You're not due for another dose for another two hours.

Patient: Are you kidding me? I'm trying to tell you that I'm in pain. And you're telling me that I have to wait for two hours. Do you know where the doctor is? Why don't you call him? You and that other nurse – I don't get it. Why did you go into nursing? You're supposed to help people.

Nurse Sarah: The pain medication that's been ordered has been given to you. I really think you should calm down. Maybe if you do, your pain would be more tolerable.

Patient: How dare you tell me to calm down? I demand to talk to your supervisor. I'm going to tell her that you're refusing to give me pain medication.

Nurse Sarah: I've already told you. There's no medication that anyone's holding. You've gotten what's written for.

INTRODUCTION

Patient: Just call the doctor. And bring the nurse supervisor in too.

Analyzing Sarah's answer

Sarah left the encounter frustrated. What went wrong? How could she have avoided this outcome? The angry patient or person scenario is frequently part of the MMI circuit. As you read through Sarah's dialogue with the patient, were you able to identify the factors that led to this unsuccessful encounter? I've listed and described these in the following box.

It was obvious that the patient was upset but Sarah **did not acknowledge the patient's emotions or feelings**. "You seem very upset" would have been one way for Sarah to do so.

Sarah never **invited the patient to share his story** and fully vent. It was clear that the patient had much on his mind. Sarah needed to make the patient feel that he was being heard.

Sarah **failed to show sympathy or regret** for the patient's situation. "I'm really sorry you had to go through all this" would have been effective.

Sarah **lost her composure.** At one point, the patient commented on her condescending tone. At another point, Sarah asked the patient to "calm down." Setting limits when someone is angry is seldom effective. In such situations, it's important to keep your cool.

Sarah **never explored any other solutions**. A particularly effective technique is to ask the patient for his thoughts on possible solutions. "Do you have some suggestions on ways to solve the problem?" Through this process, Sarah may have been able to **find an acceptable solution**. "Here's what I suggest…"

The angry patient is a common scenario in the MMI because it's such a common scenario in medicine. Patients, when faced with the stress of illness, sometimes act in uncharacteristic ways. They may lash out at their doctors and nurses for many reasons. Being sick enough to be hospitalized is frightening for most people. Patients commonly feel afraid, confused, and powerless. They feel that they have no control over what's happening to them. Physical factors, such as acute or chronic pain, may also play a role. Dealing with bad news that impacts prognosis, dealing with the risk of a disability, and the realities of living with a life-threatening illness: all of these are obviously severe stressors.

Sometimes the healthcare system itself can be the cause, as in long waiting times for a test, or an intrusive procedure, or denied insurance claims. At other times, the patient-physician relationship will cause a patient to lash out, such as when a physician is perceived as arrogant or disrespectful. Understand that there may be a number of factors at play when a patient lashes out at you, and that, in most cases, you shouldn't take it personally.

Sarah clearly didn't perform well during this scenario. Fortunately, for Sarah, this wasn't a real admissions interview. This was a mock interview experience in which I played the role of patient. After I analyzed her performance, Sarah was able to better understand where things went wrong. She was then able to implement several strategies to effectively handle this type of situation, as you'll see in the following encounter.

You are the nurse manager on a busy hospital floor. One of your nurses is upset after a difficult patient encounter. The patient was in considerable pain but the nurse was unable to give him anything because the next dose of pain medication was not scheduled for another several hours. As she tried to explain the situation, the patient became quite angry and questioned the nurse's dedication to her profession. Hurt by this, the nurse lost control of her emotions, and the situation escalated, with the patient requesting to speak with the nurse manager. The patient is now waiting for you in the room. Enter the room.

INTRODUCTION

Nurse Manager Sarah:	Hello Mr. Smith. I'm the nurse manager on the floor. I understand you wanted to speak with me. How are you feeling?
Patient:	Terrible. I'm in a lot of pain and no one seems to care.
Nurse Manager Sarah:	Can you tell me what happened?
Patient:	I just want some medication to help me with this pain. It's now so bad – nine out of ten. I've just been sitting here hoping and waiting for medication. The nurse told me that if I calmed down, that I might feel better. Can you believe that? I need some pills or even a shot. I need something. I'm really hurting.
Nurse Manager Sarah:	So let me see if I've understood the situation. You're in a lot of pain, and you don't feel like the current pain medication is providing you with enough relief.
Patient:	Yes, that's what I'm saying. I need something stronger than what I'm getting. I told the nurse this, and she kept telling me to calm down. I asked her to help me, and she kept telling me that it wasn't time for the next dose. I asked her to call the doctor, and she didn't look too happy about that.
Nurse Manager Sarah:	I'm sorry that you're in so much pain. It sounds like you would find it helpful if I reached out to your doctor. That's something I can do. I'll call and let him know that your pain medication is not keeping the pain under control. Perhaps he can make an adjustment to the medication or stop by and take a look at you.
Patient:	I would love that. I don't know why it's so hard to find the doctor.

Nurse Manager Sarah: Let me go and call the doctor. Let's see if we can come up with a plan to address this. How does that sound to you?

Patient: That sounds wonderful.

Nurse Manager Sarah: Before I take care of that, I wanted to see what else I can do for you. I know you're uncomfortable, and I apologize for that. Is there anything else I can do to help you? Are you cold? Do you need a blanket? How about a snack?

Patient: Would you mind turning the TV on for me?

In the following pages, you'll learn how to create this type of response.

A response that confirms that you have the qualities that this medical school seeks. The type of response that confirms to the interviewer that you are the perfect fit for their medical school.

In the next 200+ pages, we'll review, in depth, the multiple mini interview. You'll learn how critical the interview is in the admissions process. The Association of American Medical Colleges (AAMC) evaluated the importance of 12 variables on admissions decisions.[5] Of these, the MCAT score was rated sixth. Cumulative science and math GPA was rated third. What was the most important variable?

The most important factor in admissions decisions was, in fact, the interview.

You'll learn why the MMI is so important to admissions officers. It's widely recognized that the best physicians have more than just great scores and grades. The most effective physicians display a number of non-academic attributes. These traits are difficult to evaluate, and admissions officers rely on the MMI to help assess these traits. "Our school intends to graduate physicians who can communicate with patients and work in a team," writes Dr. Cynda Johnson, Dean of the Virginia Tech Carilion School of Medicine. "So if people do poorly on the MMI, they will not be offered positions in our class."[6]

How can you tell which qualities will be measured during your MMI? Unless you're privy to inside information at that school, you can't know for sure. However, every school will create its MMI to assess for those qualities or skills that it has deemed important in its future students. In Chapter 3, I'll show you how to determine those qualities and skills.

I also review, in detail, other important aspects of the MMI. You'll understand who the raters (interviewers) are, how they'll interact with you, and what they're looking for. In Chapter 5, you'll also learn about their pet peeves, as well as the behaviors and attitudes that would lead them to flag you as an unsuitable candidate. Will your interviewers challenge you? They absolutely will, and I'll show you how to respond to these probing questions in a compelling manner. What else do you need to be concerned about? In one study, researchers described the concerns raised by interviewers who had been tasked with asking applicants certain interview questions. A major concern involved "assessor fatigue." What is it, and how could it affect your performance?[7]

You'll also hear from interviewees. In one study, 10% of participants rated the MMI as worse than the traditional interview.[7] What were the problem areas cited by interviewees? What caused them the most difficulty? How can you avoid their mistakes?

"There are no right or wrong answers," writes one Midwestern U.S. medical school.[8] Is that true? Are there really no right or wrong answers? As reassuring as this sounds, there are clearly wrong answers. In Chapter 7, I'll present the types of answers that can remove an applicant from consideration. You'll see how such answers can easily surface in the high stakes setting of the MMI. You'll learn how to avoid these responses, and deliver answers that yield high interview scores.

I break down the process of developing and delivering powerful answers to MMI questions in chapters 8 – 11. You'll then be able to utilize these strategies with our example questions. This will help provide the practice needed to elevate your performance. With each question, task, or scenario, I provide a sample answer with a thorough explanation of what makes the response so effective.

The recommendations in this book are based on multiple sources. Throughout the book, you'll see quotes from many different admissions officers. Although the MMI is a relatively new interview technique, there's been a substantial body of research on the topic. I've included the results of these research studies, which have shaped and guided my recommendations. Lastly, the recommendations are based on extensive discussions with applicants as well as admissions faculty. I've served on the admissions committee at Baylor College of Medicine for over 10 years, and interacted with admissions officials at numerous medical schools. I now provide interview preparation services for medical school applicants. In this book, as in my previous books, I've applied a combination of evidence-based advice and insider knowledge. I've seen where students have excelled in interviews, and I've seen where they've failed. In the next 200+ pages, you'll learn how to apply these lessons to your own interview preparation. It's taken years of intense work for you to reach this point, and receiving an invitation to interview is a strong vote of confidence from the medical school. In the following pages, you'll learn how to make the most of this opportunity in order to reach your goal: medical school.

References

[1] Eva K, Reiter H, Rosenfeld J, Norman G. An admissions OSCE: the multiple mini-interview. *Med Educ* 2004; 38: 314-26.
[2] Reiter H, Eva K, Rosenfeld J, Norman G. Multiple mini-interview predicts for clinical clerkship performance, National Licensure Examination Performance. *Med Educ* 2007; 41(4): 378-84.
[3] Duke University School of Medicine. Available at: http://dukemed.duke.edu/modules/ooa_applicant/print.php?id=9. Accessed May 12, 2015.
[4] University of Nevada School of Medicine. Available at: http://medicine.nevada.edu/asa/admissions/applicants/selection-factors/applicant-interviews. Accessed May 12, 2015.
[5] Dunleavy D, Sondheimer H, Bletzinger R, Castillo-Page L. Medical school admissions: more than grades and test scores. *AIB* 2011: 11 (6).
[6] New York Times. Available at: http://www.nytimes.com/2011/07/11/health/policy/11docs.html?_r=0. Accessed May 3, 2015.
[7] McAndrew R, Ellis J. An evaluation of the multiple mini-interview as a selection tool for dental students. *Br Dent J* 2012; 212 (7): 331-5.
[8] Michigan State University College of Human Medicine. Available at: http://mdadmissions.msu.edu/applicants/mmi_faq.php. Accessed May 4, 2015.

Chapter 2

The MMI and its Importance in the Admissions Process

Rule # 1   **The medical school interview is a critical factor in the medical school admissions process.**

When applying to medical school, the admissions interview is a critical factor. In fact, at some schools it's the most important factor. In one survey of medical schools, over 60% of surveyed schools reported that the admissions interview was the most important factor in the selection process.[1]

A more recent survey provides further data. In 2011, the Association of American Medical Colleges (AAMC) published a survey that evaluated the importance of 12 variables on admissions decisions. These variables included total MCAT scores, science and math GPA, and the interview. Many students are surprised by the results.

Of the 12 variables, total MCAT score was rated sixth in importance. Cumulative science and math GPA was rated third.[2]

The most important factor in admissions decisions was in fact the interview. The interview received a mean importance rating of 4.5 (scale of 1 [not important] to 5 [extremely important]).

Did you know…

Dunleavy and colleagues examined the undergraduate grade point averages and MCAT scores of all applicants accepted into medical school in 2008, 2009, and 2010. They found that high undergraduate GPAs and MCAT scores do not guarantee admission.

Among applicants with undergraduate GPAs and MCAT total scores of at least 3.8 and 39, respectively, approximately 8% failed to gain admission to any of the medical schools to which they applied.[2]

Why is the interview considered so important, especially in relation to factors such as MCAT scores and science GPAs? "Medical educators agree that success in medical school requires more than academic competence," wrote the authors. "It also requires integrity, altruism, self-management, interpersonal and teamwork skills, among other characteristics."[2] Medical school faculty have long known that while academic variables such as scores and grades may predict preclinical performance, they're not as helpful in predicting which students will become good physicians. Studies have shown that scores and grades don't have as much predictive power, with respect to clinical performance, as do other factors.[3]

What does predict clinical performance? In one study, interview ratings of nonacademic attributes correlated strongly with subjective evaluations of clinical performance in required clerkships. These nonacademic attributes included interpersonal skills, maturity, and motivation/interest in medicine.[4]

Given these findings, med schools can't rely solely on objective data such as scores and grades. Noncognitive skills have significant value in predicting clinical performance, and since schools are limited as to how they can assess such skills, the interview takes on greater importance.

Importance of the Admissions Interview Based On Review of Medical School Websites	
Medical School	**Website Comments**
Vanderbilt University	Interviews are an important part of the application process because it provides the admissions committee with the opportunity to evaluate an applicant's interpersonal skills and intangible qualities that cannot be evaluated through MCAT scores, GPA, or other parts of the application.[5]
University of Connecticut	An important part of the admissions committee's final selections, the interview provides an opportunity to meet the applicant and to gather additional personal and supplemental data for the committee to evaluate the applicant…Interviews provide the admissions committee with personal impressions and insights on the applicant by evaluating, and putting in perspective, all aspects of the applicant's background, experiences coursework, motivations, and values.[6]
UCLA	The interview is an important and integral part of the selection process. It gives the Admissions Committee an opportunity to learn more about the candidate and their ability to be part of the entering class.[7]
Penn State University	The interview is an essential component of the selection process. It provides vital information about the applicant that is impossible to obtain by any other means. Faculty interviews with critical evaluations are the only method within the admissions process for the assessment of the important nonacademic attributes of applicants. The Selection Committee places great importance on these evaluations in making decisions on admission.[8]
LSU Shreveport	High grades and/or MCAT scores alone are never enough. For those interviewed, impressions from the personal interview are exceedingly important.[9]

IMPORTANCE OF MMI 13

Rule # 2 **Understand why some medical schools have replaced the traditional interview with the MMI**

As a faculty member who has served on the medical school admissions and residency selection committees at several U.S. medical schools, I have been privy to some interesting discussions about applicants. Here is an example of what you may hear in an admissions committee meeting at med schools utilizing a <u>traditional interview format</u>:

Did you know...

In the United States, the most common interview format is the traditional one-on-one interview. With this format, the interviewer will typically ask questions about your education, activities, and goals. Examples include:

- Tell me about yourself.
- What are your strengths?
- Why are you interested in our medical school?

Interviewer # 1: I was really looking forward to meeting Lisa. Her application indicated that she was someone who was really committed to caring for the underserved. Early in her college career, she had become involved in the local area free health clinic. Her personal statement indicates that this experience was very meaningful to her, and it certainly seems that she was highly regarded by the clinic staff. She worked there for several years, and was given increasing responsibility. In her junior year, she was given the title of Patient Assistance Representative. In this position, she had extensive patient contact, and was the point person for working with pharmaceutical companies to obtain medication free or at reduced cost for the clinic's patients. Needless to say, I wanted to learn more about all of this but when I asked her questions about her involvement, I was surprised by the superficiality of her responses. I was really looking for depth in her answers, and I couldn't find it no matter how hard I tried. Maybe it was because I was her first interviewer but I tried to get her to relax. She did seem nervous at the beginning but I would say that her answers continued to be brief and superficial throughout most of the interview. That's why I gave her the score that I did.

Interviewer # 2: We did talk about her work in the free clinic, and I got the sense that she found the entire experience very rewarding. I didn't have any trouble talking to her, and found her very easy to talk to, really quite engaging. It turns out that we went to the same college, so we had a nice discussion about the campus, what she likes to do, and so on. I have to say that I was quite impressed with her enthusiasm and her maturity. I think that her life experiences would really add to the diversity of our class. I would love to see her here.

Interviewer # 1 was clearly excited to meet Lisa but was not impressed with her interview performance. She was particularly disappointed because Lisa's answers were brief, and lacking in depth. Interviewer #2 had a very different impression. He was struck by her enthusiasm, and felt that it was easy to connect with her.

As an admissions committee member, I would often listen to these discussions, and wonder if my colleagues had interviewed the same applicant. Why would two interviewers have very different opinions of the same applicant? Studies of the traditional interview have found that interview ratings are significantly influenced by the biases, expectations, and perspectives of the individual interviewers.[10-12] While variance in interview ratings is multifactorial, research has shown that interviewer variability is a major factor, accounting for 56% of the variance in interview scores.[13] Limitations of the traditional interview are presented in the following box.

Limitations of the Traditional Interview

- Interviewer may be easily influenced by an early answer (positively or negatively)
- Interviewer brings a variety of biases into the encounter (conscious or unconscious)
- Scoring of interviewees varies from interviewer to interviewer, leading to inconsistency
- Considerable variability between interviewers
- Difficulty measuring non-cognitive qualities important in future physicians

---

The limitations of the traditional interview led researchers at McMaster University in Hamilton, Ontario to develop a new interview technique called the Multiple Mini-Interview (MMI).[14]

Admissions Officers Speak...

"Our school intends to graduate physicians who can communicate with patients and work in a team. So if people do poorly on the MMI, they will not be offered positions in our class."[15]

Dr. Cynda AnnJohnson, Dean of the Virginia Tech Carilion School of Medicine

---

"Approximately 12% of the hundreds of candidates interviewed each year at WesternU/COMP receive a 'Do not recommend' rating after their MMI performance."[16]

Western University of Health Sciences College of Osteopathic Medicine of the Pacific (in an interview with The DO)

"My bias is toward thoughtful, caring physicians who connect with the patient. We want leaders, but those with interpersonal skills and empathy. I do not want to graduate a medical student from our school who wouldn't be comfortable taking care of a patient."[17]

Dr. Charles Prober, Senior Associate Dean for Medical Education at the Stanford University School of Medicine

---

"MMI is an important tool to help the Admissions Committee gather information about the important characteristics physicians need to work effectively with patients and members of the health care team."[18]

University of Nevada School of Medicine

"The MMI and the holistic admissions model aren't just about which applicants have the best grades and MCAT scores, but which ones will make the best doctors."[19]

Dr. Nathan Smith, Assistant Dean for Admissions at University of Alabama at Birmingham School of Medicine

Rule # 3 — Understand how the MMI overcomes the limitations of the traditional interview.

"We were really dissatisfied with the process for admitting students to medical school," said Jack Rosenfeld, Professor Emeritus of Pathology and Molecular Medicine and Co-Creator of the MMI, in an interview with The Globe and Mail. "There were students that got in and maybe shouldn't have."[20]

Researchers were also driven to develop this new interview approach to ensure that desirable candidates were not removed from consideration because of the limitations of the traditional interview. "With the traditional interview process, a terrific student could have a bad interview. With the MMI, a single bad review can be neutralized by the reviews by multiple other raters," said Dr. Mariann Manno, Interim Associate Dean for Admission at the University of Massachusetts Medical School.[21]

The MMI method uses a structured and consistent approach with multiple raters, and has shown to be reliable and more predictive of future performance in medical school, especially during clinical clerkships. In a 2007 study performed by researchers at McMaster University, MMI scores correlated well with clerkship and Objective Structured Clinical Examination (OSCE) evaluations.[22]

Advantages of MMI Over the Traditional Interview

- The MMI usually has 8 to 10 stations. At each station, there will be a different interviewer (rater). Therefore, you will be exposed to far more interviewers than you would during the typical traditional interview. These interactions will yield more data, and allow for a more accurate rating.

- Every applicant encounters the same questions, scenarios, and tasks at these stations. In other words, the MMI is standardized.

- Interviewers will not have access to the GPA and MCAT score. By blinding interviewers to the academic record, the MMI allows for a more objective evaluation of the traits and behaviors the school has deemed important in their future doctors.

Established in 2002, use of the MMI in U.S. medical schools has grown rapidly.

Did you know...

In 2014 – 2015, 30 allopathic U.S. medical schools reported using the MMI approach, either alone or in combination with the traditional interview. Four osteopathic schools have also adopted this technique.

U.S. Medical Schools Utilizing MMI

Alabama

University of Alabama School of Medicine

Arizona

A.T. Still University School of Osteopathic Medicine in Arizona
University of Arizona College of Medicine

California

Stanford University School of Medicine
UC Davis School of Medicine
UC Riverside School of Medicine
UC San Diego School of Medicine
UCLA David Geffen School of Medicine
Western University of Health Sciences College of Osteopathic Medicine of the Pacific

Illinois

Chicago Medical School at Rosalind Franklin University of Medicine and Science
University of Illinois-Chicago College of Medicine

Indiana

Marian University College of Osteopathic Medicine

Massachusetts

University of Massachusetts Medical School
Tufts University School of Medicine (Maine track)

Michigan

Central Michigan University School of Medicine
Michigan State University College of Human Medicine
University of Michigan Medical School
Western Michigan University School of Medicine

Missouri

University of Missouri-Kansas City School of Medicine

Nevada

University of Nevada School of Medicine

New Jersey

Cooper Medical School of Rowan University
UMDNJ-Robert Wood Johnson Medical School

New York

Albany Medical College
New York Medical College
New York University School of Medicine
SUNY Upstate Medical University

North Carolina

Duke University School of Medicine

Ohio

University of Cincinnati College of Medicine

Oklahoma

University of Oklahoma College of Medicine

Oregon

Oregon Health & Science University

Utah

University of Utah School of Medicine

Vermont

University of Vermont College of Medicine

Virginia

Virginia Tech Carilion School of Medicine

Washington

Pacific Northwest University of Health Sciences College of Osteopathic Medicine

Canadian Medical Schools Utilizing MMI

Alberta

University of Alberta Faculty of Medicine and Dentistry
University of Calgary Faculty of Medicine

British Columbia

University of British Columbia Faculty of Medicine

Manitoba

University of Manitoba Faculty of Medicine

Newfoundland

Memorial University of Newfoundland Faculty of Medicine

Nova Scotia

Dalhousie University Faculty of Medicine

Ontario

McMaster University Michael G. DeGroote School of Medicine
Northern Ontario School of Medicine
Queen's University Faculty of Health Sciences

Quebec

Laval University Faculty of Medicine
McGill University Faculty of Medicine
University of Montreal Faculty of Medicine
University of Sherbrooke Faculty of Medicine

Saskatchewan

University of Saskatchewan College of Medicine

References

[1] Puryear J, Lewis L. Description of the interview process in selecting students for admission to U.S. medical schools. *J Med Educ* 1981; 56 (11): 881-85.
[2] Dunleavy D, Sondheimer H, Bletzinger R, Castillo-Page L. Medical school admissions: more than grades and test scores. *AIB* 2011: 11 (6).
[3] Mitchell K. Traditional predictors of performance in medical school. Paper presented at the annual meeting of the American Educational Research Association, San Francisco, California, March 1989.
[4] Meredith K, Dunlap M, Baker H. Subjective and objective admissions factors as predictors of clinical clerkship performance. *J Med Educ* 1982; 57: 743-51.
[5] Vanderbilt University School of Medicine. Available at: https://medschool.vanderbilt.edu/admissions/campus-interview. Accessed February 22, 2013.
[6] University of Connecticut School of Medicine. Available at: http://medicine.uchc.edu/prospective/apply/index.html. Accessed February 22, 2013.
[7] UCLA David Geffen School of Medicine. Available at: http://ww.medstudentucla.edu/offices/admiss/interv.cfm. Accessed February 22, 2013.
[8] Penn State University College of Medicine. Available at: http://www2.med.psu.edu/mdadmissions/interview-process/. Accessed February 21, 2013.
[9] LSU – Shreveport School of Medicine. Available at: http://www.lsuhscshreveport.edu/Admissions/ReApplicants.aspx#personal. Accessed February 22, 2013.
[10] Edwards J, Johnson E, Molidor J. The interview in the admission process. *Acad Med* 1990; 65: 167–75.
[11] Elam C, Andrykowksi M. Admission interview ratings: relationship to applicant academic and demographic variables and interviewer characteristics. *Acad Med* (Suppl) 1991; 66: 13–15.
[12] Elam CL, Johnson MM. An analysis of admission committee voting patterns. *Acad Med* (Suppl) 1997; 69: 72–755.
[13] Harasym P, Woloschuk W, Mandin H, Brundin-Mather R. Reliability and validity of interviewers' judgements of medical school candidates. *Acad Med* (Suppl) 1996; 71: 40–42.
[14] Eva K, Rosenfeld J, Reiter H, Norman G. An admissions OSCE: the multiple mini-interview. *Med Educ* 2004; 38 (3): 314-26.
[15] New York Times. Available at: http://www.nytimes.com/2011/07/11/health/policy/11docs.html?_r=0. Accessed May 3, 2015.
[16] The DO. Available at: http://thedo.osteopathic.org/2014/09/multple-mini-interviews-gains-traction-schools/. Accessed May 2, 2015.
[17] Stanford Medicine. Available at: http://med.stanford.edu/news/all-news/2011/01/on-your-mark-get-set-interview.html. Accessed May 3, 2015.
[18] University of Nevada School of Medicine. Available at: http://medicine.nevada.edu/asa/admissions/applicants/selection-factors/applicant-interviews. Accessed May 1, 2015.
[19] UAB School of Medicine. Available at: http://www.uab.edu/medicine/news/latest/item/490-mmi-added-to-admissions-process. Accessed May 4, 2015.
[20] The Globe and Mail. Available at: http://www.theglobeandmail.com/life/interview-20-theres-no-easy-way-to-ace-this-one/article1344084/. Accessed May 3, 2015.
[21] UMass Med Now. Available at: http://www.umassmed.edu/news/news-archives/2013/07/mmi-gives-students-multiple-opportunities-to-shine/. Accessed May 3, 2015.
[22] Reiter H, EvaK, Rosenfeld J, Norman G. Multiple mini interviews predict clerkship and licensing examination performance. *Med Educ* 2007; 41 (4): 378-84.

Chapter 3

Qualities Assessed by MMI

Rule # 4   Medical schools seek certain qualities in their applicants.

Each MMI station is designed to measure or assess a certain noncognitive quality or skill that the medical school has deemed important in its students and future physicians. At some stations, several qualities may be assessed. A recent survey of admissions officers, representing 90% of U.S. medical schools, provides insight about the personal qualities most commonly assessed.[1]

Personal Characteristics Assessed During the Admissions Interview	
Personal characteristics	Percentage
Motivation for a medical career	98%
Compassion and empathy	96%
Personal maturity	92%
Oral communication	91%
Service orientation	89%
Professionalism	88%
Altruism	83%
Integrity	82%
Leadership	80%
Intellectual curiosity	76%
Teamwork	74%
Cultural competence	72%
Reliability and dependability	70%
Self-discipline	70%
Critical thinking	69%
Adaptability	67%
Verbal reasoning	66%
Work habits	66%
Persistence	65%
Resilience	65%
Logical reasoning	56%

Adapted from the AAMC. Available at https://www.aamc.org/download/261110/data/aibvol11_no7.pdf.

MULTIPLE MINI INTERVIEW

Rule # 5 <mark>Ascertain qualities important to the school where you will be interviewing</mark>

How can you tell which of these qualities will be measured during your MMI? Unless you are privy to inside information, you can't know for sure. In fact, medical schools have applicants sign a Participant Agreement and Statement of Confidentiality preventing release or disclosure of MMI information to others. However, a review of the school's website can give you an idea of what is considered important, as shown below for U.S. and Canadian medical schools.

UNITED STATES

ALABAMA

University of Alabama: "We are looking for applicants who have a demonstrated commitment to becoming physicians evidenced by maturing insights into the doctor-patient relationship and a passion for service developed through experiences in a medical setting and through hands on service and volunteer activities; a demonstrated capacity for critical thinking and passion for knowledge..."[2]

ARIZONA

A.T. Still University School of Osteopathic Medicine in Arizona: "As an osteopathic medical school devoted to excellence, we value scholarship, professionalism, learning centeredness, compassion, the whole person (body, mind and spirit), teamwork, and innovation."[3]

University of Arizona: "MMIs...'test' attributes and/or traits sought in a medical student: interpersonal communication, teamwork, ethical and moral judgment, etc."[4]

CALIFORNIA

Stanford University: "...they are simply evaluating interpersonal skills, the ability to communicate clearly, to reason, to be empathic, and so on."[5]

UC Davis: "We're putting our candidates through a series of brief, but telling situations designed to illuminate key characteristic of a good physician, including resourcefulness, listening skills, and even teamwork."[6]

UC Riverside: "The stations and specific prompts used in the MMI process are...evaluating some of the applicants' personal attributes. This core set of criteria includes assessment of the following: a) integrity and ethics, b) reliability and dependability, c) service orientation, d) social and interpersonal skills, e) capacity for improvement, f) resilience and adaptability, g) cultural competence, h) oral communication, and i) teamwork."[7]

Western University of Health Sciences College of Osteopathic Medicine of the Pacific: "I think it helps identify the type of student that would be the best fit for this institution, encompassing the mission that the university has – caring, compassionate, lifelong learners."[8]

ILLINOIS

Chicago Medical School at Rosalind Franklin University of Health and Science: Core values include diversity, innovation, integrity, leadership, professionalism, service, and teamwork.[9]

INDIANA

Marian University College of Osteopathic Medicine: "The format will allow us an opportunity to gauge your non-cognitive skills such as critical thinking and communication—among other areas."[10]

In an interview with The DO, Bryan Moody, Director of Enrollment had this to say about the MMI. "In a physician, you want someone who is going to make good ethical decisions that are sound, taking in vast amounts of information and categorizing it in a way that makes sense to a patient who doesn't have all of that highly scientific knowledge. You want someone who can communicate with you, who can understand and listen and answer questions and speak with you in a way that you can relate to and feel comfortable with. Above all, you want someone who has empathy. Patients come to physicians at their lowest possible moment in life, when they are sick and tired and scared and confused and hurt. And they just want answers."[11]

MASSACHUSETTS

University of Massachusetts: According to Dr. Mariann Manno, Interim Associate Dean, "We want to be able to assess non-cognitive traits such as problem solving, communication, empathy and resilience."[12] UMMS will develop scenarios to measure certain competencies including physician as professional, scientist, communicator, clinical problem solver, patient and community advocate, and person.

MICHIGAN

Central Michigan University: The focus of the 11 stations is on teamwork, ethical and moral dilemmas. Personal and professional attributes considered important include integrity, reliability, positive attitude, adaptability, teamwork, self-discipline, responsibility, compassion, altruism, passion for medicine, communication skills, leadership abilities, personal maturity, and cultural competence.

Michigan State University: "By placing the applicant in a succession of scenarios, we'll be able to test things like a student's resilience, emotional intelligence and a team approach that we can't necessarily appropriately test in the traditional interview process," says Dr. Katherine Ruger, Director of Admissions.[11]

University of Michigan: "You'll have the opportunity to take part in a series of six, six-minute short-form interviews with a variety of people from our med school community. These interactive scenarios will challenge you to demonstrate how you work as part of team, how you think and respond to questions about an ethical or philosophical dilemma, and how you might interact with a patient in a difficult situation—all under a tight time constraint."[13]

Western Michigan University: Personal attributes considered important include teamwork, problem-solving, compassion and dedication to serve others, effective communications, and making decisions with integrity.

MISSOURI

University of Missouri – Kansas City: "...to develop the skills, knowledge, and attitudes of these students longitudinally over six years with a goal of instilling the highest standards of medical

QUALITIES ASSESSED BY MMI

professionalism, clinical competency, humanism, and altruism during a highly formative period of their lives."[14]

MISSISSIPPI

University of Mississippi: "The station scenarios do not test or assess scientific or clinical knowledge; instead, they focus on personal competencies such as oral communication skills, service orientation, respect for others including compassion and empathy, critical thinking and decision making, teamwork, awareness of ethics, maturity, coping skills and opinions on health care issues."[15]

NEVADA

University of Nevada: "Each station is designed to assess applicant communication skills, ability to solve problems and think critically, and ethics and integrity."[16]

NEW JERSEY

UMDNJ – Robert Wood Johnson Medical School: "The stations may be comprised of scenarios which do not test or assess scientific knowledge but will focus on issues such as communication, ethics, service, critical thinking and adaptability."[17]

NEW YORK

New York Medical College: "…interpersonal skills, communication, professionalism, cultural competency, and teamwork are paramount."[18]

New York University: "Scenarios may explore an applicant's communication skills, ability to work as part of a team, problem solving capabilities, integrity, ethics and judgment."[19]

SUNY Upstate Medical University: "We drive innovation and discovery by empowering our university family to bring forth new ideas and to ensure quality. We respect people by treating all with grace and dignity and embracing diversity. We serve our community by living our mission. We value integrity by being open and honest to build trust and teamwork."[20]

OHIO

University of Cincinnati: "Because physicians need good communication, critical thinking, and teamwork skills, we are very interested in evaluating these characteristics in our applicants."[21]

OKLAHOMA

University of Oklahoma College of Medicine: "These are our core values: We believe that caring for our patients must be at the center of all we do. We act with honesty and integrity. We respect our colleagues and co-workers. We magnify our effectiveness through teamwork. We improve continually through harnessing innovation and encouraging high performance. We believe in open and effective communication. We are committed to providing outstanding educational programs. We will be a leader in the advancement of basic, translational and clinical research. We embrace our social responsibilities with pride."[22]

OREGON

Oregon Health & Science University: "Attributes that enhance team-based health care, like communication skills, comfort with mutual decision-making and respect for other health professionals will be increasingly important. The MMI process will help in our ongoing goal to always be educating the types of physicians most needed by society."[23]

UTAH

University of Utah School of Medicine: "Interviewers will explore the applicant's motivation for seeking a medical degree, awareness and understanding of the medical profession, leadership, problem solving skills, understanding of medical ethics and interpersonal skills."[24]

VERMONT

University of Vermont College of Medicine: "The goal, says UVM College of Medicine Associate Dean of Admissions Jan Gallant, M.D., is to assess a student's readiness for medical school through the lens of the core personal competencies identified by the Association for American Medical Colleges (AAMC). These competencies include ethical responsibility, a capacity for improvement, cultural competence and adaptability."[25]

VIRGINIA

Virginia Tech University Carilion School of Medicine: "In the MMI process, each interviewer will pose a pre-developed scenario to each interviewee related to a single theme (such as 'Professionalism /Interdisciplinary Teamwork')...The MMI can also assess the applicant's ability to function in team settings, an important skill for our small group learning curriculum."[26]

WASHINGTON

Pacific Northwest University of Health Sciences College of Osteopathic Medicine: "Our initial College of Osteopathic Medicine has a mission to train compassionate and competent osteopathic physicians to fill the health care needs in the Pacific Northwest, especially in rural and medically underserved areas...Institutional values include mission driven (committed to create, sustain, and improve quality educational programs specifically for rural and medically underserved communities), collaborative (working together with thoughtful actions, efforts, and concerns to meet each opportunity, issue, or challenge presented), compassionate (every individual is respected and treated with consideration, kindness, and understanding), and genuine (real people providing real solutions which have direct impact on community health, resources, and outcomes)."[27]

CANADA

ALBERTA

University of Alberta Faculty of Medicine: "The questions will be designed to evaluate the interviewee's critical thinking abilities, ethical decision-making abilities, communication skills and overall performance."[28]

University of Calgary Faculty of Medicine: Seeks students who will demonstrate attributes of altruism, compassion, empathy, and integrity. Also valued are honesty, respect for others, confidentiality, self-directed learning, strong work ethic, and communication skills. "The University of Calgary aims to admit students who will demonstrate ability to manage time, tolerate ambiguity and stress, good judgment, enthusiasm for their work, pay attention to detail, and recognize and respect the roles of other healthcare disciplines."[29]

BRITISH COLUMBIA

University of British Columbia Faculty of Medicine: "The UBC MMI is designed to see how you think on your feet, how you communicate what you believe when pondering ethical, moral and other dilemmas (which are not necessarily medically-related), and to explore who you are as a person."[30]

MANITOBA

University of Manitoba Faculty of Medicine: The institution seeks students who are open to practicing medicine in urban hubs and rural parts of Canada. Also important is an emphasis on "healing through knowledge and compassion and acting as educators for patients, allied health professionals, and one another." Other points of emphasis include effective communication with other professionals, professionalism, respect, cultural safety, and compassionate care to diverse patient populations.[31]

NEWFOUNDLAND

Memorial University of Newfoundland Faculty of Medicine: "The Admissions Committee seeks in applicants the same humanistic qualities and attitudes that our medical school considers essential in a physician: integrity, a respect for others' choices and rights, compassion, empathy, personal insight, ability to communicate effectively and relate to people, maturity and motivation."[32]

NOVA SCOTIA

Dalhousie University Faculty of Medicine: "The stations are designed to assess the applicant's personal qualities, such as problem solving, thinking on your feet, leading, balance, compassion, motivation, critical thinking, awareness of societal health issues, communication skills and ethics."[33]

ONTARIO

McMaster University Michael G. DeGroote School of Medicine: "The stations deal with a variety of issues, which may include but are not

QUALITIES ASSESSED BY MMI 29

limited to, communication, collaboration, ethics, health policy, critical thinking, awareness of society health issues in Canada and personal qualities."[34]

Northern Ontario School of Medicine: The school seeks students who will be socially accountable to the needs of the population in northern Ontario, including Aboriginal, Francophone, remote, rural, and underserviced communities. Values prized include innovation, social accountability, collaboration, inclusiveness, and respect.[35]

Queen's University Faculty of Health Sciences: "The goal of using the MMI is to more effectively assess non-cognitive qualities of an applicant, which could include empathy, critical thinking, ethical decision making and communication skills."[36]

QUEBEC

McGill University Faculty of Medicine: Qualities valued include compassion, empathy, insight, judgment, honesty, adaptability, tolerance, creativity, respect for others, intellectual curiosity, reliability, teamwork, conflict or stress management, leadership, initiative, self-confidence, and professionalism.[37]

SASKATCHEWAN

University of Saskatchewan: "Station scenarios may be structured to specifically judge a candidate's ethical and critical decision-making abilities, knowledge of the health-care system, understanding of health determinants in a local or global context, commitment to helping others, non-academic achievements, or desire for studying medicine."[38]

References

[1] Dunleavy D, Whittaker K. The evolving medical school admissions interview. *AIB* 2011; 11 (7).
[2] UAB School of Medicine. Available at: http://www.uab.edu/medicine/home/future-students/admissions/welcome. Accessed May 3, 2015.
[3] School of Osteopathic Medicine in Arizona. Available at: https://www.atsu.edu/soma/about/mission.htm. Accessed May 4, 2015.
[4] University of Arizona College of Medicine. Available at: http://medicine.arizona.edu/alumni/alumni-slide/tucson-admissions-implements-new-interview-technique. Accessed May 4, 2015.
[5] Stanford Medicine. Available at: http://med.stanford.edu/news/all-news/2011/11/5-questions-prober-on-new-approach-to-admission-interviews.html. Accessed January 2, 2015.
[6] UC Davis Health System. Available at: http://www.ucdmc.ucdavis.edu/publish/news/newsroom/4447. Accessed May4, 2015.
[7] University of California Riverside School of Medicine. Available at: http://www.ucop.edu/operating-budget/_files/legreports/1314/progressreportucrsomlegrpt-4-2-14.pdf. Accessed May 3, 2015.
[8] Western University of Health Sciences. Available at: http://jprod.westernu.edu/news/nr_detail.jsp?id=13243. Accessed May 4, 2015.
[9] Rosalind Franklin University of Health and Science. Available at: http://www.rosalindfranklin.edu/Degreeprograms/corevalues.aspx. Accessed May 4, 2015.
[10] Marian University College of Osteopathic Medicine. Available at: http://www.marian.edu/osteopathic-medical-school/interview. Accessed May 4, 2015.
[11] The DO. Available at: http://thedo.osteopathic.org/2014/09/multple-mini-interviews-gains-traction-schools/. Accessed May 4, 2015.
[12] UMass Med Now. Available at: http://www.umassmed.edu/news/news-archives/2013/07/mmi-gives-students-multiple-opportunities-to-shine/. Accessed May 4, 2015.
[13] University of Michigan Medical School. Available at: http://medicine.umich.edu/medschool/education/md-program/md-admissions/interview-day/faqs. Accessed May 4, 2015.
[14] UMKC School of Medicine. Available at: http://med.umkc.edu/about_us/vision-goals/. Accessed May 4, 2015.
[15] University of Mississippi Medical Center. Available at: http://www.umc.edu/Education/Schools/Medicine/SOM_Admissions/Interviews.aspx. Accessed May 4, 2015.
[16] University of Nevada School of Medicine. Available at: http://medicine.nevada.edu/asa/admissions/applicants/selection-factors/applicant-interviews. Accessed May 4, 2015.
[17] Robert Wood Johnson Medical School. Available at: http://rwjms.rutgers.edu/education/admissions/selection_process.html. Accessed May 4, 2015.
[18] New York Medical College InTouch. Available at: http://www.nymc.edu/OfficesAndServices/PublicRelations/Assets/June2012_InTouch.pdf. Accessed May 4, 2015.
[19] NYU School of Medicine. Available at: https://www.med.nyu.edu/school/md-admissions/mmi-faqs. Accessed May 4, 2015.
[20] State University of New York Upstate Medical University. Available at: http://www.upstate.edu/excellence/pdf/values.pdf. Accessed May 4, 2015.
[21] University of Cincinnati College of Medicine. Available at: http://healthnews.uc.edu/news/?/14446/. Accessed May 4, 2015.

[22] University of Oklahoma College of Medicine. Available at: http://www.oumedicine.com/collegeofmedicine. Accessed May 4, 2015.
[23] Oregon Health & Science University. Available at: http://www.ohsu.edu/xd/education/schools/school-of-medicine/about/school-of-medicine-news/education-news/multiple-mini-interviews-4111.cfm. Accessed May 4, 2015.
[24] University of Utah School of Medicine. Available at: http://medicine.utah.edu/admissions/process/. Accessed May 4, 2015.
[25] University of Vermont College of Medicine. Available at: http://www.uvm.edu/medicine/?Page=news&storyID=19920&category=comall. Accessed May 4, 2015.
[26] Virginia Tech Carilion School of Medicine. Available at: http://www.vtc.vt.edu/education/admissions/interview_day.html. Accessed May 4, 2015.
[27] Pacific Northwest University of Health Sciences College of Osteopathic Medicine. Available at: http://www.pnwu.edu/assets/PDFs/Student-Catalog/2014-2015-Student-CatalogFinal-Contentv2.pdf. Accessed March 2, 2015.
[28] University of Alberta Faculty of Medicine. Available at: https://www.med.ualberta.ca/programs/md/admissions/applying/interview. Accessed May 15, 2015.
[29] University of Calgary Faculty of Medicine. Available at: http://www.ucalgary.ca/mdprogram/admissions/mmi-information. Accessed May 12, 2015.
[30] University of British Columbia Faculty of Medicine. Available at: http://mdprogram.med.ubc.ca/admissions/interviews/. Accessed May 12, 2015.
[31] University of Manitoba Faculty of Medicine. Available at: http://umanitoba.ca/faculties/health_sciences/medicine/education/undergraduate/ugme_mission_objectives.html. Accessed May 12, 2015.
[32] Memorial University of Newfoundland Faculty of Medicine. Available at: http://www.med.mun.ca/Admissions/ApplicationEvaluationCompetitions.aspx. Accessed May 12, 2015.
[33] Dalhousie University Faculty of Medicine. Available at: http://medicine.dal.ca/departments/core-units/admissions/application-process/interview.html. Accessed May 12, 2015.
[34] McMaster University Michael G. DeGroote School of Medicine. Available at: http://fhs.mcmaster.ca/mdprog/interviews.html. Accessed May 12, 2015.
[35] Northern Ontario School of Medicine. Available at: http://www.medicaleducationfutures.org/sites/default/files/Beyond%20Flexer%20NOSM%20Final%20Report.pdf. Accessed May 12, 2015.
[36] Queen's University Faculty of Health Sciences. Available at: http://meds.queensu.ca/education/undergraduate/prospective_students/application_process/interview. Accessed May 12, 2015.
[37] McGill University Faculty of Medicine. Available at: http://www.mcgill.ca/medadmissions/applying/selection-process/message-applicants. Accessed May 12, 2015.
[38] University of Saskatchewan College of Medicine. Available at: http://www.medicine.usask.ca/education/medical/undergrad/prospective-students/admissions/MMI%20Fact%20Sheet.pdf. Accessed May 12, 2015.

Chapter 4

MMI Format

Rule # 6 Become familiar with the MMI format

During the MMI, the interviewee moves from one station to another over about a two-hour period. At each station, the interviewee is asked to respond to one of the following:

- Short structured scenario
- Question
- Task

Trained raters (interviewers) are present to observe and score the candidate's performance. Applicants will receive the same question, scenario, or task, and this allows raters to easily compare the quality of responses among a group of candidates.

Typical MMI Format

- The typical MMI involves 8 to 10 stations.

- You'll be presented with various scenarios, usually posted on the door.

- You'll have 2 minutes to read each scenario.

- You may or may not be able to take notes.

- You'll then be prompted to enter the room, where you will respond to the scenario or task.

MMI FORMAT

SEQUENCE OF EVENTS DURING MMI STATION

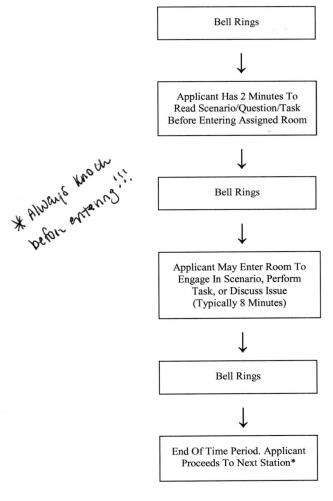

*Always knock before entering!!!

*The process continues until the applicant has completed all stations.

Rule # 7   Recognize the differences between the major types of MMI stations

There will be three main types of MMI stations you will encounter as an interviewee. These station types along with representative examples are shown below.

Question/Discussion Station

Upon entering the room, you will likely find yourself with one rater (interviewer). After your response, the rater may ask you follow-up questions. These follow-up questions will differ from one applicant to another, depending upon the content of the applicant's initial response. Question stations are designed to assess communication skills, thought processes, and professionalism.

Question/Discussion Station Examples

Dr. Cheung recommends homeopathic medicines to his patients. There is no scientific evidence or widely accepted theory to suggest that homeopathic medicines work, and Dr. Cheung doesn't believe them to. He recommends homeopathic medicine to people with mild and nonspecific symptoms such as a fatigue, headaches and muscle aches, because he believes that it will do no harm, but will give them reassurance. Consider the ethical problems that Dr. Cheung's behavior might pose. Discuss these issues with the interviewer.[1]

Recently in Congress, there has been a discussion concerning the issue of deterrent fees for all individuals on either Medicare or Medicaid (a small charge, say $20), which everyone who initiates a visit to a health professional would have to pay for every contact) as a way to control health care costs. The assumption is that this will deter people from visiting their doctor for unnecessary reasons. Consider the broad implications of this policy for health and health care costs. For example, do you think the approach will save health care costs? At what expense?[2]

Scenario/Acting Station

Prior to entering the room, you will be given a scenario to read. Inside the room, you'll find two people – rater and actor. The actor has been trained to engage in the scenario with you. The rater will observe your interactions with the actor. Scenario stations often provide information about compassion, social interaction, and problem solving.

Scenario/Acting Station Examples

The parking garage at your place of work has assigned parking spots. On leaving your spot, you are observed by the garage attendant as you back into a neighboring car, a BMW, knocking out its left front headlight and denting the left front fender. The garage attendant gives you the name and office number of the owner of the neighboring car, telling you that he is calling ahead to the car owner, Tim. The garage attendant tells you that Tim is expecting your visit. Enter Tim's office.[1]

You have a meeting set up with Frankie. He is the son of a family friend who moved to Thunder Bay about 20 years ago and so you have never met him. He has come down from Thunder Bay to look over "southern universities." He urgently needs some information on schools as he will have to make some serious decisions soon. He is happy to get this meeting as he realizes how tight your schedule is. In fact, your next meeting is in eight minutes. Frankie is in the room.[3]

Task/Collaboration Station

You will be asked to complete a task, often with another applicant. The Stanford University School of Medicine offers the following description of a task station:[2]

Two applicants participate in a scenario in which one applicant is asked to perform a complex test (such as assembling or repairing a model) with the other applicant giving directions for dealing with or assembling the model.

When you enter the room, there will be two raters, one of whom will be responsible for observing and rating your performance. The second rater will be tasked with evaluating the other applicant. Task stations are used to learn more about an applicant's teamwork, problem solving, and communication skills.

Task/Collaboration Station Example

Origami (Deliver): When you enter the room there will be a sheet of paper that illustrates how to complete an origami (paper folding) project. On the other side of the room there is another candidate who can't look at you, but who has a blank piece of paper. Verbally guide your colleague to completion of the origami project.[3]

Origami (Receive): When you enter the room there will be a blank sheet of paper in front of you. On the other side of the room there is another candidate who will provide you with instructions regarding how to turn this page into an origami (paper folding) project. Do not look at the other candidate until told to do so.[3]

Rule # 8 ==The MMI interview will differ from one school to another. Try to ascertain the particulars of the MMI format at the school were you will be interviewing.==

Although the basic structure of the MMI will be similar, there may be differences with respect to the following:

- Duration of MMI session
- Number of stations
- Duration of encounter at each station
- Number of rest breaks
- Note-taking

Acquiring this information in advance of the interview day will allow you to adjust your preparation and mindset accordingly. Begin with the school's website and written correspondence but don't be afraid to contact the school for more information. Schools may share this information if you ask. This approach will help you avoid common pitfalls:

- I remember one applicant who had interviewed at a school where interviewees were given 8 minutes to address the question, task, or scenario at each station. She assumed that she would be given the same chunk of time at her next MMI interview. On the day of her interview, she was thrown for a loop when the school informed her that she would have only 5 minutes per station.

- Another applicant was surprised to learn that she would not be able to jot down notes during the two minutes she had before entering the room. This school's policy was a departure from the MMIs she had taken part in at two other schools. She struggled to adapt, and felt that her answers lacked structure and organization.

Did you know…

If the medical school's website does not provide details about the logistics or structure of the MMI, ask the admissions office for this information. Admissions offices may provide an overview of the interview day and details about the MMI format. "A week in advance, we e-mail applicants detailed instructions explaining how our MMI works," said Gurmeet Rai, Manager of the Office of Education at UC Davis.[4]

Admissions Officers Speak...

"The MMI is a series of 8 interview stations consisting of timed interview scenarios. Applicants rotate through the stations, each with its own interviewer and scenario. The MMI session lasts approximately 72 minutes."[5]

New York University School of Medicine

"There will be a two-minute break between each station. The MMI session lasts approximately 100 minutes. Yes, you will have at least one to two rest breaks during your MMI session."[6]

Michigan State University College of Human Medicine

"You will interact with the interviewers for seven minutes. You will be informed when time is up. There will be a two minute break between stations. The MMI itself, including all the mini-interview stations, lasts approximately 90 minutes."[7]

University of Arizona College of Medicine

"The MMI is a series of approximately six to eight interview 'stations' or encounters that last eight to 10 minutes and are centered on a scenario. Each station has its own interviewer (rater); consequently, each student is evaluated by approximately six to eight different individuals."[8]

University of Cincinnati College of Medicine

"Applicants will participate in each MMI station for seven minutes. Students are informed when time is up. There will be a one-minute break between stations."[9]

University of Nevada School of Medicine

> **Did you know...**
>
> You may be wondering how schools develop their MMI scenarios. In some cases, these scenarios are licensed from other institutions like McMaster University where the MMI was founded. Schools may even rely on faculty and students for development. "Each year faculty, students and community members are invited to assist with developing scenarios for the interview process...Once the 2015 interview process is complete, you will be informed whether or not your scenario was selected for use. Those chosen will be awarded a $ 50 honorarium."[10]

References

[1] Eva K, Rosenfeld J, Reiter H, Norman G. An admissions OSCE: the multiple mini-interview. *Med Educ* 2004; 38 (3): 314-26.

[2] Stanford Medicine. Available at: deansnewsletter.stanford.edu/word_docs/DeanNews11-08-10.doc. Accessed May 4, 2015.

[3] Eva K, Reiter H, Rosenfeld J, Norman G. The relationship between interviewers' characteristics and ratings assigned during a multiple-mini interview. *Acad Med* 2004; 79 (6): 602-9.

[4] UC Davis School of Medicine. Available at: https://www.ucdmc.ucdavis.edu/facultydev/pdfs/FacDevNLDec10_Jan11_pages.pdf. Accessed May 29, 2015.

[5] New York University School of Medicine. Available at: https://www.med.nyu.edu/school/md-admissions/mmi-faqs. Accessed May 4, 2015.

[6] Michigan State University College of Human Medicine. Available at: http://mdadmissions.msu.edu/applicants/mmi_faq.php. Accessed May 4, 2015.

[7] University of Arizona College of Medicine. Available at: http://medicine.arizona.edu/admissions/application-process/interviews. Accessed May 4, 2015.

[8] University of Cincinnati College of Medicine. Available at: https://med.uc.edu/medicalstudentadmissions/apply/MMI. Accessed May 4, 2015.

[9] University of Nevada School of Medicine. Available at: http://medicine.nevada.edu/asa/admissions/applicants/selection-factors/applicant-interviews. Accessed May 4, 2015.

[10] University of Saskatchewan. Available at: http://usaskmedalumni.com/2014/09/04/help-our-admissions-office-develop-scenarios-for-testing-students-applying-for-medicine-in-2015/. Accessed May 4, 2015.

Chapter 5

MMI Interviewers

Rule # 9   **Understand who the raters are**

To administer the MMI, the medical school must have one or more raters at each of 8 to 10 stations. A sufficient number of raters must be available for multiple interview dates. Therefore, schools generally train a large number of raters to accommodate their needs. Within several years of instituting the MMI process, Stanford University had recruited 250 raters.[1]

As you would expect, raters are often faculty physicians but the group tends to be heterogeneous at most schools. MMI raters at Stanford University and UC Davis are also lawyers, nurses, former patients, administrators, and residents.

At the McMaster University Michael G. DeGroote School of Medicine in Hamilton, Ontario where the MMI was developed, raters also include students and community members. These have included the former mayor of Hamilton and a copy editor for the *Hamilton Spectator*, Ross Longbottom. Having a variety of stakeholders involved allows the group to bring different perspectives to the interview process. "I take it very seriously," says Mr. Longbottom. "You are actually getting to choose someone who could be standing over you with a scalpel one day."[2]

Unlike the traditional interview where names of interviewers are disclosed to applicants on the interview day, you won't know who your MMI interviewers or raters are until you enter the room to address the MMI question, scenario, or task. Even then, interviewers are often instructed to not indicate their title or position in the medical school. Irrespective of whether your interviewer is a faculty member, student, or community member, rest assured that each rater has been trained to deliver similar interview experiences to every applicant.

Admissions Officers Speak...

"Interviewers are NYU faculty, staff, and students who have been trained specifically for the MMI process at NYU School of Medicine."[3]

New York University School of Medicine

"Interviewers and raters are administrators, faculty, staff, and students who have been trained specifically for the MMI process at the College of Human Medicine. You will not know in what capacity each interviewer/rater is affiliated with the College."[4]

Michigan State University College of Human Medicine

"The 'raters' are actually the individuals who will be positioned at the individual stations. With the MMI process, they are referred to as 'raters' rather than 'interviewers.' The raters are members of the School of Medicine Admissions Committee which includes administrators, faculty, staff, and students and have been trained specifically for the MMI process at Duke."[5]

Duke University School of Medicine

"These people are alumni and community physicians, and members of the larger health care community including nurses, social workers, child health workers, department managers, as well as OHSU faculty, residents and fellows, and students. We have a pool of about 100 that we draw upon..."[6]

Dean Cynthia Morris (Oregon Health & Science University)

Did you know...

During a recent application cycle, the Virginia Tech Carilion School of Medicine received 2,700 applications. From this pool of applicants, 239 were invited to participate in the MMI. Interviews took place over six weekends. The medical school had trained 80 people to serve as interviewers, including doctors and businesspeople from the community.[7]

Rule # 10   Recognize how raters will interact with you.

The way in which interviewers interact with you will differ based on the station type. In a question-based station, you will be given the freedom to address the issue as you see fit. Upon entering the room, you will begin the discussion. At the end of your response, one of two things will happen:

- The interviewer will ask you follow-up questions or;
- The interviewer will inform you that he has all the necessary information.

If the latter occurs before time has run out, you may have to remain in the room until the bell rings.

In a scenario-based station, you will interact with an actor while the interviewer evaluates your performance. The interviewer will function as an observer, and your focus should be entirely on the actor. Don't be surprised or offended if the interviewer doesn't speak or interact with you. It's his or her role to observe.

In a task-based station, you may be paired with another applicant, and the two of you will be assigned a task. As with the scenario-based station, the interviewer will observe your interactions with the other applicant, and rate you accordingly.

Did you know...

During your MMI, your interviewer may ask you probing questions. Some applicants have been unnerved by the aggressiveness of these follow-up questions. Remember that schools may purposely instruct their interviewers to aggressively ask questions as a means to assess your composure and ability to adapt and think quickly on your feet. In some respects, this is similar to the stress interviews that more commonly took place years ago. The advice offered by Dr. Steven Hausrath, a former member of the admissions committee at the University of Texas Medical Branch at Galveston, for stress interviews is certainly applicable to the MMI:[8]

These are stress interviews – we're taught how to give an interview to put some people under stress. Why is that? Because how one reacts to stress is very stereotyped. One reacts to stress in the same way whether it's traffic, a money problem, or whether it's a dilemma at work or in the laboratory. So by provoking a stress response in someone, you get a sense of how they're going to approach a problem or a hurdle. If they become unglued, then that's not a good thing.

Rule # 11   Beware of assessor fatigue.

Even in the MMI, it's common for schools to incorporate questions typically asked during traditional interviews at one or two stations. For example, you may be asked, "Why do you want to be a doctor?" or "Why are you interested in our medical school? In preparing for such questions, work hard to develop answers that would make you stand out from other applicants. This would be of importance even in a traditional interview but MMIs require interviewers to interact with many more applicants. At schools with traditional interviews, the interviewer may have only 3-4 interviews on any given day. Contrast this with the MMI where the interviewer may have to ask the same question to 20 applicants in a short period of time.

As you might expect, interviewers may quickly tire of hearing the same type of answer again and again. This has been termed "assessor fatigue," and has been reported as a concern by MMI interviewers. In one study, researchers described concerns raised by interviewers tasked with asking applicants traditional interview questions. Some representative comments include:

- "It is an essential station, however, after 40 candidates I found it a little tedious."
- "It does allow the prospective student to merely quote prepared answers, often (as many were so similar) written by careers school staff."[9]

Did you know...

In a KevinMD article, I wrote about how applicants often sound the same. Here's an excerpt:[10]

"After a month of interviews, applicants start to blend together. Actually, this starts to happen after a day of interviews. You may provide heartfelt responses, but if you sound like every other applicant, you've lost an important opportunity to stand out and impress. My mantra is: 'If you can imagine another applicant saying the same thing, then your answer isn't good enough.' At a recent symposium, I asked over 300 students to write down their response to this question: 'What are your strengths?' Here are typical answers:

'I am very team oriented and work well with others. I am a calm person who can work well with obstacles that come up, and I am a good listener.'

'My strengths are working well with others, strong listening skills, and work ethic.'

'I have a positive attitude, and constant willingness to learn. I'm easy to work with.'"

> **Did you know...**
>
> Interviewees have been known to ask interviewers for feedback on their performance following their answer. Don't be one of these applicants. ==Asking for feedback is a huge no-no.==

References

[1] Stanford Medicine. Available at: http://med.stanford.edu/news/all-news/2011/11/5-questions-prober-on-new-approach-to-admission-interviews.html. Accessed May 4, 2015.
[2] Globe and Mail. Available at: http://www.theglobeandmail.com/life/interview-20-theres-no-easy-way-to-ace-this-one/article1344084/. Accessed May 4, 2015.
[3] New York University School of Medicine. Available at: https://www.med.nyu.edu/school/md-admissions/mmi-faqs. Accessed May 4, 2015.
[4] Michigan State University College of Human Medicine. Available at: http://mdadmissions.msu.edu/applicants/mmi_faq.php. Accessed May 4, 2015.
[5] Duke University School of Medicine. Available at: http://dukemed.duke.edu/modules/ooa_applicant/index.php?id=9. Accessed May 4, 2015.
[6] Oregon Health & Science University. Available at: http://www.ohsu.edu/xd/education/schools/school-of-medicine/about/school-of-medicine-news/education-news/qa-cynthia-morris.cfm. Accessed June 1, 2015.
[7] New York Times. Available at: http://www.nytimes.com/2011/07/11/health/policy/11docs.html?_r=0. Accessed May 4, 2015.
[8] SUNY Plattsburgh. Available at: http://www.plattsburgh.edu/academics/prehealthadvising/insiderhausrath.php. Accessed May 5, 2015.
[9] McAndrew R, Ellis J. An evaluation of the multiple mini-interview as a selection tool for dental students. *Br Dent J* 2012; 212 (7): 331-5.
[13] KevinMD. Available at: http://www.kevinmd.com/blog/2013/07/medical-school-interview-strategies-admissions-officer.html. Accessed May 3, 2015.

Chapter 6

MMI Experiences of Prior Interviewees

Rule # 12 | Most interviewees like the MMI. Take comfort in that.

Multiple studies have shown that most interviewees view the MMI favorably. In a study of 100 applicants who interviewed at the McGill University Faculty of Medicine, researchers found that participants rated the MMI more highly than the traditional interview.[1] Applicants felt that it was fair and enjoyable. Similar results were found in a study of dental students in the United Kingdom with 65% indicating that the MMI was better than the traditional interview.[2]

Medical School Applicants Speak...

"I loved the fact that the MMIs tested to see the type of person you were. The interview process definitely illuminated different characteristics that were necessary for working in the medical field. The different prompts that were given were meant to display your problem-solving abilities, your public health approach, as well as testing your ethics. I feel that having those qualities are crucial to becoming a good physician because it gives you a more holistic view of the patient."[3]

Amy Merino

Did you know...

In a study performed at Chicago Medical School, the MMI was viewed by applicants as a positive interview experience. One hundred percent of the interviewees enjoyed their time on the campus, and the school received positive comments about the MMI.[4]

Medical School Applicants Speak…

"I thought the whole process was more geared toward problem-solving than to me talking about who I was as an applicant. And I liked that."[5]

Andrew Snyder

"You're asked to discuss a given scenario with your interviewer, which I thought was a comparatively objective way to evaluate applicants. Although the combined time is similar to that of the combined time of interviews at other schools, it's a bit more draining since you're constantly being confronted with a new scenario and new interviewer."[6]

Hilary Lin

"Every situation they gave you was very different, including the personal and the ethical. It was better at getting who you are as a person than at other schools. It's part of the reason I picked Robert Wood Johnson."[7]

Bridget Hottenstein

"The scenarios help provide more of a conversation rather than the awkward question-and-short answer situations I found myself in during other interviews. And having multiple interviewers is another aspect of the MMI that I preferred. Each faculty member's impression is considered. I found the MMI to be much less subjective than a single interviewer, who may not consider a student after one wrong answer."[8]

Cory Banaschak

"Prior to my interviewing at Marian, I had experienced a panel interview as well as longer one-on-one interviews. Those interviews were intimidating and felt very formal…it was refreshing to be presented with multiple opportunities to share my interests, my values and my experiences in a unique format. And I felt more at ease knowing that if one station didn't go as well as I had hoped, I still had several others I could excel at."[8]

Heather Chouteau

Rule # 13   Some applicants are not fans of the MMI. Understand why.

Although multiple studies have shown that most interviewees view the MMI favorably, a significant percentage of students have expressed concerns. In a study of interviewees at Cardiff University, 10% of participants rated the MMI worse than the traditional interview.[2] As part of this study, qualitative analysis of written comments was performed, and comments were categorized in several themes. Problems cited by interviewees included lack of control, anxiety, and nervousness.

Concerns of Interviewees Following MMI[2]	
Candidate Concern	**Representative Comments**
Lack of control	"…didn't get chance to talk about stuff I wanted to – work experience, personal interests, etc."
	"I felt like it was difficult to express myself at times and put forward my strongest qualities."
	"…five minutes was not enough to fully complete what I had to say."
Anxiety and nervousness	"I was very nervous and did not communicate my thoughts as effectively as I could have."
	"Not calm enough to logically answer the tasks."
Inability to move past poor performance on previous station	"…if the previous station was bad I was nervous for the next one."
Approach taken by interviewers	"Some interviewers were quite aggressive."
McAndrew R, Ellis J. An evaluation of the multiple mini-interview as a selection tool for dental students. *Br Dent J* 2012; 212 (7): 331-5.	

Another concern has to do with the relationship between personality type and MMI scores. In a study performed at UC Davis, researchers had nearly 450 applicants who participated in the MMI process complete a questionnaire. The questionnaire was designed to measure agreeableness, conscientiousness, extroversion, neuroticism, and openness. Of these personality types, conscientiousness had previously been shown to be the personality factor predictive of better performance as a medical student and physician. However, in the study, conscientiousness was not associated with better MMI scores. Instead, researchers found that candidates with higher extroversion scores performed better during the MMI.[9]

EXPERIENCES OF PRIOR INTERVIEWEES

> **Did you know...**
>
> In one study, concerns and comments were obtained from MMI interviewers and interviewees during focus group sessions. Some interviewers reported "responding more to the candidates who were confident." This raised concerns among both groups that "students who are more nervous...a little bit shyer" or "less empathic" may be "negatively discriminated against."[10]

> **Did you know...**
>
> In one study, 33% of interviewees considered the MMI to be more stressful than the traditional interview.[11]

Rule # 14   **Practice but be careful not to offer rehearsed answers.**

In preparing for the MMI, we do recommend that you read different scenarios and practice by developing responses to these situations. However, some applicants have run into trouble when they offer a rehearsed answer as the response to a similar but not identical scenario. The key is to utilize the knowledge you have gained through preparation, and apply it to the scenario at hand. This will yield a more spontaneous response, and one that will make sense to the interviewer.

> **Admissions Officers Speak...**
>
> "Take time to think about the scenario. Sometimes candidates over-rehearse and don't listen. They answer the question that they've prepared for, rather than responding to what we've said. Quite a few candidates fall down on that."[12]
>
> Micki Regan, Admissions Officer at St. Georges University of London

> **Did you know...**
>
> A particularly nice touch is to incorporate information from your background into your answers. For example, if the interviewer asks you about euthanasia and you spent a summer studying the ethics of euthanasia in the Netherlands, work that into your answer. Keep in mind that this is not necessary and you shouldn't overthink this.

References

[1] Razack S, Faremo S, Drolet F, Snell L, Wiseman J, Pickering J. Multiple mini-interviews versus traditional interviews: stakeholder acceptability comparison. *Med Educ* 2009; 43 (10): 993-1000.

[2] McAndrew R, Ellis J. An evaluation of the multiple mini-interview as a selection tool for dental students. *Br Dent J* 2012; 212 (7): 331-5.

[3] Umass Med Now. Available at: http://www.umassmed.edu/news/news-archives/2013/07/mmi-gives-students-multiple-opportunities-to-shine/. Accessed May 4, 2015.

[4] Rosalind Franklin University of Health and Science. Available at: http://www.rosalindfranklin.edu/Portals/0/Documents/Faculty%20Affairs/Faculty%20Development/ERSIG/MMI-ERSIG.pdf. Accessed May 4, 2015.

[5] New York Times. Available at: http://www.nytimes.com/2011/07/11/health/policy/11docs.html?_r=0. Accessed May 4, 2015.

[6] The Stanford Daily. Available at: http://www.stanforddaily.com/2011/07/21/med-school-adopts-multiple-mini-interview-process/. Accessed May 4, 2015.

[7] NJ.com. Available at: http://www.nj.com/news/index.ssf/2011/08/new_interview_process_for_umdn.html. Accessed May 4, 2015.

[8] The DO. Available at: http://thedo.osteopathic.org/2014/09/multple-mini-interviews-gains-traction-schools/. Accessed May 4, 2015.

[9] Jerant A, Griffin E, Rainwater J, Henderson M, Sousa F, Bertakis K, Fenton J, Franks P. Does applicant personality influence multiple mini-interview performance and medical school acceptance offers? *Acad Med* 2012; 87: 1250-59.

[10] Kelly M, Dowell J, Husbands A, Newell J, O'Flynn S, Kropmans T, Dunne F, Murphy A. The fairness, predictive validity and acceptability of multiple mini interview in an internationally diverse student population-a mixed methods study. *BMC Med Educ* 2014; 14: 267.

[11] Dowell J, Lynch B, Till H, Kumwenda B, Husbands A. The multiple mini-interview in the U.K. context: 3 years of experience at Dundee. *Med Teach* 2012; 34 (4): 297-304.

[12] The Guardian. Available at: http://www.theguardian.com/education/2013/oct/07/interview-for-medical-school. Accessed May 4, 2015.

Chapter 7

Evaluating Your Performance

Rule # 15 Understand how the interviewer will evaluate your MMI performance.

The MMI was pioneered by researchers at the Michael G. DeGroote School of Medicine of McMaster University. University officials have visited institutions across the world offering guidance to medical schools seeking to implement the MMI approach in their own admissions process. To facilitate this process, McMaster University has made several documents public. In the publication *Manual for Interviewers*, you can view the evaluation form used by MMI interviewers at McMaster University.[1] On this form, you will see that the interviewer is asked to rate the applicant's overall performance on a scale of 1 (unsuitable) to 10 (outstanding) relative to the pool of all applicants. The school urges interviewers to carefully consider the following in determining the interview score:

- Communication skills
- Strengths of arguments displayed
- Applicant's suitability for the medical profession

At the bottom of the form is space for the interviewer's comments. Although each school will have its own evaluation form, these criteria will be important to all schools.

Did you know…

"After each six-minute interview is complete, the interviewer gives the candidate a score from one to ten and writes comments on his or her performance. Later, when the executive admissions committee reviews the candidate's full application, they'll be able to see both a composite score and the individual comments and scores from all eight interviewers the candidate met with during his or her MMI session."[2]

New York Medical College

Rule # 16 — Medical schools consider communication to be a vital skill, and will evaluate your proficiency during the MMI.

"We are trying to weed out the students who look great on paper but haven't developed the people or communication skills we think are important," said Dr. Stephen Workman, Associate Dean for Admissions at the Carilion School of Medicine at Virginia Tech University. "Candidates who jump to improper conclusions, fail to listen or are overly opinionated fare poorly because such behavior undermines teams. Those who respond appropriately to the emotional tenor of the interviewer or ask for more information do well in the new admissions process because such tendencies are helpful, not only with colleagues but also with patients."[3]

If you think about your encounters with doctors, either as a patient or through shadowing, you know that the basis of every physician – patient encounter is a symptom or concern.

To establish the diagnosis, the physician must start by listening carefully and effectively to the patient's story. He then has to ask insightful questions to elicit key information. He must be able to explain even complex diagnoses in terms that are easily understood by the patient. He also has to communicate a treatment plan, and he has to ensure that patient understands and is able to comply with the recommendations.

"Communication skills are important, not only for physicians in their consultations with patients and their families, but also in their contacts with all members of the health care team," writes Dr. Carol Elam, Associate Dean for Admissions at the University of Kentucky College of Medicine.[4]

Given the importance of communication skills in the practice of medicine, medical schools routinely assess for these skills in the admissions interview. In a recent survey of admissions officers, oral communication was assessed at the time of the interview by 91% of schools.[5]

In assessing your communication skills, interviewers seek to answer some very important questions. Are you a good listener? How well do you express yourself? Can you easily engage in conversation? Do you connect with people? The answers to these questions help the interviewer answer the most important question of all: If I were a patient, how would I feel if this person in front of me was my doctor?

EVALUATING YOUR PERFORMANCE

Did you know...

Research indicates that patient satisfaction is closely linked to communication behaviors demonstrated by the physician during the physician – patient encounter. Behaviors associated with satisfaction include active listening, responding empathically, and showing concern. Nonverbal communication behaviors shown to be strongly associated with satisfaction include eye contact and listening attentively.

Common Communication Problems Encountered During the MMI

Poor listening skills

In mock and real interviews with med school applicants, I frequently encounter poor listening skills. At question-based stations, after you deliver your initial response, the interviewer will often ask follow-up questions. These may be prompts designed to lead you in a particular direction, and it's up to you to listen carefully to these cues. You may be given new information, and your ability to respond appropriately will yield you extra points. Be sure that you understand the new information. Don't be afraid to ask for clarification if necessary.

Poor nonverbal communication

Don't forget that you'll be communicating in two ways at each station – verbally and nonverbally. Your interviewer will pay close attention to not only what you say but also how you say it. To make a strong favorable impression on your interviewer, be sure to maintain eye contact, display good posture, and avoid distracting behaviors. As obvious as this may seem, I can't tell you how often I encounter applicants who make poor eye contact, slouch in their seats, play with their hair, and fiddle with their pens. Remember that nonverbal communication is important in the physician – patient encounter. Research on the nonverbal behavior of physicians has shown that a comfortable degree of eye contact, head nodding, forward lean, and more direct body orientation with uncrossed arms and legs is viewed positively by patients.

Failure to acknowledge and respond to emotions

In scenario-based stations, there will be times when the actor shows emotion. Many interviewees fail to acknowledge and respond to these emotions. Failure to do so will definitely affect your interview score. Why? Many physicians aren't comfortable with patient emotions, and some even demonstrate blocking behaviors. These include switching topics, ignoring the expressed emotion to focus solely on the physical aspects of the illness, and explaining away distress as normal. If a patient expresses an emotion, it should be acknowledged and further explored. If you put yourself in your patient's shoes, you can imagine how you would feel if your doctor ignored or minimized your fear, sadness, frustration, or anger.

MULTIPLE MINI INTERVIEW

Rule # 17   ==You will be told that there are no right or wrong answers. Don't believe that for a minute.==

"There are no right or wrong answers, but instead the MMI gives insight into critical thinking, communication, and decision-making skills."[6]

- Robin Lorenz, M.D., Ph.D., MSTP Director, University of Alabama at Birmingham

"Oftentimes there are no right or wrong answers to the scenarios posed..."[7]

- New York University School of Medicine

"There are no right or wrong answers. Instead, the MMI's purpose is to give insight on the applicant's thought process and interpersonal skills as well as individual values and ideals – qualities beyond grades and scores."[8]

- Michigan State University College of Human Medicine

Is it true? Are there really no right or wrong answers? As reassuring as that sounds, there are clearly wrong answers, and these answers, for the most part, have to do with professionalism. What is professionalism? ==The foundation of the medical profession rests upon the trust that patients place in their physicians. Professionalism focuses on this foundation of trust.== Although it's been defined in many ways, the core values and elements agreed upon include ==honesty, integrity, compassion, empathy, the ability to communicate effectively with patients, and respect for others.==
  Although we think of physicians as highly compassionate and ethical individuals, lapses in ethics and professionalism can affect every level of our profession. These lapses can certainly occur in med school. The evidence indicates that unprofessional behavior in medical school is associated with subsequent disciplinary action of physicians by state medical boards.

EVALUATING YOUR PERFORMANCE

In the pressure-packed, high stakes environment of the MMI, behaviors and attitudes easily surface, particularly when applicants are challenged by interviewers. Your suitability for a career as a physician will be called into question if you:

- Share a belief considered to be unsuitable for a physician. These include, but are not limited to, prejudicial, sexist, or racial comments, statements, or views.

- Choose a position or take a stance that would be considered unethical, highly inappropriate, or immoral for a physician.

- Fail to demonstrate empathy during scenario or task-based encounters with actors or other applicants.

- Lie or cheat

Other ethically inappropriate behaviors and attitudes are presented in the following table.

Ethically Inappropriate Medical Student Behaviors And Attitudes[9]	
Arrogant	Insensitive
Brash	No give and take
Antisocial	Defensive
Rude	Indifferent
Condescending	Prejudiced
Power-seeking	Self-centered
Egocentric	Cocky
Amoral	Dishonest
Rigid attitudes	Selfish
Inflexible	Flippant
Isolated	Uncaring
Devious	Judgmental

It's not always professionalism that calls into question an applicant's suitability for a career in medicine. Responses that convey a lack of understanding about the medical profession or commitment to the field are also concerning to interviewers.

Did you know...

"The system is designed to address the most frequent issue regarding patient complaints. When a licensing or regulatory body reviews the performance of a physician subsequent to patient complaints, the most frequent issues of concern are those of the non-cognitive skills, such as interpersonal skills, professionalism and ethical/moral judgment...The interviewer receives background information on the question or scenario, which assists them in challenging the applicant's ideas or positions. A successful applicant will therefore be one who has used their own body of knowledge effectively and demonstrated a high degree of professionalism in addressing the presented scenario and can deal with the challenges from the interviewer or situation as it develops."[10]

Academy of Medicine

Admissions Officers Speak...

"As a MMI grader, I've seen a couple of people who did pretty bad. One that I interviewed was so nervous she didn't really answer the question. She kept on asking me to give her a minute to think about what she wanted to answer. The other one that stood out the most to me was a girl with that death stare. It's that look when you get into trouble with your significant other but she won't say anything but you know he/she is super pissed."[11]

MMI Interviewer (Student Doctor Network)

Success Tip

In interacting with MMI interviewers at meetings and conferences, I have found that lying or bluffing is particularly concerning. If you encounter a question or scenario that you don't understand, it's always best to ask for clarification.

Did you know...

MMI interviewers have space on the evaluation form to add comments. This space may be used to address concerns about an applicant. In a study done at one school, researchers wrote that "if candidates made one or more inappropriate remarks during the course of any of the station interviews then a 'red flag' option could be employed, indicating that the interviewer had very serious concerns regarding the candidate's suitability for the course and profession."[12]

EVALUATING YOUR PERFORMANCE

Rule # 18 ==The MMI reduces bias in the interview process but doesn't eliminate it.==

Unlike the traditional interview where the interviewer has access to all or part of your application, MMI interviewers have no knowledge of you as an applicant, including your credentials, background, and accomplishments. "The raters do not know the candidates at all, they have not seen their files, they do not know which undergraduate school they went to, they don't know anything other than their name, and that's because the candidate's wearing a name tag," said Dr. Charles Prober, Associate Dean for Education at Stanford University School of Medicine. "We don't want any bias whatsoever to be introduced into the process."[13]

With no prior knowledge of your background, concerns about introducing bias are lessened. However, bias still remains an issue. Potential sources of bias are described in the following table.

Potential Biases of the Multiple Mini-Interview	
Bias	**Description**
Hawk/dove effect	The evaluator is extremely harsh ("hawk") or lenient ("dove") in his assessment regardless of performance.
Halo effect	The applicant is rated higher across the board because the interviewer permits one factor to overshadow or have an effect on everything else.
Horn effect	The applicant is rated lower across the board because of one factor that is particularly bothersome to the evaluator.
Order effect	Order of interviewees affects evaluation of performance (e.g., scoring an applicant lower or higher because he was interviewed earlier or later among a group of candidates)

Medical school admissions committees work hard to mitigate the effects of any potential bias by training MMI interviewers. As an interviewee, there is little that you can do with respect to the above biases. You can do even less about unconscious biases that some interviewers may have due to stereotypes about race, gender, national origin, sexuality, and disability.

One potential bias deserves further mention because applicants actually have some control over it. This bias has to do with the ==power of first impressions==. We've all heard about the importance of the first impression in making hiring decisions outside of medicine. Is there any evidence to suggest that first impressions are also crucial in medical school interviews? In an interesting study, University of Kentucky anesthesiology residency interviewers made note of their overall impression of applicants within 30 seconds of meeting them, and then determined if these snap judgments correlated with final overall faculty interview scores.[14] A good correlation was indeed found. Although this study was not performed for medical school admissions, residency interviewers often serve on medical school admissions committees. It wouldn't be a stretch to believe that they would be influenced similarly by first impressions when interviewing medical school applicants.

Why do some people make a better first impression than others? "I think a lot of it is a person's interpersonal communications, how they come across," said Dr. Fragneto, lead author of the study. "Do they look you in the eye when they come in? Do they have a firm handshake? Things like that."[14] In my experience conducting mock interviews with medical school applicants, I find that applicants focus almost exclusively on developing answers to questions. Few applicants give considerable thought to the opening of an interview. Since we rarely receive feedback about the first impression we make on others, practice the opening of your interview through role play with others.

Did you know…

The snap judgment an interviewer makes based on their first impression of you can significantly affect your interview score in a positive or negative manner. Your eye contact, posture, smile, attire, and handshake are major determinants of the first impression you will make on the interviewer.

Did you know…

Dr. Charles Prober, Senior Associate Dean for Medical Education, offered some insight into how the medical school reduces interviewer bias in the MMI process. "The structure of MMI mitigates any effect of 'tough scorers' or, at the other extreme, 'rosy-eyed scorers…Because raters see at least eight students on each recruitment day, they serve as their own controls. That is, those raters regarded as being 'tough' are 'tough' for all applicants they see in a given day and their scores are all corrected for their 'toughness.' And because the overall score of each applicant is derived from the score of all eight raters, the effect of a single rater is diluted. Finally, because raters are not given the applicants' files, they are blinded to all prior history and accomplishments and therefore not susceptible to the biases that may arise from a file review."[13]

EVALUATING YOUR PERFORMANCE

Rule # 19 ==Be reassured by the fact that one bad performance will not destroy your chances.==

In a traditional medical school interview, the applicant typically has several one-on-one interviews with members of the admissions committee. Each interview is immensely important, and one bad interview can torpedo an applicant's chances of admission. Each MMI interview is also important but the applicant is exposed to 8 to 10 interviewers, and the opportunity to be evaluated by multiple raters offers applicants an advantage. "Students like the MMI because they have multiple opportunities to shine," said Dr. Mariann Manno, Interim Associate Dean for Admissions at the University of Massachusetts School of Medicine. "With the traditional interview process, a terrific student could have a bad interview. With the MMI, a single bad review can be neutralized by the reviews by multiple other raters."[15]

Tip #

You must understand that poor performance at a single MMI station can be overcome but only if you're readily able to move past it. Interviewees who dwell on their suboptimal performance often perform poorly on subsequent stations. This is an incredibly important point, and your ability to embrace and internalize this advice can help you deliver a winning performance.

Medical School Applicants Speak…

"While at first the new MMI format can seem longer and more grueling than the typical interview day, it's important to remember that more interviews means more opportunities to display your personality and interact with representatives from Duke Med. More interviews also means that making one or two mistakes has less of an impact in the overall process."[16]

Hannibal Person, MSIII

Success Tip

Panic is an interviewee's biggest enemy. Nervousness is to be expected but anxiety and panic can cause well-qualified applicants to act or behave uncharacteristically. Controlling your nerves will allow you to process scenarios and tasks more clearly, and deliver concise and insightful answers that interviewers will find compelling.

Rule # 20 **Show interviewers the strength of your arguments**

In addition to communication skills, interviewers will evaluate the strength of your responses. To show interviewers the strength of your arguments, you must:

- Establish the focus of the topic. Your ability to grasp the underlying issue is very important.

- Identify your own point of view or position. It's important to take a position on the issue. Without it, your argument or discussion will lack clarity and direction. The position you choose should be consistent with the values and characteristics of physicians.

- Present your point of view as a well-reasoned argument. Use compelling reasons to support what you're saying.

- Show the interviewer that you've considered other points of view, and why some might make an argument for these alternative views.

- Deliver your message in a structured way. A well-reasoned argument will not be viewed as such if it is delivered in a disorganized manner. Aim to present your position in a clear and logical way.

Did you know…

"Articulate your thinking process as it is helpful for the interviewer to hear how you arrived at your conclusion and demonstrate that you fully considered all of the information, stakeholders and implications," writes the University of Toronto.[17]

Did you know…

After you've taken a stance and offered reasons for your position, you may find that your interviewer disagrees with you. Don't be surprised by this. Go into every interview expecting to be challenged. As long as you offer reasons for your point of view, you have shown the strength of your argument.

EVALUATING YOUR PERFORMANCE

> **Did you know...**
>
> A study of the MMI process performed at the University of Calgary shed some light on how applicants are assessed. The school asked raters to assess interviewees on 5 criteria using a 10-point scale. These criteria included:
>
> - Ability to understand and address the objectives of the scenario
> - Communication skills
> - Strength of arguments
> - Suitability for a career in medicine
> - Overall performance
>
> At each station, applicants could be given a maximum of 50 points.[18]

> **Did you know...**
>
> The evaluation form at one medical school allows the rater to express concerns about an applicant's suitability. After ticking the "red flag" box, the rater must describe the concern. Among the examples were rudeness to the rater or another candidate and bizarre statements or mannerisms "suggesting they are unable to conduct themselves in a professional manner."[19]

References

[1] McMaster University. Available at: http://fhs.mcmaster.ca/mdprog/documents/InterviewerManualFull2012-13forWEBSITE.pdf. Accessed May 5, 2015.
[2] New York Medical College. Available at: http://jenuscher.com/static/media/portfolio/transformingbetter.pdf. Accessed May 5, 2015.
[3] New York Times. Available at: http://www.nytimes.com/2011/07/11/health/policy/11docs.html?_r=0. Accessed May 4, 2015.
[4] Elam C, Burke M, Wiggs J, Speck D. the medical school admission interview: perspectives on preparation. *NACADA Journal* 1998; 18 (2): 28-32.
[5] Dunleavy D, Whittaker K. The evolving medical school admissions interview. *AIB* 2011; 11 (7).
[6] UAB School of Medicine. Available at: http://www.uab.edu/medicine/mstp/images/October_2014.pdf. Accessed May 4, 2015.
[7] New York University School of Medicine. Available at: https://www.med.nyu.edu/school/md-admissions/mmi-faqs. Accessed May 4, 2015.
[8] Michigan State University College of Human Medicine. Available at: http://mdadmissions.msu.edu/applicants/mmi_faq.php. Accessed May 4, 2015.
[9] Lowe M, Kerridge I, Bore M, Munro D, Powis D. Is it possible to assess the "ethics" of medical school applicants? *J Med Ethics* 2001; 27 (6): 404-8.
[10] Academy of Medicine. Available at: http://www.academyofmedicine.org/Portals/0/MMI%20Description.pdf. Accessed May 4, 2015.
[11] Student Doctor Network. Available at: http://www.studentdoctor.net/. Accessed May 3, 2015.
[12] Perkins A, Burton L, Dray B, Elcock K. Evaluation of a multiple mini-interview protocol used as a selection tool for entry to an undergraduate nursing program. *Nurse Educ Today* 2013; 33 (5): 465-9.
[13] The Stanford Daily. Available at: http://www.stanforddaily.com/2011/07/21/med-school-adopts-multiple-mini-interview-process/. Accessed May 4, 2015.
[14] Anesthesiology News. Available at: http://www.anesthesiologynews.com/ViewArticle.aspx?d=Ad+Lib&d_id=384&i=September2011&i_id=760&a_id=18916. Accessed May 5, 2015.
[15] UMass Med Now. Available at: http://www.umassmed.edu/news/news-archives/2013/07/mmi-gives-students-multiple-opportunities-to-shine/. Accessed May 4, 2015.
[16] DukeMed. Available at: http://www.dukedavisoncouncil.org/?page_id=258. Accessed May 5, 2014.
[17] University of Toronto. Available at: http://www.utsc.utoronto.ca/aacc/sites/utsc.utoronto.ca.aacc/files/u5/PreparingforMMI.pdf. Accessed May 4, 2015.
[18] Lemay J, Lockyer J, Collin V, Brownell A. Assessment of non-cognitive traits through the admissions multiple mini-interview. *Med Educ* 2007; 41 (6): 573-79.
[19] Dowell J, Lynch B, Till H, Kumwenda B, Husbands A. The multiple mini-interview in the U.K. context: 3 years of experience at Dundee. *Med Teach* 2012; 34 (4): 297-304.

Chapter 8

Basics of Preparation

Rule # 21   **Don't buy into the belief that you can't prepare for the MMI.**

You'll hear that it's difficult to prepare for the MMI, and schools may even urge you to not prepare in certain ways. "It is not recommended that you try to prepare for specific MMI questions," writes the University of Nevada School of Medicine.[1] "Reviewing or going through a list of 'practice' questions is not applicable because the MMI does not use the same questions as a standard interview," writes the University of Cincinnati College of Medicine.[2]

The truth is that it's important to prepare because preparation can help you in a variety of ways:

- It takes poise and presence to deliver strong answers to MMI questions, and practicing will help you develop the confidence needed to tackle these challenging situations.

- Moving from one station to another requires you to be flexible and open to encountering new situations, and practicing through a circuit of stations allows you to more easily adapt to MMI questions and scenarios.

- Communication skills will be assessed at each station, and the feedback you receive through practice will leave you better informed about your ability to speak articulately.

- Like other types of medical school admissions interviews, the MMI is a high stakes interview, and applicants will understandably by anxious. Practicing will help you handle the "nerves," and show you how to channel this energy to elevate your performance.

Admissions Officers Speak...

"Because you will be rotating through several different stations and because the MMI does not use the same questions you might experience during a traditional interview, we do not recommend that you attempt to rehearse answers ahead of time. Instead, we recommend you practice expressing yourself verbally to someone else to ensure that you can provide thorough, logical answers within a short time frame."[3]

New York University School of Medicine

"As with any human interaction, practice is helpful. It could identify nervous habits, and it may help you feel more comfortable and relaxed. Participate in a mock interview event through your school's career development office, have a friend ask questions and give you feedback, or use a webcam to record your own practice responses. All of these may help you find ways in which you might improve your interview performance."[4]

Michigan State University College of Human Medicine

"The strongest advice is to understand the basic structure, time limit, and number of stations. Listen carefully to any prompts directed to you."[5]

Duke University School of Medicine

"The purpose of the MMI is not to test your scientific or clinical knowledge. However, you may find it helpful to be familiar with current events and policies in health care."[6]

University of Arizona College of Medicine

"Your time is best spent learning how to discuss you thoughts and ideas in a brief timeframe so you can provide the most logical and thorough answers at each station. Recording your answers can help you improve your performance."[1]

University of Nevada School of Medicine

BASICS OF PREPARATION

Rule # 22   **Become knowledgeable about current events, ethical issues, and social policies.**

"We recognized that our biggest problem is not in evaluating the cognitive domain - it's not about knowledge," says Dr. Jack Rosenfeld, Professor Emeritus of Pathology and Molecular Medicine and Co-Creator of the MMI. "It's the interpersonal domain: the way of dealing with people. It's about ethics and it's about judgment."[7] You will hear that MMI stations are not designed to be a test of your scientific or pre-existing medical knowledge, and that is true. However, some stations have a medical aspect, often dealing with current events, ethical issues, or social policies. Ethical issues are particularly common.

What are your thoughts about the role of the pharmaceutical industry in medical practice? How would you handle a case of witnessed medical negligence by a colleague? Have you thought about the ethics of end-of-life care?

You need to.

You must be prepared to respond to ethical dilemmas during an interview. In an analysis of interviewee experiences, researchers found that approximately 10% of interview questions focused on resolving an ethical dilemma. The authors wrote that "admissions committees and faculty physicians deem it important to query prospective students about ethical issues."[8]

"Controversial and ethical topics have become somewhat standard among medical school interviews. They are worth researching in advance, and thus a word to the wise is: DO YOUR HOMEWORK."[9]

> Dr. Norma Wagoner
> Former Dean of Students
> University of Chicago Pritzker School of Medicine

Interviewers may present you with a difficult scenario, and ask how you would resolve it. You're more likely to respond well if you have a basic understanding of the issues surrounding the dilemma. You'll need to become well read on common controversies in medicine.

Since it's not possible to prepare for every possible scenario, we recommend that when you're faced with questions about a difficult and complex ethical situation you:

- Pause to gather your thoughts. What do you know of the situation based on your experiences and reading?

- Ask for clarification or further information, if needed.

- Share your knowledge of the topic with the interviewer.

- Discuss, out loud, the steps you would take to resolve the situation so the interviewer can assess your analytical and reasoning skills.

- Provide an answer or present options, and explain your rationale.

You won't simply be judged on the content of your answer. Questions about ethical scenarios are used to assess your poise under stress. Interviewers also assess your ability to "think on your feet," and they'll evaluate your approach to a difficult situation. Do you ask for more information if you feel that something is missing? Are you open to seeking input from others?

You should avoid being "quick to judge, quick to respond without gathering data, or imposing your opinion on the patient when your opinions differ," writes Dr. Carol Teitz, Associate Dean for Admissions at the University of Washington School of Medicine. Dr. Teitz finds it acceptable to say, "I don't know," but this should be followed with "Here's how I would go about making a decision."[10]

How will your response to an ethical issue be evaluated?

Interviewers will look to answer the following questions in assessing your response:

- Did the interviewee identify the specific ethical issues or problems?

- Was the interviewee able to analyze the issues?

- What was the strength of the argument?

- Did the interviewee consider other viewpoints or perspectives?

- How well did the interviewee express his ideas or thoughts?

- Was the applicant's viewpoint or recommendation suitable and reasonable?

BASICS OF PREPARATION

Common Ethical Dilemmas Asked of Medical School Applicants

- Doctor – patient relationship

  - Confidentiality
  - Informed consent
  - Patient rights
  - End-of-life decisions
  - Patient autonomy
  - Truth telling/disclosure

- Professionalism/professional misconduct

- Medical negligence/mistakes

- Relationship with pharmaceutical industry

- Issues related to reproductive health

- Issues related to treatment of HIV/AIDS

- Genetics/stem cell

- Issues related to treatment of mentally ill patients

- Performing procedures/tests not medically indicated for reasons for defensive medicine

- Disagreements between patients/families and physicians about treatment decisions

- Treatment with placebo

- Transplantation/organ donation

- Research ethics

- Abortion

- Physician-assisted suicide

- Physician impairment (alcohol, drugs, or illness)

- Conflicts of interest

- Health care rationing

- Introducing medical students as doctors

- Practicing procedures on anesthetized or dead patients

Rule # 23   Practice makes perfect.

Many applicants have a difficult time discussing issues logically and coherently. In the following box, we've presented some ways for you to improve your skills in this area. Our recommendations begin with becoming more knowledgeable about ethics, current events, social policies, and the health system. With knowledge in hand, you'll be ready to practice expressing your ideas about these issues with others. Your ability to form and verbalize your thoughts will improve. "Practice with someone you don't know, as that'll help you to get used to an interview situation and to role plays," says Kim Piper, Lecturer at Queen Mary University. "Any student who practices questions with an adult they don't know well will find it easier. Doing that can help to get rid of nerves."[11] Utilize the feedback you receive to make your presentations even better.

How should I prepare for the MMI?

- Read about ethics.
- Become well informed about the health system.
- Gather MMI questions and scenarios from the Internet, and practice delivering timed presentations to a partner or friend.
- Pay close attention to the news, and practice debating issues with family and friends.
- Read the Op-Ed section of the newspaper to understand how an argument or persuasive piece is presented.
- Learn from the opinions and viewpoints of others.
- Encourage others to present to you a topic, and then deliver an impromptu discussion.
- Consider taking a public speaking class.
- Join Toastmasters.
- Attend MMI sessions conducted by your premedical advising office.
- View videos of MMI encounters developed by medical schools. These videos are available at school websites and YouTube.
- Record yourself answering questions to assess your verbal and nonverbal communication.

BASICS OF PREPARATION

Rule # 24   <mark>Respect the power of voice.</mark>

You've reviewed the school's mission statement and philosophy. You feel confident about your attire. Your mock interviewer was impressed with the quality of your handshake. You've prepared exhaustively for ethical questions. What have you overlooked? Chances are you haven't given any thought to your voice.

As an exercise, listen to the speaking voices of others in public, particularly people whom you've never met. You'll find that you quickly draw impressions of people based on the quality, volume, pitch, and pace of their speaking voice. In the MMI process where your encounter with the interviewer will last no longer than 8 minutes, your voice will have considerable impact on the way in which you are perceived. You can say all the right things but if your voice is not consistent with your message, you'll fail to inspire confidence in the interviewer. As far as voice is concerned, here's what I commonly encounter in mock interviews:

- Weak or timid voice

    Your goal is to project your voice strongly. Unfortunately, the high stakes setting of the interview can easily make your voice sound weak.

- Speaking too loudly

    This tends to be less common in my experience but could communicate an overbearing or aggressive nature.

- Speaking too fast

    Nervousness and concern about running out of time can cause applicants to speak too quickly. The end result is stumbling over words.

- Trailing off at the end of a response

- Pronouncing statements as if they were questions ("uptalk")

    Uptalk occurs when speakers end their sentences with rising inflection, making it seem as if the statement is a question. Believed to have originated in the Valley Girl culture of California, it was popularized in the movie *Clueless*. Although more common in women, it's not at all unusual in men. In an interesting study, contestants on the game show *Jeopardy!* used uptalk 37% of the time.[12] Unfortunately, in interview settings, uptalk has been found to be detrimental.

- Vocal fry

  Vocal fry is different than uptalk, and refers to a low-pitched, creaky-sounding speech infection. You can easily find examples of vocal fry on YouTube. It's become a common type of speech, and research indicates that women who demonstrate vocal fry come across less competent.

Did you know...

How important is the sound of your voice? In an analysis of speeches delivered by 120 executives, researchers at Quantified Impressions determined that the sound of a speaker's voice accounted for 23% of listeners' evaluations. Of note, it was rated more important than the content of the message (11%). "We are hard-wired to judge people," says Lynda Stucky, president of ClearlySpeaking. "You hear somebody speak, and the first thing you do is to form an opinion about them."[13]

If you're like most people, you've probably never received any feedback on your voice. In your interview preparation, seek opinions about your voice quality from others. An especially effective but underutilized technique is to videotape your mock interview so that you can hear what you sound like. Was your voice rough or weak? Were you speaking too fast? Don't fret if you discover any problems. Knowing about problems in advance of your interview will allow you to take the steps needed to convey calmness and strength through your voice. Although many applicants assume that nothing can be done to change voice quality, that's not at all true. You can strengthen or improve your voice with coaching.

Did you know...

It can be hard for many applicants to avoid fillers, such as "uh" and "um." With practice, however, you can replace these fillers with brief pauses. Take several seconds to gather your thoughts before you continue. Initially, this pause may seem like an eternity but it won't be perceived as such by the interviewer. Effective utilization of pauses shows confidence and adds variety.

BASICS OF PREPARATION

UNDERSTAND WHAT THE INTERVIEWER IS SEEKING

Rest assured that your interviewer does not expect you to be well versed in the nuances of healthcare reform. With that being the case, what is the purpose of these questions?

"This interaction tells the interviewers that the candidate has some awareness of the wider world and that she or he is cognizant of the changes in the health care system that may have complex implications for practitioners," writes Dr. Carol Elam, Associate Dean for Admissions at the University of Kentucky College of Medicine. "Neither is the applicant expected to have extensive knowledge of the subject. Rather, this discussion gives the interviewer a chance to see that the candidate, in preparing for a career in medicine, is aware of the issues confronting the profession."[21]

With the changes that are occurring in our health care system, schools seek to identify students who have an interest in finding solutions to our nation's health care problems. "Just as we learn to diagnose diseases and develop treatment plans for individual patients, we must also learn to diagnose and treat problems in the systems," writes Dr. Paul Rockey, former Associate Dean for Clinical Affairs at the Southern Illinois University School of Medicine. "Too often our profession has left this task to administrators, regulators, and insurers. Medical care doesn't end when we leave the patient's bedside or exit the examining room."[22]

BECOME WELL INFORMED OF HEALTHCARE ISSUES

If you're feeling unprepared to handle these questions, take comfort in knowing that others feel the same. University of Michigan researchers surveyed more than 58,000 graduating U.S. medical students from 2003 – 2007. Nearly half of the students felt inadequately prepared in understanding the health care system, health economics, managed care, or managing a practice.[23] In another survey of over 800 medical students in Minnesota, researchers sought to determine knowledge of the 2010 Affordable Care Act. Less than half reported understanding the law's basic components.[24] To increase knowledge of health care issues, schools have incorporated coursework into their curricula. "Ten or 15 years ago, most schools did not have anything involving health care policy," said Dr. Matthew Mintz, Associate Professor of Medicine at George Washington University in an interview with Slate. "Medicine was medicine and policy was policy and why would doctors want to learn anything about policy?"[25] Today, most medical schools include health policy, business and/or delivery teaching along with traditional subjects like anatomy and pathology.

Medical students have also taken the initiative to develop resources to enhance understanding of complex issues in the health care system. One such text is the *Health Care Handbook* written by Elisabeth Askin and Nathan Moore, students at the Washington University School of Medicine. "We wanted to write a book that would be like giving people little floaties to help them learn to swim through the vast and confusing ocean that is health care," said Elisabeth in an interview with the *New York Times*.[26] Other recommended resources to help you become well informed include American Medical News, AMSA The New Physician, Virtual Mentor, KevinMD, and the New York Times Health Section.

With your interview invitation in hand, you are one step closer to your goal: medical school. Although developing an understanding of the health care system may seem daunting, now is the time to recognize current healthcare issues, identify gaps in your knowledge, and take steps to expand your understanding. It's well worth the effort.

Some Additional Tips On Handling Interview Questions About The Affordable Care Act

- Understand that the Affordable Care Act (ACA) may be an emotionally charged topic for interviewers. Physicians will have varying opinions about the ACA.
- Some physicians are strong proponents of the ACA while others are fierce opponents. A 2015 survey showed that 44% of physicians were opposed to the ACA prior to implementation. The percentage opposed rose to 58% one year after its implementation.[27]
- Therefore, you must be delicate in how you answer questions. Fortunately, you can provide an informed response without indicating a strong political preference. To do so, be sure to include both pros and cons in your answer.
- In the aforementioned survey, positives included increased access to care for patients, coverage for children under 26, reduced costs of end-of-life care, emphasis on preventive medicine, and no insurance denials for pre-existing conditions.
- Negatives included reduced reimbursement to physicians, increased patient debt due to high-deductible plans, and practice burdens related to administrative hassles.
- A particularly useful strategy is to become informed about how the ACA is being implemented in the state in which the medical school you will be visiting is located. You can then utilize this knowledge in your MMI answer.

References

[1] University of Nevada School of Medicine. Available at: http://medicine.nevada.edu/asa/admissions/applicants/selection-factors/applicant-interviews. Accessed May 8, 2015.
[2] University of Cincinnati College of Medicine. Available at: https://med.uc.edu/medicalstudentadmissions/apply/MMI. Accessed May 7, 2015.
[3] New York University School of Medicine. Available at: https://www.med.nyu.edu/school/md-admissions/mmi-faqs. Accessed May 4, 2015.
[4] Michigan State University College of Human Medicine. Available at: http://mdadmissions.msu.edu/applicants/mmi_faq.php. Accessed May 4, 2015.
[5] DukeMed. Available at: http://www.dukedavisoncouncil.org/?page_id=258. Accessed May 5, 2014.
[6] University of Arizona College of Medicine. Available at: http://medicine.arizona.edu/admissions/application-process/interviews. Accessed May 4, 2015.
[7] The Globe and Mail. Available at: http://www.theglobeandmail.com/life/interview-20-theres-no-easy-way-to-ace-this-one/article1344084/. Accessed May 7, 2015.
[8] Rippentrop A, Wong M, Altmaier E. A content analysis of interviewee reports of medical school admissions interviews. Available at: http://www.med-ed-online.org. Accessed May 5, 2015.
[9] Association of American Medical Colleges. Available at: https://www.aamc.org/students/aspiring/basics/284816/interview6.html. Accessed May 5, 2015.
[10] University of Washington School of Medicine. Available at: http://www.uwmedicine.org/education/Documents/md-program/TheInterview%2014.pdf. Accessed May 4, 2015.
[11] The Guardian. Available at: http://www.theguardian.com/education/2013/oct/07/interview-for-medical-school. Accessed May 4, 2015.
[12] Linneman T. Gender in *Jeopardy!* Intonation variation on a television game show. *Gender & Society* 2013; 27 (1): 82-105.
[13] The Wall Street Journal. Available at: http://www.wsj.com/articles/SB10001424127887323735604578440851083674898. Accessed May 5, 2015.
[14] Student Doctor Network. Available at: http://www.studentdoctor.net/2014/12/discussing-obamacare-in-your-med-school-interviews/. Accessed May 22, 2015.
[15] PreMedLife (September/October 2013). Available at: http://www.premedlife.com/feature-articles/how-to-nail-interview-questions-about-health-care-1459/. Accessed May 22, 2015.
[16] Dr. Gregory Polites (personal communication).
[17] University of Washington School of Medicine. Available at: http://www.uwmedicine.org/education/md-program/admissions/applicants/pages/interview.aspx. Accessed June 16, 2013.
[18] Florida State University College of Medicine. Available at: http://med.fsu.edu/?page=mdAdmissions.interview. Accessed June 17, 2013.
[19] Texas Tech University School of Medicine. Available at: http://www.ttuhsc.edu/som/admissions/umsi.aspx. Accessed June 17, 2013.
[20] Dr. Will Ross (personal communication).
[21] Elam C, Burke M, Wiggs J, Speck D. The medical school admission interview: perspectives on preparation. *NACADA Journal* 1998; 18 (2): 28 – 32.
[22] Rockey P, Winship M. Nurturing leaders for an environmental change. Available at: http://virtualmentor.ama-assn.org/2009/11/pfor1-0911.html. Accessed June 15, 2013.

[23] Patel M, Lypson M, Davis M. Medical student perceptions of education in health care systems. *Acad Med* 2009; 84 (9): 1301-6.
[24] Winkelman T, Antiel R, Davey C, Tilburt J, Song J. Medical students and the Affordable Care Act: uninformed and undecided. *Arch Intern Med* 2012; 172 (20): 1603-5.
[25] Beam C. Is our doctors learning? Why aren't medical students taught about health care policy? Available at: http://www.slate.com/articles/news_and_politics/prescriptions/2009/06/is_our_doctors_learning.html. Accessed June 15, 2013.
[26] Chen P. Two medical students navigate the health care maze. Available at: http://well.blogs.nytimes.com/2012/07/12/two-medical-students-navigate-the-health-care-maze/. Accessed June 17, 2013.
[27] LocumTenens.com Survey. Available at: http://www.prnewswire.com/news-releases/66-percent-of-physicians-feel-the-affordable-care-act-should-be-repealed-300044607.html. Accessed May 22, 2015.

Chapter 9

Question/Discussion Station Preparation

In this chapter, I'll present a question/discussion station approach that will significantly increase your chances of making a favorable impression on the interviewer. In later chapters, I'll address approaches for scenario- and task-based stations. I discussed the differences between these three types of MMI stations in Chapter 4.

Rule # 26   Set the stage for success by making the most of your first two minutes.

In the typical MMI format, you'll be presented with a question posted on the door. You'll typically have **two minutes** to read this information and gather your thoughts. An alarm will then ring, signaling that it's time for you to enter the room where you will respond to the question. These can be complex issues to address, and candidates often wonder if it's possible to deliver a cogent response in a time-limited manner. Without a doubt, you can, and making the most of these two minutes will set the stage for a successful encounter.

In these precious two minutes, I recommend that you begin by focusing on the topic. As obvious as this may seem, in my MMI mock interview sessions, I have seen how easy it is for applicants to squander this time by allowing the mind to wander or become overwhelmed with feelings of nervousness. Begin by determining the focus of the scenario or question. Is it an ethical scenario about confidentiality? Is it a scenario assessing your integrity or professionalism?

> **Did you know…**
>
> "I have been an interviewer during an MMI for a healthcare institution…the best thing I can tell you is *read the question and read it again*. Applicants occasionally came in to my room having not the faintest clue what the parameters were, and came prepared to follow some instructions in their head that were nothing like what they were supposed to be doing. That always left me underwhelmed."[1]

Rule # 27 — Define the structure of your response.

Once you've identified the topic, it's time to develop your plan or approach. By defining a structure to what you will say, you'll enter the room with a more organized approach. This will help prevent rambling, one of the most common mistakes interviewees make. The response you give at a question station should include an introduction, body, and conclusion. Think of it as a speech, granted an impromptu one. All good speeches have these three parts. I recommend that you:

- Lead with a compelling introduction.

- Select an appropriate approach for the body of your discussion.

    - Discuss 3-4 important points that come to mind about the topic.

    - Discuss the pros and cons of an issue, or talk about two sides of the issue.

    - State your point of view and give the reason that you feel this way, providing support for your views. Show that you've considered other points of view.

    - Think of the past, present, and future. There was a time when…but now we find that…in the future I expect…

    - Ask yourself who, what, when, where, why and how and focus on the response to those questions in your discussion.

    - Discuss how the topic affects you personally or how it affects the world in general.

- End with a strong conclusion.

Did you know…

On your notepad or card, quickly write down an introduction, two or three supporting points, and a conclusion, or use another approach as shown above. If you're not permitted to use notes, learn how to organize your thoughts in your mind.

Rule # 28   **Manners can make all difference.**

Not long ago, I came across an interesting discussion in an online patient forum. Although contributors to the discussion felt that doctors generally knocked before entering rooms, some were miffed by what sometimes happened next. Rather than waiting for permission to open the door, doctors sometimes just barged right in after knocking. For the busy physician trying desperately to stay on schedule, this breach in door-knocking etiquette may seem trivial. However, it's an important part of the first impression that we make on our patients, and can set the stage for a satisfying and positive physician-patient encounter. Some other reasons why patients appreciate this behavior:

- The patient may not have disrobed or fully changed into the gown.

- The patient may be anxious about the visit. A few seconds may allow the patient to regain composure.

- While waiting, the patient may have chosen to make a phone call or read a book. Waiting for permission to enter the room permits the patient to end a phone conversation or set aside a book.

"Basic etiquette-based communication makes a difference in patient outcomes, but it doesn't appear that these strategies are being used to the extent that they should be," says Dr. Leonard Feldman, Assistant Professor of Medicine at Johns Hopkins University School of Medicine. "These communication strategies matter to patients and are relatively easy to do."[2] As an aspiring physician, you can demonstrate proper etiquette in the MMI, starting with knocking on the door and waiting for permission to enter the room.

Did you know...

"I believe that medical education and postgraduate training should place more emphasis on this aspect of the doctor–patient relationship — what I would call 'etiquette-based medicine.' There have been many attempts to foster empathy, curiosity, and compassion in clinicians, but none that I know of to systematically teach good manners. The very notion of good manners may seem quaint or anachronistic, but it is at the heart of the mission of other service-related professions."[3]

Michael Kahn, M.D.

Rule # 29   Buy yourself some extra time if necessary

"At one MMI station, I got confused about the wording of the question and realized that I read the question wrong 20s after I started to reply. I stumbled around for a bit trying to sneak extended glances at the prompt, so I could figure out what the heck was going on in the scenario! The interviewer had to ask me clarify what I meant a couple of times. By the time I figured it out, time was just about up."[4]

- Medical School Applicant (Student Doctor Network)

If you find yourself struggling after the two minutes elapse, consider one of the following approaches assuming that the MMI process at the school permits it:

- Enter the room and ask for clarification if there is something you don't understand.

- Enter the room and ask if you can have a moment before you speak.

- Enter the room and look over the scenario or question again. Often, there will be a second copy of the instructions inside the room.

Although any one of the above approaches will cut into the time you have available to address the issue, the time you have bought may be just what is needed to help you gather your thoughts and regain your composure. This may be all that is required for your great answer to surface. Although this is an effective strategy, refrain from utilizing it too often since schools are assessing you on your ability to think on your feet.

Try not to start any discussion with "I'm really not good at this," "I don't know where to begin," or "I don't have a clue how to answer this." These are comments that I frequently encounter in mock interview situations, and you may be able to avoid saying something to this effect if you can buy yourself some additional time.

If you just don't have any experience or knowledge of the topic…

Think about your knowledge or experience in a similar area, and consider offering it instead.

Admit that you don't have the answer but then describe how you would solve the problem. "Although I don't know the answer to the question, I'd like to tell you how I would go about finding the answer…"

QUESTION/DISCUSSION STATION PREPARATION

Rule # 30   **Set the tone for the rest of the encounter.**

Never underestimate the power of the first impression. As soon as you enter the room, pause to introduce yourself unless you've been given instructions not to do so. Your appearance, attire, smile, posture, eye contact, and handshake are all components of the first impression. We generally make assumptions about the first impressions that we make on others, and it's rarely based on feedback. It's wise to practice the opening of an interview with a mock interviewer so that you develop an understanding of how you come across when you're meeting someone new. Do you walk with confidence? Are you standing tall? Do you have a nice, engaging smile? Are you making good eye contact?

Did you know…

When meeting someone for the first time, 93% of the first impression you make will be based on nonverbal communication (e.g., body language, attitude, demeanor, etc.). Only 7% of your first impression is based on what you say.

Body Language Tips Following The First Impression

What should I do with my hands?

Rest your hands in your lap. It's acceptable to clasp your hands together, but don't clasp them too tightly or make a fist. Avoid folding your arms across your chest. This can create an impression of rigidity, unapproachability, or even dishonesty. Do not cover your mouth or touch your face while you speak. Avoid touching your tie, tugging at your collar, or straightening your clothing. We also recommend that you not hold your pen in your hand. Many applicants end up fiddling or tapping with it.

How should I sit?

Posture can weigh heavily in how others perceive you. Maintain an alert, straight posture while you sit, stand, and walk. Leaning forward slightly while sitting demonstrates interest but don't lean on the table or desk. Applicants who slouch can appear lazy, unmotivated, or disinterested.

What should I do with my feet?

Keep your feet flat on the floor. You may cross your legs at your ankles. Do not rest your ankle on the opposite knee.

Rule # 31   ==Start with a strong introduction==

Starting with a strong introduction is not as hard as some applicants believe. If you are able to ==grasp the meaning or significance of the issue==, you can certainly craft a strong opening. You can build momentum for the rest of your response with a strong opening. In the event that you lose your train of thought during the discussion, you can ==return to what you've said in the opening to redirect yourself.== Consider the following MMI scenario:

> Mr. C, a 72-year old male with mild dementia, diabetes and elevated cholesterol, is admitted to the hospital with right leg pain and swelling following a long plane trip. The emergency medicine physician has made the diagnosis of deep vein thrombosis (DVT), a condition that poses considerable risk to the patient's health. The danger with this condition is that the blood clot that has formed within the veins in the patient's leg could travel to the blood vessels supplying the lungs, causing a potentially life-threatening condition termed pulmonary embolism (PE). The treatment of DVT is the blood thinner heparin. Despite the best efforts of the medical team, the patient is steadfast in his refusal to start heparin or any other blood thinner. He simply states, "If my time has come, then I'm ready to accept it." Unwilling to accept the patient's decision, the intern says, "We need to find a way to force this patient to take this medication." Discuss the ethical issues involved.

A particularly effective technique is to ==enter the room and summarize the question, issue, or scenario in your own words:==

> *In this particular case, the patient has been diagnosed with a serious condition. He has been found to have a blood clot. If it travels to the lungs, he could become seriously ill or even die. The treatment for the clot is a blood thinner but the patient refuses to take the medication despite the pleas of the medical team. This has frustrated the intern, and he wants to find a way to make the patient take the medication. Do you feel that I have a good understanding of the situation?*

==Beginning with a summary of the issue is similar to what physicians do during patient encounters.== After we take a history, we will often ==check the accuracy of what we've heard== by offering ==the patient a summary== and an opportunity to correct any errors in our history taking. "Let me see if I have this right...Your symptoms started...You first noticed..." You can do the same during the MMI, and it will be viewed favorably.

After checking in with the interviewer to verify your understanding of the issue or question, continue with your introduction.

> *The issues here have to do with the patient's decision-making capacity and the physician's desire to act in the best interests of the patient. The scenario raises some important questions. Does this patient have the capacity to make decisions about his health care? How should a physician who clearly disagrees with the patient's decision handle such a situation? Should a patient ever be forced to take a medication? I'll discuss these ethical issues in more detail.*

QUESTION/DISCUSSION STATION PREPARATION

Rule # 32 <mark>Use clear transitions between your points.</mark>

Your interviewer will do his or her best to follow what you're saying. You will undoubtedly have a number of points to make, and it's important that your interviewer stays with you. Every time you make a new point or change ideas, use transitions. The use of transition words tells your interviewer that you're moving from one point to another or when you're emphasizing something. Without transitions, your discussion can easily become choppy, or appear unorganized. Here are some examples of transitions:

- Now that I've discussed the importance of confidentiality, I'd like to move on to...
- The second point I'd like to make...
- We've look at [point # 1] but now let's move on to [point # 2]
- Finally...

I recommend that you use transitions between the introduction and first point, between each point, and before the conclusion. In the following table, you will find specific words and phrases you can use to make transitions.

Transition Words or Phrases To Help Your Interviewer Understand Your Message	
Situation	**Transition words or phrases**
If you need to elaborate on a point or idea	Furthermore In addition Also Moreover
If you need to transition between similar points or ideas	Likewise Similarly
If you need to transition between contrasting points or ideas	On the other hand However Conversely
If you want to show cause-effect relationship	As a result Consequently Therefore
If you want to provide an example for support	For example As an example To illustrate this
If you want to transition from the body of your discussion to the conclusion	In summary In conclusion

Rule # 33 ==Don't feel compelled to use all 8 minutes.==

There's a belief among some applicants that points will be deducted from the interview score if the candidate does not speak for the allotted time. That's not at all true. Remember that schools are looking for evidence of the following in your responses:

- Can you ==apply your general knowledge to a variety of iss==ues?
- Are you able to ==think on your fee==t?
- Can you ==communicate your ideas in an articulate manner==?
- Can you ==adopt a position== or viewpoint?
- Can you ==defend your position or ideas clearly==?

So long as you demonstrate the above, you will have successfully delivered a winning response regardless of whether you speak for 5 minutes or 8 minutes. Finishing your answer before the alarm bell rings also allows the interviewer to ask you follow-up questions. In the event that your original answer was lacking in some respect, the follow-up question may allow you to bring forth important information that elevates your final interview score. If you speak for the entire time, it's possible to rob yourself of this potentially important opportunity.

Did you know…

Many interviewees have difficulty effectively addressing the issue in the allotted time. You will not be permitted to complete your answer once the bell rings. To avoid running out of time, practice making presentations in a timed manner. Note that interview rooms may not have clocks. Although you may choose to wear a watch, I've seen many applicants repeatedly check time remaining on their watch. This can affect the rapport you establish with the interviewer, and, of course, your final interview score.

Admissions Officers Speak…

"Just say what you have to say. If it takes the whole time, fine, but I will probably get bored interviewing you. Once you've said your piece, I'll ask follow up questions. The worst thing you can do is make a strong argument, then weaken it by rambling nervously trying to take up time."[4]

MMI Interviewer (Student Doctor Network)

QUESTION/DISCUSSION STATION PREPARATION 83

EFFECTIVELY MANAGING TIME AT A QUESTION-BASED STATION (8-MINUTE ENCOUNTER)

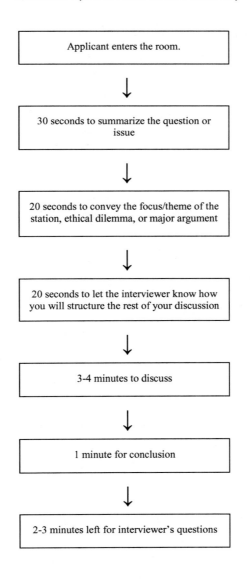

Rule # 34   Leave a lasting impression.

The most common reason for a lackluster ending is poor time management. Poor pacing often finds applicants in the middle of a sentence when the bell rings. At most MMI interviews, you will be given a warning that the interview is drawing to a close. Conclude by:

- Reviewing or reinforcing the key points or ideas you have discussed.

- Finishing with a strong sentence that links back to your introduction.

- If the question calls for it, you should have already taken a position on the issue. Restate your opinion or point of view in the conclusion.

When the interviewer has no further questions or the bell rings, you have come to the end of the interview. Let the interviewer know that you enjoyed meeting him, and thank him for his time.

Did you know...

Applicants who end their response before time runs out may be asked follow-up questions. If no follow-up questions are asked, consider what you have said so far. Is there an additional point you would like to make? Do you feel that you can elaborate on a point that you made earlier? If so, you can always say, "I was just thinking about a point I made earlier, and I realized that there's something I'd like to add. Is it okay if I bring it up now?" If you have nothing else to say, embrace the silence. Remember that there is nothing wrong with silence, and this time can be used to mentally prepare for the next station.

While going through this thought process, remember that you are being observed. Whatever you do, do not let your guard down in the remaining time that you have. There have been situations where candidates have said or done something inappropriate while making small talk. Do not feel the need to initiate small talk but do politely engage in it if the interviewer wishes to do so. Keep whatever you say 100% positive. Remember that the evaluation form has a comments section, and anything you say or do that is viewed as concerning will be documented. Points may be deducted from your overall score, and applicants can even be removed from consideration.

Did you know...

Earlier we discussed the importance of making a good first impression. You also need to leave the interviewer with a good lasting impression. You can do so by telling the interviewer you were glad to meet her. Thank her for this opportunity to meet, and for considering you for one of their positions. Leave with a smile, direct eye contact, and a firm handshake if the interviewer extends her hand to you.

QUESTION/DISCUSSION STATION PREPARATION

Rule # 35   You would like to know how well you're doing in the interview. Pay close attention to the nonverbal cues of the interviewer but recognize that there are pitfalls in this approach.

The interviewer's body language may be your only clue as to how well you're doing. Most interviewers won't interrupt you to tell you that you're rambling. They won't tell you that your last response came across as very defensive. Better than words, their posture, movements, facial expressions, and tone of voice can indicate their reactions.

However, you should realize that MMI interviewers are instructed to give no feedback whatsoever to interviewees. Some take these instructions very seriously, and purposely stifle their nonverbal communication. They may sit rigidly in their chairs and never crack a smile. If you sense that you're losing your interviewer, try to reconnect but if your efforts don't succeed, don't get flustered. In mock interview sessions, I always tell applicants to not put too much stock on the interviewer's look and demeanor. Of course, it's human nature for us to take notice of such things but, in an MMI, you can't be sure that the interviewer's body language is a true reflection of what he or she thinks about you.

Interviewers are also asked to challenge applicants and, at times, may come across more aggressive than you would expect or like. Rest assured that they're treating all applicants in the same manner. The work of a physician is fraught with challenges and frustrations, and how you handle difficult situations in the interview setting may give the school an idea of your poise under pressure.

Medical Students Speak...

"One other thing - I thought two of my MMI interview days went HORRIBLY and I got into both of the schools. You really can't tell how you're doing, so just try to relax and have fun."

"My experiences have definitely been a lot closer to this where my raters are stone-faced and often look disinterested in what I'm saying which throws me off as I try to re-engage their interest."

"Finally, keep in mind that some interviewers may be less engaging or responsive than others. Assume that they are doing this on purpose and are trying to see how you react under stress etc. Don't let them mess with your head."[4]

Medical School Applicants (Student Doctor Network)

References

[1] AskMetaFilter. Available at: http://ask.metafilter.com/257166/Help-me-prepare-for-a-Multiple-Mini-Interview. Accessed May 5, 2015.
[2] Physicians Weekly. Available at: http://www.physiciansweekly.com/medical-training-etiquette/. Accessed May 5, 2015.
[3] Kahn M. Etiquette-based medicine. *NEJM* 2008; 358 (19): 1988-9.
[4] Student Doctor Network. Available at: http://www.studentdoctor.net/. Accessed May 4, 2015.

Chapter 10

Scenario/Acting Station Preparation

Rule # 36 Understand what you're likely to encounter at scenario-based stations.

At a scenario-based station, you will be presented with a difficult or challenging situation to address, navigate, or resolve. What makes this type of station even more challenging is that you will have to address the scenario by engaging in dialogue with an actor waiting for you in the room. Your interaction with the actor will be evaluated by a rater (interviewer). The following is an example of a scenario station:[1]

The parking garage at your place of work has assigned parking spots. On leaving your spot, you are observed by the garage attendant as you back into a neighboring car, knocking out its left front headlight and denting the left front fender. The garage attendant gives you the name and office number of the owner of the neighboring car, telling you that she is calling ahead to the car owner, Tim. The garage attendant tells you that Tim is expecting your visit. Enter Tim's office. Tim will be played by an actor.

Common scenarios that candidates may encounter include:

- Breaking bad news to another person
- Managing a conflict situation
- Taking responsibility for an error
- Comforting a friend, colleague, or family member in distress
- Dealing with someone who is upset

Success Tip

Reflect on your life experiences, and recall situations when you had to break bad news, take responsibility for a mistake, comfort a friend, or pacify an angry person. What did you find to be effective in those situations? What are some things that didn't work?

Rule # 37 — Empathy is important in the physician-patient relationship. Find ways to show empathy in the MMI.

Consider the following exchange between patient and doctor:

Patient: "I have to tell you I'm in bad shape. Last few days, my knees have hurt me so much. I can hardly make it out of the house. The pain is killing me. I can't get any sleep."

Doctor: "Okay, when did it start?"

Patient: "It's been going on for some time but the last few days have been something else. If I don't get this fixed, I don't know what I'm going to do. You know how my job is. I got to be on my feet all day. If I can't work, I'm going to be in trouble."

Doctor: "I see. Does it hurt all the time?"

Patient: "It won't stop hurting. I can't even play with my grandson. It rips me apart when I tell him I can't throw the football around like we used to."

Doctor: "Have you tried taking anything for it?"

As you read the above exchange, did you feel that something was lacking in the doctor's response? The patient was sharing his concerns but the doctor seemed fixated on only gathering information. There was no acknowledgment of the patient's worries or emotions, nothing to suggest that the doctor understood the patient's concerns. Research indicates that patients are more satisfied with care when they feel a strong emotional connection with their physician. Patients are also more likely to follow through on physicians' advice and have better outcomes when their physicians demonstrate empathy.

Given the importance of empathy in the physician-patient relationship, medical schools often assess for empathy in the MMI through the use of scenario-based stations. Failure to show empathy during scenario-based stations can easily remove an applicant from further consideration. These scenarios will test your ability to remain empathetic with actors who display strong emotions. In such situations, some applicants may become frustrated, and demonstrate unsuitable behavior. "At one of my stations, when the actress kept crying and I could not think of anything else to say, I tapped my laps and said to her "STOP CRYING!"[2]

SCENARIO/ACTING STATION PREPARATION

Medical Students Speak...

"I had a hypothetical comfort situation in my MMI...kept changing the story to keep the conversation going into a tricky direction. Basically, every time I did/said the right thing, they moved it into a direction to try to trick me into saying something thoughtless."[2]

Breaking Bad News Scenario: Tips and Recommendations

- Use the two minutes you have before you enter the room to think about your general approach.

- As you process the information, ask yourself whether the person is or isn't expecting bad news.

- If the person is expecting bad news, begin your conversation by finding out how much he or she already knows. This will allow you to assess how much the person understands, and his or her emotional state.

- Prepare the person for the bad news with an appropriate phrase.

    - "I have some sad news to share with you."
    - "There's no easy way to say this but..."
    - "I just received a call from..."

- Come right to the point. This is not the time for small talk or speaking in a roundabout manner.

- Always look the person right in the eye.

- Be gentle in your approach.

- Avoid rigidity in your approach. Show flexibility and adaptability as you respond to the actor's cues.

- Give an account of what has happened so that the person understands.

- Expect to encounter emotions. These may include anger, shock, disbelief, sadness, or distress. As emotions arise, react appropriately to them. Acknowledge and address these emotions. "I can see that you're really upset about this."

- If they respond with intense emotions, such as anger, remain calm. If they cry, be there to comfort them.

- If the recipient remains silent, don't feel compelled to fill up the silence. While letting the news sink in, simply sit with them in a sympathetic manner.

- Decide the next action step when the time is right.

Managing Conflict Scenario: Tips and Recommendations

- Use the two minutes you have before you enter the room to think about your general approach. In any conflict situation, remember that your goal is not to win but rather find a solution that is satisfying to both parties.

If it's your fault…

- If it's an obvious issue where you have erred, then you have to acknowledge your error and apologize.
- In your apology, let the other person know that you understand the problems that have resulted from your words or actions.
- Do not make excuses or offer explanations. Simply take full responsibility for your error and inform the other party of your intent to resolve the situation.
- If you are not sure how to rectify the situation, consider several options, present them, and come to some agreement on which is best.

If it's not clear where the fault lays or if both parties share blame…

- Start by informing the person of why you wish to speak, the issue at hand, and how you feel. Phrase feelings with "I" rather than "You." "I feel ___ when you…" is better than "You make me ___ …"
- Listen carefully to the other person's perspective. Avoid interrupting. After hearing the person's point of view, restate it in your own words to make sure you understand both views.
- Conflict often arises from miscommunication, incorrect assumptions or incomplete information. For example, we may assign motives for someone's behavior based on incorrect assumptions.
- By listening carefully, you are better able to understand where the other person is coming from. Don't be afraid to ask questions to better understand the other person's perspective.
- As you discuss the situation, don't overreact. If the other person is angry, allow him to vent his anger.
- Even if you feel angry, remain poised and calm. Choose your words carefully, avoiding any language that may further inflame the situation.
- Propose some solutions, and invite the other party to do the same. Discuss these in more detail, and come to some compromise. If you're unable to find a solution, consider meeting again to continue the discussion.
- Remember that your goals are to resolve this conflict by finding a fair solution. If it's someone you must continue to work with, do what you can to preserve the relationship.

Dealing With An Upset Person: Tips and Recommendations

- Set the stage for the encounter. "Is it okay if I sit next to you? We can talk about what's happened, and the best way for me to help you."

- Begin by acknowledging how the person appears to you. "You seem to be very upset."

- Ask the person to tell you what happened, how they feel, and how you can best help.

- Allow the person to speak without interrupting.

- Make appropriate eye contact.

- Show that you are actively listening. "Uh-huh" and "Go on" invites the person to continue.

- Reflecting out loud what has been said shows that you have understood the person. "If I understand you correctly, you're really concerned that…"

- Use a calm voice.

- Don't offer false reassurances. Applicants sometimes have the tendency to say, "It is okay. Everything will be alright." The problem with this statement is that you don't know that for sure. Therefore, it's best to refrain from making such reassurances.

- "I know how you're feeling. I've been in the same situation." These words may seem empathetic to you but can be very irritating to the person. When people are acutely distressed, hearing that others have gone through similar situations doesn't feel comforting.

- Some applicants resort to humor to diffuse the emotional tension. There may be a role for humor later but right now the emphasis should be on acknowledging and respecting how the person is feeling and helping him handle it.

- Recognize that your approach should not be rigid. Show flexibility and adaptability as you respond to the actor's cues.

- Expect to encounter other emotions. These may include anger, shock, disbelief, sadness, or distress. As emotions arise, react appropriately to them. Don't get to a point where you can no longer accept the emotion.

- If they respond with intense emotions, such as anger, remain calm. If they cry, be there to comfort them. You may be tempted to give the person a hug but not everyone responds positively to touch in these situations. You may feel that touch shows genuine concern and willingness to help but some people will find it awkward or even uncomfortable.

- Decide the next action step but don't hurry it. Decision-making can be difficult for a distressed person.

Rule # 38 Avoid clichés.

In role playing scenarios with mock interviewees, I've come across a number of clichés and statements that may seem appropriate but could easily be taken the wrong way. I would urge you to avoid these statements.

Statements To Avoid In Scenario-Based Stations (Comfort/Bad News)	
Statement	Reasons To Avoid
You have to be strong now.	It's not helpful to tell someone who is grieving that they shouldn't grieve anymore. People have to express their grief before the healing process can begin.
I know exactly how you feel.	Even if you've suffered a loss, you can't know exactly how the person is feeling. Relating what they are going through to something you've experienced takes the focus off of them and places it onto you.
You need to put this behind you.	The grieving process can take varying amounts of time.
Everything happens for a reason.	After a loss, it's difficult for people to believe that what occurred is part of a grand plan.
He/she is in a better place now.	Many people believe that those who suffered before passing away are now in a better place. However, not everyone shares these beliefs.

Dos and Don'ts For Scenario-Based Stations	
Do…	Don't…
Acknowledge how the actor is feeling	Reveal your own discomfort with the situation
Validate the actor's experience	Tell the actor how you think he should feel or urge him to get over it
Be patient and allow the actor to speak	Fill up the silence, even if you're feeling uncomfortable or the actor's taking too long to respond.
Ask the actor questions	Admonish the actor for not getting over the emotion
Encourage the actor to take whatever time is necessary to deal with his feelings	Talk about how you felt when you were in a similar situation. The focus should be on what the actor is going through and how he feels.

SCENARIO/ACTING STATION PREPARATION

Rule # 39 **Ask for specific feedback following scenario-based station practice**

The following evaluation form can be used to provide valuable feedback about your scenario-based station performance during mock interviews.

Feedback Evaluation Form for Scenario-Based Station		
Statement	Yes	No
I greeted the actor warmly.		
I sat, leaned in, and adopted an open, receptive posture.		
I gave the actor my undivided attention.		
I listened to the actor without interruption.		
I encouraged the actor to share his feelings.		
I acknowledged the actor's feelings in an empathetic way.		
I validated or confirmed the legitimacy of the actor's feelings.		
I communicated empathy for the actor's feelings through my words.		
I showed empathy through my nonverbal behavior (e.g., nodding, looking concerned, etc.).		
I invited the actor to share his ideas and viewpoints (thoughts, worries, feelings, expectations) before making any suggestions.		
I was approachable, friendly, and respectful.		
I showed genuine concern for the actor.		
I sought to determine the next step or action based on partnership.		

Medical Students Speak…

"The first was an actor that played the part of a mentally disabled teen that needed me to teach him how to tie his shoelaces. It was pretty challenging especially because the actor's role was to get very frustrated and verbally upset during the process. I couldn't have prepared for this scenario at all other than remembering to stay calm, act with kindness, and do my best to keep 'teaching' him how to tie his shoes."[3]

References

[1] Eva K, Rosenfeld J, Reiter H, Norman G. An admissions OSCE: the multiple mini-interview. *Med Educ* 2004; 38 (3): 314-26.
[2] Student Doctor Network. Available at: http://www.studentdoctor.net/. Accessed May 4, 2015.
[3] Mindful of Medicine. Available at: http://mindfulofmedicine.com/2014/12/28/med-school-interviews-mmi/. Accessed June 3, 2105.

Chapter 11

Task/Collaboration Station Preparation

Rule # 40   **Task-based stations test your ability to stay poised under pressure while working as part of a team to complete a complex task.**

At a task-based station, you will be asked to complete a task, often with another applicant. The Stanford University School of Medicine offers the following description of a task station:[1]

> *Two applicants participate in a scenario in which one applicant is asked to perform a complex test (such as assembling or repairing a model) with the other applicant giving directions for dealing with or assembling the model.*

When you enter the room, there will be two raters, one of whom will be responsible for observing and rating your performance. The second rater will be tasked with evaluating the other applicant. Task stations are used to learn more about an applicant's teamwork, problem solving, and communication skills.

    The task will often be complex, difficult to complete within the time allotted, or even impossible. Emily Aaronson, a graduate of the McMaster University Michael G. DeGroote School of Medicine, recalls a particularly memorable task-based scenario she encountered. After entering the room, she found two chairs placed back to back. She was asked to sit in one while another person sat in the other. Both were given a piece of paper covered in small dots. "My partner's dots were numbered and mine were not," said Ms. Aaronson. "He had to talk me through how to connect the dots." Later, she discovered that the dots on each page were not identical. "My knee-jerk reaction was, 'Are you kidding me?'"[2] Faced with such a daunting task, applicants under pressure to complete the task in a time-limited manner may demonstrate behaviors and attitudes considered unsuitable in future physicians.

Rule # 41 **Prepare for the task-based station by delivering instructions to someone else.**

Now that you know the type of situation you may encounter in a task-based scenario, practice by performing similar tasks with a partner under the same conditions. Some examples include:

- Print out the instructions to build a paper airplane. Then arrange the furniture so that you and your partner are sitting back to back. Give your partner a blank piece of paper, and guide him through the process of making the paper airplane.

- A similar exercise can be done with origami. Origami instructions and designs are easily available on the Internet, and it's not necessary to have origami paper. Start with easy to make shapes but be sure to challenge yourself with harder designs.

- Use Lego models. Give instructions to your partner on how to build a Lego model. You can sit back to back, and your partner should not see the model. He will take direction from you.

If you're giving instructions…

- Inform your partner of the task ahead of you. "The point of this exercise is to build a paper airplane…" Check to make sure your partner understands the task.

- Set the stage for a positive encounter by encouraging your partner to ask for clarification or help whenever needed. "If anything I say is unclear, please tell me."

- Indicate that you will break down the task into a series of small steps.

- Before taking an action step, make sure your partner is holding the paper, model, or other prop the same way you are. In other words, identify the present position and orientation of the prop before providing the first set of instructions. Then do the same after each step is completed.

- If you sense that your partner is frustrated, offer words of encouragement and support. Show empathy. Remember to be nonthreatening if you must repeat instructions or correct a misstep. Be tactful and delicate when you point out a mistake.

- Encourage your partner to provide updates on his progress and when the step has been completed.

TASK/COLLABORATION STATION PREPARATION

Rule # 42   **Prepare for the task-based station by receiving and following through on instructions given by someone else.**

If you're receiving instructions in a task-based scenario, much of your success will hinge on your ability to listen carefully. Over a century ago, Sir William Osler uttered a dictum which is arguably his best-known saying. "Listen to your patient, he is telling you the diagnosis." Although these words continue to have as much meaning today as they did then, research indicates that physicians are lacking in their listening skills. "Studies show that the clinician's ability to explain, listen and empathize can have a profound effect on biological and functional health outcomes as well as patient satisfaction and experience of care," writes the Institute for Healthcare Communication. "Further, communication among healthcare team members influences the quality of working relationships, job satisfaction and has a profound impact on patient safety."[3]

If you're receiving instructions...

- Your partner will be giving you instructions periodically. Remember to let your partner speak without interruption.

- Offer facilitating remarks to indicate that you are listening. Examples include "Uh-huh" and "Go on."

- There may be times when your partner is silent. Perhaps she is thinking about the best way to explain something. Silence often feels uncomfortable, and it's common for people to fill it up with words. However, a good listener is comfortable with silence.

- After receiving instructions, provide a recap to your partner to ensure that you have correctly understood the instructions.

- If you sense that your partner is frustrated, show empathy. Offer words of encouragement and support.

- Remember to be nonthreatening if you must ask for the instructions to be repeated or clarified. If you have questions, ask your partner one question at a time.

- Provide your partner with updates on your progress and when the step has been completed.

Rule # 43 — Ask for specific feedback following task-based station practice

The following evaluation form can be used to provide valuable feedback about your task-based scenario performance during mock interviews.

Feedback Evaluation Form for Task-Based Station (Giving Instructions)		
Statement	Yes	No
I gave an overview of the task that we were expected to accomplish as a team.		
I encouraged my partner to ask for clarification or help if needed.		
I listened with an open mind to my partner's point of view.		
I acknowledged and appreciated my partner's efforts, and provided encouragement during the task.		
If my partner was frustrated or had an issue with me, I listened and carefully considered his point of view without becoming defensive.		
I kept an open mind to my partner's ideas even if he disagreed with me.		
I offered empathy during the encounter when needed.		
I acted as a positive role model for collaboration and teamwork.		

Feedback Evaluation Form for Task-Based Station (Receiving Instructions)		
Statement	Yes	No
I listened to my partner without interruption.		
I restated the instructions to make sure that I correctly understood my partner.		
I asked for clarification if needed in a gentle manner.		
If I had questions, I asked one question at a time.		
I acknowledged and appreciated my partner's efforts, and provided encouragement during the task.		
If my partner was frustrated or had an issue with me, I listened and carefully considered his point of view without becoming defensive.		
I offered empathy during the encounter when needed.		
I acted as a positive role model for collaboration and teamwork.		

Did you know…

As the founder of F Cancer, Yael Cohen deals with the emotions of cancer on a daily basis. She learns so much about her employees during times of hardship. "Everyone we hire works for free as an intern for a month first and I will give them tasks that are impossible on purpose just to see what happens. Do they lose their s---? Do they blame themselves? Do they take it out on someone else? You need to see what happens when they fail. As a team, we're going to fail. As individuals we're going to fail."[4] That's precisely what task-based MMI stations are designed to assess – your ability to remain poised at times of great stress.

References

[1] Stanford School of Medicine. Available at: http://deansnewsletter.stanford.edu/archive/11_08_10.html. Accessed May 4, 2015.

[2] The Globe and Mail. Available at: http://www.theglobeandmail.com/life/interview-20-theres-no-easy-way-to-ace-this-one/article1344084/. Accessed May 4, 2015.

[3] Institute for Healthcare Communication. Available at: http://healthcarecomm.org/about-us/impact-of-communication-in-healthcare/. Accessed May 3, 2015.

[4] 99U. Available at: http://99u.com/articles/7247/want-better-employees-give-them-an-impossible-task. Accessed May 22, 2015.

Chapter 12

MMI Scenarios

In this chapter, you will find MMI scenarios and questions which you can use in your preparation. Since most schools will allow you 2 minutes to read the case, gather your thoughts, and establish your approach, I recommend that you do the same with each case in this chapter. Then answer the question in the same length of time you will have for each station at the school where you will be interviewing.

If possible, practice with a partner. Consider recording your encounter. Together, you can review the interview, critique your performance, and use this information to make improvements in your verbal and nonverbal impressions.

For each case, we have developed a sample response with detailed analysis. The analysis focuses not only on content but also structure and organization. Below are some important points to consider as you work through these cases:

- Although you'll be most concerned about how to answer the question, don't minimize the importance of making a favorable first impression. Remember to knock on the door, and wait for permission before entering. Manners are important in medicine. Assuming your attire is impeccable, the first impression you make will largely be based on your posture, eye contact, smile, and handshake.
- You will undoubtedly be nervous at the start but most candidates are able to relax. Remember that one bad performance won't hurt you. However, if you're not able to move past the experience, it may affect your performance at other stations. Learn to let the past go.
- Compassion and empathy are important to all schools. If there is an opportunity to demonstrate these traits, by all means, do so.
- It's often preferable to end your answer several minutes before the encounter ends. This will allow the interviewer to ask you follow-up questions. Your answers to follow-up questions can yield extra points. Don't rob yourself of this important opportunity.

MMI SCENARIOS

- As you practice, you'll develop an approach or method that is most comfortable for you. We discussed possible approaches in Chapter 9.
- Don't be surprised to encounter MMI stations with medical scenarios. After all, you're interviewing for a career in the health professions. Remember that MMI stations are not designed to be a test of your scientific or pre-existing medical knowledge. However, some stations have a medical aspect, often dealing with current events, ethical issues, or social policies. Ethical issues are particularly common.
- You don't have to be an expert in medical ethics to make a favorable impression but it does help to have an understanding of important ethical dilemmas in medicine (see Chapter 8).
- You may also encounter a question about the health care system. Although you're not expected to be an expert, you should have a basic understanding of the system. See Chapter 8 for more information on what interviewers are looking for in your answers to these questions.
- Interviewees should expect to receive some traditional interview questions (Why do you want to be a doctor?). The number of MMI stations of this sort will vary from school to school.
- Don't let the attitude, look, or demeanor of the interviewer affect your performance. Interviewers are trained not to show emotion, give feedback, or divulge their thoughts.
- When the final bell rings, remember to smile again and thank the interviewer for his or her time.

Case # 1

While on a cruise, Mr. C developed flu-like symptoms. He felt too ill to go on a prepaid shore excursion. Upon returning home, he is informed by the travel company that the money spent for the excursion can only be refunded with a signed doctor's note. He asks his physician to write a note indicating that he was ill. How would you handle this situation if you were the physician?

Sample Answer

If I understand the situation correctly, the patient became ill while vacationing on a cruise ship. He had paid for a shore excursion. Because of his illness, he was unable to take part in the excursion, and now seeks a refund. The travel company has informed him that a refund can only be given if he has a signed doctor's note. He has asked his physician to write this note. Do you feel that I have a good understanding of the scenario?

Physicians are motivated to act in the best interests of their patients. Sometimes, they may be placed in positions in which they are called upon to deceive others. I would imagine that some situations would be more difficult to handle than others, especially if the patient stands to gain medical or social benefits. However, in this particular case, I believe that there are strong reasons not to write this note.

Lying and deception undermine social trust. If a physician lies, what reason would anyone have to believe him later? That's a real problem for physicians because the relationship between doctors, patients, and society depends on trust. Physicians have to routinely deal with third parties, and there is an expectation that the physician will be truthful.

In terms of how I would handle this situation if I were the physician, I would initially consider whether an important health benefit is at stake. In this case, health care isn't an issue. The patient wants a refund. Since it's not a medical issue, I don't think I have an obligation as a physician to help the patient.

Analysis

Note how the student provides a summary of the case. At the end, the interviewee asks if he has a solid grasp of the scenario. As physicians, we often do the same after we take a patient history. We check in with the patient to make sure we have an accurate understanding.

In the introduction, the student acknowledges the difficulty of the situation. Of note, he ends the introduction with a statement indicating his position. Now the interviewer will expect to hear the reasons why the interviewee feels this way.

Here the interviewee offers the reasoning behind the position he has taken.

Now the interviewee applies his thought process to the scenario, making sure to answer the question, "How would you handle this situation if you were the physician?"

MMI SCENARIOS

Before I present my position to the patient, I would first inquire about the patient's health. How is he feeling? Is he over the flu-like illness? How did the rest of the trip go?

The interviewee shows concern for the patient, an important quality to demonstrate during the MMI.

After doing so, I would explain to the patient why I'm unable to write the note. I would remind the patient that I have two ethical duties – to help him and be truthful. If I mislead the travel company, how would my patients trust me not to mislead them in other situations? I would also point out problems that will occur if the travel agency makes further inquiries. This has ramifications for both the doctor and the patient.

After showing concern, he explains the approach he would take with the patient.

However, I would help the patient find other solutions. If the patient had seen the ship's doctor, I would encourage him to contact the cruise line to obtain the proper documentation. If the patient had not visited the doctor, perhaps the ship can still provide documentation that would be accepted by the travel company. Maybe the patient could speak with a manager at the company who might be able to award him credit for future travel.

Recognizing that this is something important to the patient, the interviewee continues to show concern for the patient by exploring other options.

In summary, although it would be unethical for me to write a note for this patient, I would do whatever I could to help the patient find another solution.

The interviewee closes with the summary statement.

Case # 1: Key Points

- Patients seeking benefits frequently ask physicians to communicate with third parties. These parties include employers, schools, and insurance companies.
- At times, physicians may be tempted to deceive third parties in an effort to secure benefits for their patients.
- In one study, 39% of physicians reported one or more of the following tactics within the past year:
    - Exaggerating severity of patients' conditions
    - Changing billing diagnoses
    - Reporting signs or symptoms not present to secure patients coverage for needed care

---

To Deceive or Not Deceive...

Reasons for Deception

Deception is in the best interests of the patient (e.g., "I did it because I felt that it was unfair for the insurance plan to deny a test which was necessary.")

Benefits outweigh the harms

Reasons against Deception

Deception is problematic because it undermines social trust.

Harms outweigh benefits

Approach to Handling Deception Situations Involving Third Parties

Step 1: Is there a health benefit at stake? If so, how important is the benefit?

Step 2: Can the situation be resolved without deception?

Step 3: Consider other options carefully.

Step 4: Gently discuss the situation with the patient, including the consequences of deception for all parties involved, including patient, physician, and third party.

> **Similar MMI Scenarios**
>
> For the past month, a pediatrician has been evaluating a child for abdominal pain. Tests have been normal, and the cause of the abdominal pain is not yet clear. The parent calls the office asking for a note from the pediatrician. The child has not been able to participate in weekly swimming lessons because of the pain. The aquatics center will allow make-up classes if the parent is able to provide a doctor's note indicating that illness prevented the child from participating. Discuss how you would handle the situation if you were the pediatrician.
>
> One of your patients asks you for a disabled parking permit. He does not have a medical indication for a permit. It turns out that his mother is visiting him from China. She has severe arthritis, and finds it difficult to walk long distances. He is hoping that you will sign the permit application so that he can take trips to the store more easily with her. Discuss how you would handle the situation.

References

Wynia M, Cummins D, VanGeest J, Wilson I. Physician manipulation of reimbursement rules for patients: Between a rock and a hard place. *JAMA* 2000; 283: 1858-65.

MULTIPLE MINI INTERVIEW

Case # 2

Mr. J is a 62-year-old man who returns to his physician for a follow-up appointment. At the last appointment, he had reported upper abdominal pain and weight loss. Tests were ordered, and the results raised concern for possible cancer of the pancreas. The diagnosis can be established by needle biopsy. As the physician prepares to disclose the test results, the patient says, "The Missus and I are getting ready to take an Alaskan cruise. I sure hope that the news is good." The physician silently debates whether to delay this discussion until after the cruise. Should the physician inform the patient of his concerns about possible cancer?

Sample Answer

I can imagine that the patient and his wife have been really looking forward to this trip. From what I've heard, an Alaskan cruise is an amazing experience. I can see how the physician would be concerned that disclosing his fears about possible pancreatic cancer could affect the patient's travel plans, including cancellation of the trip. That said, I believe there are strong reasons for the physician to be truthful.

First, I believe that a physician has a strong moral duty to tell the truth since trust is at the heart of the doctor – patient relationship.

Second, the patient has to make some important decisions regarding diagnosis and treatment. He needs to know the truth so he can make informed decisions.

Third, if the physician conceals the truth, how will this affect their relationship moving forward? It seems as if the patient's life will change significantly, and it will be important for the patient to have confidence in the physician and their relationship.

Fourth, if physicians begin concealing the truth, then the public would lose faith in the medical profession. This could prevent people from seeking care when it's needed.

Finally, I would say that illness may not be convenient. The timing can never be predicted. Although the doctor may be uneasy about disclosing this information prior to the patient's cruise, there may never be a good time to have such a discussion.

Analysis

It is clear that the interviewee understands the physician's dilemma. He ends the introduction by taking a position. The interviewer will now expect to hear the reasons why the interviewee has chosen this position.

By using transition words ("First") between major points, the interviewee makes it easier for the interviewer to follow his line of reasoning.

In presenting your position, consider the consequences of your position with respect to all stakeholders. Here the interviewee addresses the potential impact on the public.

In summary, I would favor being truthful. This would allow both parties to discuss options for diagnosis and treatment. Although it may lead to a delay or even cancellation of the trip, it gives Mr. J an opportunity to make informed decisions.

Case # 2: Key Points

- Honesty in all professional interactions is recommended by major organizations, such as the American Medical Association and United Kingdom's General Medical Council.

- Under certain circumstances, however, some physicians believe that deceiving patients is morally acceptable.

- There are no guidelines available to help physicians determine when deception is morally acceptable.

To Deceive or Not Deceive…

Reasons Why Physicians Deceive Patients

Avoid physical or psychological harm to the patient
Maintain hope
Lessen stress or anxiety
Patient does not wish to know the information
Patient is unable to handle the information (emotionally or cognitively)
Temporary deception to avoid great distress

Reasons Why Physicians Should Not Deceive Patients

Violates physician code of ethics
Patient will lose trust in physician
Public will lose trust in physician and profession
Emotional distress caused by discovery of deception
Failure to respect or enhance patient's immediate autonomy
Initial deception may lead to further deception

Sokol D. Can deceiving patients be morally acceptable? *BMJ* 2007; 334 (7601): 984-6.

Case # 3

Near the end of a 24-hour shift, you realize that your fellow intern is in a state of distress. During rounds, the supervising physician asked her to begin a blood pressure medication on Mr. Smith. Several hours after writing the medication order, she realized that she wrote the order in the wrong patient chart. By the time she caught her mistake, the nursing staff had already administered the medication to Mr. Jones. After receiving the blood pressure medication, his blood pressure fell and IV fluids had to be given to normalize the blood pressure. After she tells you what happened, she urges you to not share this information with the supervising physician. Discuss how you would handle this situation.

Sample Answer

From what I gather, this is a case involving an intern who has made a medical error. His intent was to treat a patient with a blood pressure medication. Unfortunately, the wrong patient was given the medication, and he suffered a drop in his blood pressure. Fortunately, the blood pressure improved with fluids. After making this mistake, the intern is understandably upset. She is urging me not to share this information with our superior. Do you feel that I have a good understanding of the situation?

Seeing how distressed she is, I would begin by offering her emotional support. I'd let her express her feelings for as long as she needs to, and acknowledge how she's feeling. When it's appropriate, I would tell her that we all make errors. I might even share with her some of my own errors so that she realizes that he isn't alone. I would hope that through this conversation she would realize that it can be difficult to admit fault but it shows that we are responsible and caring physicians.

After offering her my support, I would ask her why she doesn't want to discuss this with the supervising physician. She may be concerned about her grade. Perhaps she really needs a recommendation from our supervising physician. There may also be concerns about what impact this mistake may have on her future job prospects. She may be fearful that our attending physician would be harsh and judgmental rather than supportive. I would remind her that our attending physician is ethically and legally responsible for our patient's care. If we don't tell him what happened, he can't do

Analysis

By providing a summary of the case, the interviewee demonstrates an understanding of the situation. He invites the interviewer to correct any misunderstandings on his part. This is an effective way to make sure you're headed in the right direction.

The discussion continues with an emphasis on the intern's emotional well-being. It's clear that the interviewee is showing empathy. Empathy is defined as the ability to imagine what it's like to be in another person's situation.

He tries to place himself in the intern's shoes, and comes up with a number of reasons for the intern's reluctance to share the error. The interviewee recognizes that the intern has an ethical duty to inform the supervising physician of the error. He knows that the patient should come first.

his job properly and that has the potential to impact the patient's care.

Plus, there's a good chance he's going to learn about it. If he does, it will be a lot worse than if we bring it up. It's one thing to make an error. It's a very different thing to hide it. If we do hide it, it'll raise questions about our reliability, trustworthiness and character.

> Failing to disclose the error has consequences that extend beyond patient care.

I would also say that disclosing the error to our attending physician allows for a discussion about the reasons why the error took place. From this, we can learn how to perform better as individuals and also identify ways to avoid such errors in the future.

> The interviewee raises a very important point about learning from errors.

In conclusion, I believe that it is important for my fellow intern to inform our supervising physician of this error in patient care.

Case # 3: Key Points

- When a physician colleague makes a patient care error, there should be concern for both the patient and physician.
- Although physicians have a professional duty to address errors with colleagues, research indicates that this often does not occur.
- Begin such conversations in a gentle and non-confrontational manner. "I was hoping to talk with you about Mr. Smith's care. There's something that I'm concerned about. Do you have time to talk about it?"
- Remember to be emotionally supportive. This is undoubtedly an emotional time, and your support can help set the tone for the ensuing conversation.
- Try to delicately uncover professional or personal (high stress, depression, relationship issues, family issues, substance abuse) factors that may have led to the error.
- Explore ways to prevent such errors in the future, and discuss the importance of disclosure to superiors and patients.

How Do Residents Respond To Mistakes Made In Patient Care?

In a survey of over 250 internal medicine residents, researchers asked participants about major mistakes made in medical care, and how they responded to these errors:

- The mistake was discussed with the supervising attending physician in only 54% of cases.
- Residents discussed the mistake with the patient or patient's family in only 24% of cases.
- 5% of residents reported not telling anyone about the error.
- Making an error in patient care was emotionally distressing for residents.
- 81% of residents reported feeling remorseful.
- 72% of residents reported feeling guilty.
- 60% of residents reported feelings of inadequacy.
- 79% of residents reported feeling angry.

Wu A, Folkman S, McPhee S, Lo B. Do house officers learn from their mistakes? *Qual Saf Health Care* 2003; 12: 221-8.

Case # 4

At a party, you're surprised to see one of your physician partners. He is on call but is at the party with a glass of wine in hand. As the evening progresses, your colleague continues to drink and it's clear that he is now tipsy. Having taken call before for your group, you know how busy it can be, and you worry about your colleague's ability to provide care to patients in this state. How would you handle this situation?

Sample Answer

My biggest concern would be the danger my impaired colleague presents to our group's patients. I would also be concerned about what's going in my colleague's life and his overall mental state. Drinking on call is obviously not the best choice, and raises concerns about his emotional well-being. This is a very difficult situation with the potential to impact the lives of our patients, my colleague, and, of course, myself.

Before I took any action, I would need to be sure that patients are at risk. Although it appears that he is under the effects of alcohol, I would need to confirm this. There's a lot at stake here – the health of our patients, and his reputation, livelihood, and privacy, my relationship with him, and what others might think.

I'd also worry about the repercussions of my actions as it relates to my own career. If I pursue this, there is a possibility that I may damage my relationship with him. The partners in the group may be forced to take sides, and some may be very disapproving of the choices that I make. I could be accused of having my own agenda, and this could all affect my career.

Although my actions could threaten my own career, nothing would trump the dangers to patient care that this situation presents. I would have a duty to prevent harm and protect patients from impaired colleagues. There may also be legal precedents requiring me to report my impaired colleague.

I could also see that intervening now in my colleague's health might allow him to fix

Analysis

The interviewee shows concern for the safety of her group's patients. She also expresses concern for her colleague. She recognizes that her actions or inactions could have a significant impact on all parties involved.

Since so much is at stake, she takes a cautious approach.

She considers the potential harm to her own career.

Although the situation poses risk for her professional career, she indicates that she will place patients above everything else.

things before it got even worse. He may not see it that way of course.

In terms of how I would handle the situation, I would take immediate action. I would urge the colleague to have me or one of my partners take call for him. If he doesn't agree, I would notify our chief medical officer or partners to arrange for someone else to cover him. I would ask our office to review any calls that he received from patients to make sure that no harm will come to them from his actions.

She now addresses the key question, "How would you handle this situation?" Again her position shows that patients come first.

After preventing immediate harm, I would talk with my colleague. I would encourage him to seek help. If he agrees and follows through, then I would support him. If not, I would have to contact the chief of service and seek guidance on how to proceed. Perhaps there is a program in the hospital to help physicians struggling with these issues.

She continues to show concern for her partner's emotional well-being and expresses the desire to help him. She's even willing to take it a step further if he does not agree to seek assistance. Research indicates that a significant percentage of doctors feel unprepared to report or deal with an impaired colleague.

The bottom line is that I would do whatever is necessary to ensure that our patients received the best possible care.

Case # 4: Key Points

- Impairment may occur because of a physical, mental, or substance-related disorder. The end result is interference with the physician's ability to deliver safe patient care.
- A physician who is concerned about an impaired colleague has an ethical and legal responsibility to address the issues. Failure to do so puts the safety of patients at risk.
- Once impairment is recognized, meet with the physician to offer support and share concerns. This conversation should not become a personal attack or confrontation. Remember that impairment affects everyone, including the physician, his or her family, colleagues, and, of course, patients.
- Discuss potential options with the impaired physician.
- If the physician is not open to any reasonable option, it may be necessary to notify the clinic, practice, or hospital where the physician practices. States and licensing boards may have reporting requirements, and physicians should be familiar with these guidelines.

References

Mossman D, Farrell H. Physician impairment: When should you report? *Current Psychiatry* 2011; 10 (9): 67-71.

Yancey J, McKinnon H. Reaching out to an impaired physician. *Fam Pract Manag* 2010; 17(1): 27-31.

DesRoches C, Rao S, Fromson J, Birnbaum R, Iezzoni L, Vogeli C, Campbell E. Physicians' perceptions, preparedness for reporting, and experiences related to impaired and incompetent colleagues. *JAMA* 2010; 304 (2): 187-93.

Case # 5

You are the nurse manager on a busy hospital floor. One of your nurses is upset after a difficult patient encounter. The patient was in considerable pain but the nurse was unable to give him anything because the next dose of pain medication was not scheduled for another several hours. As she tried to explain the situation, the patient became quite angry and questioned the nurse's dedication to her profession. Hurt by this, the nurse lost control of her emotions, and the situation escalated with the patient requesting to speak with the nurse manager. The patient is now waiting for you in the room.

Sample Answer

Nurse Manager: Hello Ms. Smith. I'm the nurse manager on the floor. I understand you wanted to speak with me. How are you feeling?

Patient: Terrible. I'm in a lot of pain and no one seems to care.

Nurse Manager: Can you tell me what happened?

Patient: I just want some medication to help me with this pain. It's now so bad – nine out of ten. I've just been sitting here hoping and waiting for medication. The nurse told me that if I calmed down, that I may feel better. Can you believe that? I need some pills or even a shot. I need something. I'm really hurting.

Nurse Manager: So let me see if I've understood the situation. You're in a lot of pain, and you don't feel like the current pain medication is providing you with enough relief.

Patient: Yes, that's what I'm saying. I need something stronger than what I'm getting. I told the nurse this, and she kept telling me to calm down. I asked her to help me, and she kept telling me that it wasn't time for the next dose. I asked her to call the doctor, and she didn't look too happy about that.

Nurse Manager: It sounds like you would find it helpful if I reached out to your doctor. That's something I can do. I will call and let him know that your pain medication is not keeping the pain under control. Perhaps he can make an adjustment to your medication or stop by and take a look at you.

Analysis

In a MMI scenario with an angry person or patient, sit if you can. Sitting gives the person the feeling that this is important to you and that you have the time to address it.

The nurse manager invites the patient to tell her how he's feeling and describe the events that transpired. Listening patiently to an angry patient or person will often help diffuse the situation. Remember to let the person talk.

No matter how difficult the person is, you must be professional in your interactions. Although you may not agree with his comments, refrain from responding with your own harsh comments.

To ensure that she has understood the situation, the nurse manager provides a summary and looks for corroboration. It is clear that she now understands the source of the patient's concern.

Sometimes patients will offer a potential solution. If it's reasonable or appropriate, you can agree to it. If no solutions are offered, ask the patient what he would like for you to do.

Perhaps he can make an adjustment to the medication or stop by and take a look at you.

Patient: I would love that. I don't know why it's so hard to find the doctor.

Nurse Manager: Let me go and call the doctor. Let's see if we can come up with a plan to address this. How does that sound to you?

Patient: That sounds wonderful.

Nurse Manager: Before I take care of that, I wanted to see what else I can do for you. I know you're uncomfortable, and I apologize for that. Is there anything else I can do to help you? Are you cold? Do you need a blanket? How about a snack?

Understanding that the situation has been difficult for the patient, the nurse manager looks for ways to make the patient feel comfortable.

Patient: Would you mind turning the TV on for me?

Case # 5: Key Points

In any unhappy or angry person scenario, you can utilize the mnemonic BLAST to diffuse the emotions and resolve the situation.

Using the BLAST Mnemonic with Angry or Unhappy Patients	
B	**Believe** in the patient's concern and distress, even if the patient is irrational, incorrect, exaggerating, or lying.
L	Actively **listen** to the patient. Allow the patient to vent. Remain calm and be sure your nonverbal communication communicates attentiveness and understanding. Show understanding by clarifying and repeating the patient's concerns.
A	**Apologize** to the patient. This does not mean you to have accept responsibility if you didn't do anything wrong. You are simply apologizing to the patient for what he's going through.
S	**Satisfy** the patient by offering several solutions.
T	**Thank** the patient for sharing concerns, and the opportunity to make things better.
From Dermatology Times. Mnemonics help to keep patient satisfaction levels high. Available at: http://dermatologytimes.modernmedicine.com/dermatology-times/content/tags/aesthetic-procedures/mnemonics-help-keep-patient-satisfaction-levels-?page=full. Accessed May 12, 2015.	

Case # 6

You are the doctor in a busy medical practice. Today, you are running 1.5 hours late. Earlier in the day, a patient came to see you, and you realized that she was having a heart attack. Concerned for her, you stabilized the situation, made arrangements for transfer to the hospital, and called the cardiologist to let him know of the patient's situation. Your next patient is waiting for you. Before you enter the room, your nurse informs you that he is very angry about waiting so long to see you.

Sample Answer

Patient: You're finally here.

Doctor: It sounds like you're feeling frustrated.

Patient: I've been waiting for well over an hour. When I spoke to your office staff this morning, I told them that I needed my blood pressure medication refilled. They told me that you wouldn't be able to refill it unless I came in to the office. I told her about my busy day, that I would be leaving for an overseas trip tomorrow. That didn't seem to matter to her. Then when I got here, I asked the receptionist if they knew whether you were running behind schedule. She looked at me and said she had no clue. How rude is that?

Doctor: Well, it sounds like my front office staff didn't give you the information you were looking for.

Patient: No. They didn't. Was I really asking too much? All I wanted was some idea of how long you would be so I can plan my day better. I'm leaving for this last-minute work trip. It's going to be stressful, and on top of that I'll be missing my daughter's birthday. I was hoping to spend some time with her before I left.

Doctor: I know you've waited a lot longer than you wanted to. Then you tried hard to find out when I would see you but the staff didn't tend to your concerns. I can see how upsetting that would be, especially with you getting ready for a trip, and having to miss your daughter's birthday. I know how much your daughter means to you.

Analysis

It's very important to acknowledge a patient's emotion.

No matter how difficult the person is, you can't take what he's saying personally. Remember to listen and communicate with respect. Above all, guard against saying anything negative even if the situation escalates.

Although you will feel the pressures of time, you will score points for listening. By letting the actor say what he must say, you're showing the interviewer that you're a patient listener.

Don't forget the importance of body language. If you're saying the "right things" but your nonverbal communication says something entirely different, points may be deducted from your interview score. Nonverbal behaviors to avoid include crossing your arms, scratching your hands or face, tapping hands against your lap, or shaking your foot.

Patient: I just thought that I could be in and out of here quickly. I mean, it's just a refill. Now my day is all out of whack.

Doctor: You know how hard I try to stay on schedule. What I can never predict is when I may encounter a patient emergency. It just so happened that earlier today, I saw a patient with severe, crushing chest pain. It turned out she was having a heart attack. So I had to do a lot to get her stabilized and in a safe place. That's what made me so late for your appointment. I do apologize for making you wait as long as you have. Your time is precious, and important to me. I hope you can understand why things happened the way they did today.

Patient: Boy, I had no idea. I sure hope that your other patient does okay. Thanks for explaining everything to me.

Long wait times are a common cause of patient anger. How should anger be addressed in such situations? In one study, participants were shown a video tape of an angry patient and asked to rate 12 physician responses. Highest scores were given to an <u>apology</u> combined with an <u>explanation</u> of the reasons for the delay (see reference below).

References

McCord R, Floyd M, Lang F, Young V. Responding effectively to patient anger directed at the physician. *Fam Med* 2002; 34 (5): 331-6.

Case # 7

As the manager of on an electronics superstore, you are in charge of 10 employees. One of your employees, Larry, has been receiving and sending texts regularly during work hours. He has even done so while providing service to customers. Today, you noticed that a customer became visibly upset when Larry pulled out his cellphone in the middle of their conversation. You are puzzled by Larry's behavior because up until this started two weeks ago, he had been one of your best employees. You have decided to discuss the situation with Larry. Larry is waiting for you in your office.

Sample Answer

Manager: Thanks, Larry, for meeting with me today. Lately, I've noticed that you've been using your cellphone during the workday. You've been sending and receiving texts, even in front of customers. Today, one of our customers was upset when you checked your phone. Is there a reason for this behavior?

Larry: I'm very sorry. My wife and I are really concerned about my son. You see, he's been skipping class, and getting into fights. We had to sit him down to talk, and things really didn't go well. My wife's taking this especially hard, and I wanted to reassure her that everything will be fine. I'm also concerned about my son. I don't want anything bad to happen to either one of them.

Manager: Thank you for sharing all that with me, Larry. It does sound like you're going through a lot at home. This must be a very difficult time for you, and I certainly hope that everything works out. If you'd like to take some time off to resolve these issues, that would be just fine with me. Just let me know.

Larry: I appreciate your support. I think that would be a good idea. Some time off may be just what I need to get things back on track.

Manager: Meanwhile at work, I believe it's important for all of us to deliver the highest quality customer service. Can I ask you to please leave your cellphone in your locker during the workday? Of course, I don't mind at all if you take it out during lunch or breaks.

Analysis

Notice how the manager focuses on Larry's actions at work rather than Larry as a person. This approach makes it less threatening for Larry, and increases the chances that this will be a productive exchange between the two parties.

Here the manager expresses concern for Larry, recognizes that this is a trying time in Larry's life, and expresses hope for a positive outcome.

After providing support, the manager returns to the work issue at hand. Here she offers a possible solution.

Larry: That's sounds fine to me.

Manager: Larry, you've always received high marks for your customer service. We appreciate the ways in which you make our customers feel special, and that's what we're looking for in our team members. You know that you're a big part of the impression that we make on our customers, and it's crucial that we provide the service that our customers want. Do you feel that this is a reasonable request?

The manager now reaffirms her faith in Larry. At the end, she seeks Larry's input and confirmation.

Larry: Yes. It's quite fair. I had no idea that my texting was causing so many problems. I guess I was so caught up in what's been going on at home. I promise you, from now on, I'll keep my phone in the locker. I'll only access it during breaks.

Although the manager was able to arrive at a definitive solution in this case, remember that some MMI situations may not have a solution. If you're involved in such a scenario, you will be mainly evaluated on your ability to show empathy and make the actor feel comfortable enough to discuss the situation with you.

Case # 8

Mr. T, a 75-year-old Mandarin-speaking man, has just been diagnosed with colon cancer. The son asks the doctor to not disclose the diagnosis to his father. He maintains that people from China of that generation are not told they have cancer. The son says Mr. T will lose hope if he's told he has cancer. How would you handle this situation if you were the physician?

MULTIPLE MINI INTERVIEW

Sample Answer

To begin with, I would like to summarize the case to make sure I fully understand it. This is a difficult situation in which a patient has been diagnosed with cancer. The physician has been asked to not inform the patient of this new diagnosis. The family indicates that people of their father's generation from China are not told of a cancer diagnosis. There is concern that the patient may lose hope if he's told that he has cancer. Do you feel that I have a good understanding of the situation?

This case really brings up some important issues, including trust in the doctor – patient relationship and how cultural values can impact the way in which physicians care for patients. I would like to discuss these issues, and then end with how I would approach this particular situation.

The first point I'd like to make is that trust is essential in the doctor – patient relationship. Lying and deception undermine trust, and I would worry that not being truthful to the patient would make him feel that he has been betrayed.

However, I recognize that there are cultural issues in play here. In some cultures, it might be standard practice to not disclose a diagnosis of cancer or other serious illness. Disclosing the information may cause the patient to suffer, and I can see how some patients would be more hopeful if information was withheld. Even in a culture, there will be some people who would want to know, and I think that's the key here. Would this patient want to know?

Analysis

Begin with a summary of the case. Check in with your interviewer to make sure you have a good grasp of the situation. This will increase the likelihood that you will address salient points.

In the introduction, provide the listener with a blueprint to follow. The interviewer now knows the issues that will be discussed, and the order in which the information will be presented.

Be on the lookout for cultural issues in the MMI. The United States has a multicultural population, and our physicians must be sensitive to different cultural beliefs and practice.

Never assume that all patients would behave in the same manner.

There are other situations in which I might not share information. If a patient was severely depressed or suicidal, I might worry about the consequences of disclosure. In these cases, I would consult with psychiatry to assess likelihood of harm. If the patient was a danger to himself, I might wait until his mental health improves.

It's important not to be too rigid during the MMI. In medicine, there are often exceptions that need to be made based on the situation.

If I were the physician, I would ask the patient how he would like me to proceed. Would he like to know the diagnosis or would he prefer that I discuss the diagnosis only with his family? If the patient said, "I don't want to know," I would have to respect his wishes.

In summary, I think that there are many reasons to tell patients the truth. I believe most patients in the U.S. would want to know so that they can understand treatment options, ask appropriate questions, and make informed decisions about their health. However, I do recognize the importance of being sensitive to patients' cultural beliefs and practices, and I would take that into account in my decision-making.

Many interviewees end their response with a whimper rather than a bang. Close with a strong summary statement.

Case # 8: Key Points

- In some cultures, families withhold bad medical news out of concern that disclosure will lead to feelings of despair in patients.
- Since the United States is such a culturally diverse nation, physicians will sometimes encounter situations in which families make requests outside of the norm.
- Truth telling, as highlighted in this case, is one such example. In this case, the patient's son felt that it was his responsibility to protect the patient from distressing news.
- This poses problems for physicians in the United States who are accustomed to having patients make their own health decisions. Physicians prefer to keep patients informed so that they can make educated decisions about their health (patient autonomy).
- Such situations require physicians to be sensitive and delicate in their approach. It's important to show respect for the perspectives of all family members.
- Ask family members about their concerns. What do they fear will happen if the patient is told the truth? Although the family may want to protect their loved one, the patient may wish to be actively involved in the process. It's never wise to assume that everyone within a culture would want to be treated the same way.
- Determine what the patient would like. It's up to the patient to decide whether he wants to be involved in the decision-making.

Case # 9

An attending physician is in the habit of introducing third-year medical students rotating with him in the hospital as "Doctor." Discuss the ethical issues raised by this practice.

Sample Answer

I believe there are strong reasons to be truthful in these introductions.

First, it's important that patients trust their doctors. If the doctor misrepresents who the student is, the patient may feel betrayed when he discovers the student's true status. I feel that patients might perceive this practice as deceptive.

Second, doctors have the responsibility to reveal pertinent information to patients. It would be important for the patient to know who is involved in their care, their precise roles, and their responsibilities. Knowing all this may very well have an impact on the patient's decision-making. For example, let's say the patient needs a procedure. It would be well within his rights to refuse to have the procedure done by a student but he would only be able to express that sentiment if he knew the student's true status.

Third, there may be legal requirements for students to inform patients of their educational status. Even if there are no legal requirements, there may be policies that have been put in place by the state medical board, hospital, or medical school. It would be important to adhere to these rules.

In trying to understand this from the doctor's perspective, I wonder if he's concerned that the patient may not allow the student to participate in his care if he knows the student's status. Or perhaps he feels that learning opportunities will be compromised if he uses the term "medical student." Although I can understand these concerns, I don't believe that they override the importance of maintaining trust.

Analysis

The interviewee takes a position from the start.

Each point offered to support the position is introduced by number ("first"), making it easier for the interviewer to process the information.

An example is offered to provide more strength for the point.

In concluding the response, the interviewer tries to understand the perspective of the doctor before leaving the interviewer with his final thoughts. His last words remain consistent with the position taken at the beginning.

Challenge Question

You are the medical student working with this attending physician. After entering the patient's room, you are introduced as "doctor." The attending physician decides that a knee aspiration is needed for diagnosis. This is a procedure in which a needle is inserted into the joint space, and fluid is removed for testing. You have only seen the procedure performed once, and now your attending physician would like you to perform the procedure. How do you proceed?

Case # 10

At a party, a group of medical students lament the good old days of medicine in which doctors were wined and dined, and sent on lavish trips at the expense of pharmaceutical companies. "I don't get it," said one student. "We should still be able to receive gifts from drug companies." Discuss reasons for and against accepting drug company gifts.

Sample Answer

Although I understand reasons why some may feel that it's acceptable to receive gifts, I believe there are compelling reasons why doctors should not accept gifts.

I'd like to start with reasons to accept gifts. I've heard that education courses and meetings are sometimes subsidized by drug companies. In these situations, an argument can be made that this practice provides an important educational benefit. In working in free health clinics, I've also seen how many patients can't afford medications. In these cases, medications received as gifts allow for the proper treatment of these patients' medical conditions.

Reasons to not accept gifts have to do with objectivity. If drug companies fund educational conferences, I would be concerned that this might influence speakers and their slides. The material presented may be slanted towards a medication produced by the drug company. I would even worry about low-cost items like pens and notepads because if it's in front of you, you may be tempted to prescribe that medication.

I would also worry about how gifts would be viewed by patients. If it affects the trust patients have in their physicians, then it's a significant problem. Patients need to be confident that their doctors' behavior and practices are not being influenced by drug companies.

I have read that physician organizations have been enacting strict policies on the ways in which physicians interact with pharmaceutical companies. I would be in favor of policies that place the patients' best interests above other factors. For these reasons, I would not favor accepting gifts.

Analysis

As the interviewee offers reasons to accept gifts, he is effectively able to incorporate what he has observed as a volunteer in free health clinics. If you have personal experience related to the MMI scenario, consider weaving it into your discussion. This has the potential to elevate the strength of your answer.

In 2003, drug companies spent over $25 billion dollars promoting their drugs. Money was used to give doctors gifts and sponsor informational lunches. Although many physicians don't believe that this affects their prescribing practices, research has shown that these interactions often do.

Case # 11

You are an employee working in the shoe section of a major department store. A customer returns to the store upset about a problem with shoes she bought five weeks ago. The store policy allows for returns with full refund within 30 days of purchase. For older items purchased from the store, employees can issue store credit, exchange items, or arrange for repair when items are defective.

Sample Answer

Employee: Hello. My name is _____. How can I help you today?

Customer: I bought these shoes for my daughter's prom. Yesterday, when she tried them on, the heel immediately broke. It's three days before prom and my daughter is so upset because she doesn't have shoes.

Employee: You must be very upset. I'm so sorry this happened.

Customer: Well, sorry won't cut it. My daughter's prom is a big deal, and she's upset about the shoes. How does a heel break when it has never been worn? What kind of shoe department is this? You should be concerned about quality.

Employee: I'm going to do whatever I can to make this right for you.

Customer: I'm just so angry. I really didn't need this.

Employee: You know, I would be too if I were in your position. Is it okay if I ask you a couple of questions? Let me start by asking you when you bought these shoes? Do you have a receipt?

Customer: Yes, I have a receipt. I bought these shoes, let me see, it looks like five weeks ago.

Employee: I see. According to this receipt, it has been about five weeks since your purchase.

Customer: That's what I said.

Analysis

In any MMI scenario where you have to interact with an actor, focus entirely on the actor. Do not concern yourself with the rater who will be sitting in the corner of the room evaluating your performance. Remember that your goal is to connect with the actor.

Acknowledge emotion and express belief in what the person is feeling or saying. This helps to build trust.

Allow the person to vent their feelings.

These can be intense encounters but you must remember to remain calm and composed. Maintain eye contact, remain attentive, and offer expressions of understanding.

MMI SCENARIOS

Employee: I can imagine how upsetting this is for you. I'm sure you have so much to do for your daughter's prom, and you didn't need this to happen.

Customer: Yes. There's a lot to do, and I want to make this prom a special day for her.

Employee: So, you bought these shoes five weeks ago. Your daughter tried them on yesterday, and the heel broke. You only have three days before prom and you need shoes before then. You must also be concerned about whether these shoes are returnable.

Clarify and repeat back what you've heard to show the person you truly understand the situation.

Customer: Yes, I am.

Employee: Well, I wish we could refund your money. But our store's policy only allow for full refunds within 30 days of purchase. Here's what I can do for you though. I can give you credit for the shoes that you can apply to another purchase or allow you exchange them for another pair. Another option available to us is repair of the heel. Of course, this would be at no expense to you. Which would you prefer?

You should explore possible solutions but don't agree to something that you can't offer. At some point, you may need to call on someone else to help you resolve the situation. Remember that a physician should be able to recognize his limitations, and call upon others if need be.

Customer: If I had the heel repaired, would it be available before the prom date?

Employee: Yes. We have a relationship with the shoe repair service in this mall. If you give me the go ahead, I'll take these shoes myself to their store, and make sure they're ready for you in two days.

Customer: That would be great. Let's do that.

Case # 12

Following the death of their 17-year-old daughter in a car accident, the parents donated her organs and received permission from the courts to remove and freeze their daughter's eggs. Their intent is to have the eggs fertilized with donated sperm. Discuss the ethical issues involved.

Sample Answer

My heart really goes out to the parents of this 17-year-old who was killed in a car accident. Donating her organs has the potential to benefit other patients but removing and freezing her eggs for fertilization raises some important ethical concerns.

In this situation, I would imagine that the parents are distraught. By harvesting and the fertilizing the eggs with sperm, they might feel that the child born would be one way to keep the memory of their daughter alive.

I wonder if the daughter had expressed a desire to have children before her death. Even if she had, I wonder if she was mature enough to truly understand what it means to be a mother. Since she would be unable to provide consent, the doctors involved would have to rely on the parents to make suitable decisions on her behalf.

Then I realized that the bigger issue is that any child conceived from fertilization of her eggs will never know her mother. Would the daughter have wanted a child to be born after she passed away? If she did, would she have wanted her own parents to raise her child? And what impact would this have on the child years later when she fully understands how she came into this world?

I'm not sure there are any easy answers to these questions. However, I might be inclined to encourage families to wait until enough time passes before making these important decisions. With time, the emotions which are so raw initially may lessen to some extent, and allow loved ones to make a sound choice.

Analysis

The interviewee begins by showing concern and compassion for the parents who have just lost their child.

Benefits to the parents are discussed. A useful approach with ethical scenarios is to consider the perspectives of all stakeholders.

Interviewee discusses the situation from the perspective of the deceased. Also raised are important issues related to informed consent.

Additional concerns from the perspective of the deceased are presented. The interviewee also considers what effect this may have on the child conceived.

Interviewee recognizes the difficult issues raised, and does not profess to have all the answers. She ends with a very mature response on how she might guide such families dealing with the loss of a loved one.

Case # 13

In 2005, after having her feeding tube removed by court order, Terri Schiavo passed away at the age of 41. She had been in a coma for fifteen years. During the last seven years of her life, there was a fierce battle between her husband and parents. Referring to conversations he had with Terri, the husband indicated that she never wanted to be kept alive artificially. Terri's parents were skeptical of his claims, and argued vehemently to keep her alive. They remained hopeful that she would recover despite the fact that doctors disagreed. Terri's parents appealed to the governor, state legislature, and even the President of the United States. However, the courts consistently backed her husband's right to let his wife die. Discuss the issues involved.

Sample Answer

I remember being in high school at the time when the Terri Schiavo case gripped our nation. My heart really goes out to both her husband and parents. I can't imagine what it must have been like for them to go through all of it. From my perspective, I believe that the case highlighted some very important issues about advanced directives and who should make medical decisions for family members when they're not in the position to do so.

If I remember correctly, she had no written advanced directives. Without a living will, it can be difficult to know for sure what someone would want in an end-of-life situation. The living will would also make clear who she would have wanted to speak for her on her behalf if she became incapacitated. Unfortunately, the lack of advanced directives led to considerable emotional distress for all those involved.

Had a living will been present indicating that she wanted her husband to make decisions on her behalf, it's possible that her parents would have respected her wishes. This would have prevented the battle in the courts that was waged for so many years.

In my own family, I know that the case spurred us to have a conversation that we may not have had otherwise. It led my parents to prepare their advance directives, and have these crucial conversations with their doctors. I hope that one of the lasting legacies of this sad case is to foster greater public awareness of the importance of living wills.

Analysis

The interviewee recalls the case, remembers feeling affected by it, and shows her human side. She then reveals the issues she will discuss, readying the interviewer for what's to come.

She identifies the central issue. She goes on to discuss how the lack of advanced directives led to the problems.

She offers her thoughts on what might have happened had Terri Schiavo documented her wishes.

Here the interviewee relates the case to her own life.

During my oncology shadowing experience, one of the things I learned was the importance of having end-of-life discussions early on. My physician preceptor told me that it's important that we speak to families about these issues well in advance of when these decisions have to be made. That way, when the time does occur, the family will know that they are making a decision that is consistent with what their loved one wanted.

The interviewee very effectively relates the case back to her own experiences shadowing. In doing so, she clearly conveys exposure to the medical profession.

In summary, as distressing as this case was, there's so much that we can learn from the events. I know my family and I benefitted from it, and I do hope others did as well. In the future, I hope to be like my oncology preceptor, someone who handles these important conversations in a delicate manner.

She provides an effective close to her discussion, focusing on what she's learned from the case, and how it will shape her future.

Case # 13: Key Points

- When a patient lacks the capacity to make personal health decisions, physicians rely on surrogates to do so.
- Be familiar with the legal hierarchy of surrogate decision-makers.
- At the top of this hierarchy are court-appointed guardians and surrogates selected by patients (health care proxy). The latter becomes official when the patient completes a form designating the person as the health care proxy, and then has the form witnessed and notarized.
- If there is no court-appointed guardian or health care proxy, then family members may serve as surrogates in the following order: spouse, adult child, parent, sibling, and other relative.
- Note that domestic partners in some states are considered on the same level as spouses.
- If there are no family members, a close friend may serve as a surrogate.
- If no one is available, then the physician can make decisions on behalf of the patient, preferably after consultation with other physicians or the hospital ethics committee.

Challenge Questions for Surrogate Decision Making

What if the patient is a minor?

If it is a non-emergent medical decision involving a minor, the physician must secure consent from the minor's parent or guardian. In some states, certain medical treatments may be offered to minors without parental permission. These include prescriptions for birth control, abortion, and treatment of sexually transmitted diseases. Before your MMI, become familiar with the laws in the state you will be visiting.

What if the patient's adult children are the decision-makers but they don't agree?

In these cases, consensus is preferred. Some states will allow physicians to rely on a majority decision or ask adult children to identify one person to be the key decision-maker.

What if the physician doesn't agree with the ethical or legal appropriateness of a surrogate's medical decision?

Hospitals often have an institutional ethics committee, and physicians can consult with these committees when there is dispute over treatment decisions. If an appropriate resolution still can't be reached, a judicial review may be requested.

Case # 14

A 38-year-old banker informs his physician that he recently tested positive for HIV. "Doc, you have to promise me not to tell anyone. I don't want to lose my job." The physician urges the patient to disclose the diagnosis to his wife. After a long conversation, the patient adamantly refuses to do so. "Doc, this will end my marriage," he says. How should the physician proceed?

Sample Answer

In this situation, the patient recently discovered he was positive for HIV. He is concerned that this information may be shared with others. He is worried about losing his job. He also fears that telling his wife will destroy his marriage. This brings up important issues related to patient confidentiality. Among the points I'd like to address are the importance of confidentiality, consequences of breaking a patient's trust, and reasons why physicians may have no choice but to do so.

I'd like to begin by discussing why confidentiality is so important. At the heart of the physician-patient relationship is trust. Trust may be lost when personal health information is divulged without the patient's consent. If there is lack of trust, patients may be less inclined to seek care and share important health information. This could certainly affect the quality of care delivered.

Although personal health information should only be released if the patient provides consent, I believe that there are several exceptions to this rule.

The first exception involves concern for the safety of others. I believe that a physician may have to breach confidentiality if the patient informs the physician that he or she intends to harm others. In these situations, the physician's duty to prevent harm trumps the mandate to maintain confidentiality.

Confidentiality must also be breached when there is a legal requirement to do so. I know that, with some communicable diseases, physicians are required to notify the public

Analysis

The interviewee provides a summary of the case, and identifies the key issue (confidentiality). The last sentence in this paragraph gives the listener an idea of where the interviewee will take the discussion.

Note the interviewee's use of transition statements ("I'd like to begin..."). These help the interviewer process the information more easily.

Interviewee recognizes that there are limits to confidentiality.

With every ethical scenario involving patient confidentiality, always be vigilant for exceptions to the rule which would require physicians to breach confidentiality. The exceptions fall under concern for the safety of others and legal requirements.

health department. In these cases, the physician has a duty to protect public health, and this duty supersedes the mandate to maintain confidentiality.

In this case, I believe that the physician has compelling reasons to not maintain confidentiality. First, I would worry about his wife being infected with HIV. If she knew that her husband was HIV-positive, she could take proper steps to protect herself from harm. Second, if a diagnosis of HIV requires notification of public health authorities, I would be legally mandated to inform them.

Interviewee now returns to the question posed in the scenario.

I realize that my actions would have serious consequences for my patient's life. For that reason, I would explain all of this to the patient in a sensitive and respectful manner. It would be my hope that we could come to some agreement. I would do my best to address his concerns, and support him. In terms of his job situation, I don't see why I would need to disclose this to his employer in the banking industry.

If you must break confidentiality, be straightforward with the patient. Let the patient know that you're obligated to do this, and offer reasons why this is the case. Offer an apology, and then the opportunity for the patient to disclose the information on his own. If the patient refuses, then inform the patient that you must disclose the information.

In conclusion, I believe that physicians should maintain confidentiality. However, there are some exceptions to this rule, and this case is a good example of that.

Challenge Questions for Confidentiality

Is it ever appropriate for the physician to breach confidentiality?

With every ethical scenario involving patient confidentiality, always be vigilant for exceptions to the rule which would require physicians to breach confidentiality. The exceptions fall under concern for the safety of others and legal requirements. If there are no exceptions, then always maintain confidentiality.

What if a family member wants to discuss the patient's health?

If you're presented an ethical scenario where a family member is asking about their loved one's health, remember to seek permission from the patient before disclosing any personal health information. If, however, the patient has suffered an injury or illness and can't make his or her own medical decisions, then the physician may discuss the situation with the next of kin. The physician will need a family member to make informed decisions on the patient's behalf. Appropriate individuals would be those named in a living will or healthcare power of attorney.

What if the patient is an adolescent?

Trust in the physician-patient relationships is important to adolescents. Many adolescents are afraid that their health concerns will be disclosed to their parents. These fears can prevent adolescents from seeking care, sharing sensitive information, and returning for follow-up. In one study of adolescent girls, nearly 60% reported that they would cease to use sexual health services or delay testing/treatment for sexually transmitted illnesses if this sensitive information was divulged to parents (Reddy). Laws regarding confidentiality with adolescents vary from state to state. In some states, sensitive issues (sexually transmitted illnesses, contraception, pregnancy) can be kept confidential if the patient is able to provide informed consent.

What if you have to break confidentiality?

If you must break confidentiality, be straightforward with the patient. Let the patient know that you're obligated to do this, and offer reasons why this is the case. Offer an apology, and then the opportunity to disclose the information on their own.

References

Reddy D, Fleming R, Swain C. Effect of mandatory parental notification on adolescent girls' use of sexual health services. *JAMA* 2002; 288 (6): 710-14.

Case # 15

Ms. F is a 60-year-old woman who recently suffered a heart attack. After an extensive evaluation, her cardiologist has recommended bypass surgery to restore normal blood flow to the heart. The surgery has traditionally required the patient's breastbone to be split for access to the heart. A new technique, termed "mini" bypass, is now available and can be done by just making several smaller incisions. This technique causes less pain and is associated with a shorter recovery period. The cardiologist has referred Ms. F to a cardiothoracic surgeon who will perform the bypass surgery. This particular surgeon prefers traditional surgery over "mini" bypass, and does not perform the newer procedure. Should he even discuss "mini" bypass with Ms. F? Explain your reasoning.

Sample Answer

Having just had a heart attack, I imagine that this is a difficult time in this patient's life. Now her cardiologist, after evaluating her, has recommended bypass surgery. The cardiothoracic surgeon seems skilled in the traditional method of performing bypass. However, there is a new method that apparently has some benefits, which include less pain and shorter recovery time. Since the surgeon doesn't perform this new surgery, should he even discuss it with the patient? If I understand the situation, that's the central issue here. Do you feel that I have a good grasp of the case?

Before I address whether the surgeon should inform the patient about the new surgical approach, I will say that patients need to know the nature of any surgery planned, how it will benefit them, the associated risks, and alternatives to surgery. With this knowledge in hand, the patient can then make an informed decision about what she would like. That's the basis of informed consent, and the focus of this case.

In this case, it seems clear that surgery is needed. If the patient understands that and wishes to proceed with surgery, then a more detailed discussion about surgical approaches would seem reasonable. I realize that the surgeon doesn't perform the "mini" bypass but I do believe that it's important that he discuss this new technique with her.

If the patient knows that the new procedure is less painful and leads to faster recovery, then she may be more inclined to have it done in this manner. Not being told of this option would prevent her from making an

Analysis

Informed consent is legally required. Doctors have an obligation to inform patients who are deemed competent of the proposed plan. This includes surgery, test, procedure, or medication.

The applicant's position is very clear.

informed decision, and could lead to suboptimal care.

From the surgeon's perspective, he may have some concerns about the procedure. Perhaps he's concerned about outcomes. Maybe long-term data is lacking, and that's why he prefers the traditional approach. It may be that he's simply more comfortable with the traditional surgery. I think it would be okay to talk about these concerns, and the patient would probably welcome his perspective.

Always try to consider the other side of the argument.

If this new approach had no scientific basis or evidence to support it, then I could understand not bringing it up. But it seems like there is some research to back up this new technique, and I feel like other physicians in the field might recommend it.

If alternative treatment options have no scientific support and are not effective, the doctor does not need to mention these treatments.

In closing, I believe the surgeon should discuss both surgical approaches. My feeling is that the patient should have the right to choose among these feasible options. It's the physician's job to educate the patient and make recommendations. Only after that can the patient make an informed decision that's in accordance with her goals and values. Even if it leads her to have the surgery done by someone else, it still seems the right way to handle things.

Case # 16

Family members and friends often ask physicians for medical opinions, prescriptions for medication, and other types of treatment. Discuss the ethical issues raised by such situations.

Sample Answer

I would expect that physicians are often asked to dispense medical advice and prescribe treatment outside of the office or hospital. Although I can see why physicians would do so, I believe that physicians should refrain from this practice with few exceptions.

To begin with, I'd like to offer some reasons why physicians might want to treat their family members or friends. Physicians are well-qualified to diagnose and treat, and it may be more convenient for them to do so. For family members, setting up an appointment, waiting for the appointment, and taking time off from work are all hassles. And so it can be less time consuming if they simply turn to the physician who is already in their life.

What would concern me most about physicians treating family members is whether the personal relationship could impact the care that the doctor delivers. For example, what if it's a touchy issue or problem? The physician may be reluctant to explore certain parts of the history or even perform aspects of the physical exam. The same could be said about patients. I would worry about the family member or friend's degree of comfort sharing information or allowing an examination.

In the hospital or office, the physician may not have any trouble setting limits on what he would be willing to do. With a family member or friend, would the doctor feel inclined to handle problems that fall outside the scope of his training or practice? If so, that would pose a danger to the patient.

Analysis

A very clear position has been taken by this interviewee. Now the interviewer will expect to hear her reasoning.

Before offering support for her position, she describes why physicians may be inclined to treat family and friends. It shows that she understands different perspectives.

According to AMA Code of Medical Ethics, self-treatment or treatment of non-patients, including family and friends, is not recommended because professional objectivity may be compromised.

Another concern has to do with the outcome of any recommendation or treatment. You would hope that nothing bad would come of it but what if something's missed or the patient doesn't do well. What repercussions would that have on their relationship?

An exception I would make is for emergencies or when medical care can't be easily accessed. In these situations, I believe it makes sense for the doctor to diagnose and treat a family member or friend.

One thing I'm not sure about is whether there are any state laws or licensing body guidelines regarding this practice. I would certainly consult with these authorities when making any recommendations.

> This is an excellent point. Don't hesitate to consult with others who may know more than you. A good physician always recognizes his limitations.
>
> Note that some states require physicians to maintain written records of treatment for non-patients.

In summary, I don't believe that physicians should help their family members or friends with medical issues unless it's an emergency situation. The physician may feel pressured to do so but with a gentle explanation, I believe that most people would understand.

Challenge Questions for Treatment of Friends and Family

You're at Disney World on vacation with your family. Shortly after arriving in Orlando, your cousin develops an upper respiratory tract infection with fits of coughing that she fears will keep her awake at night. She asks you to prescribe a narcotic cough syrup. How do you proceed?

Physicians should not prescribe controlled substances for non-patients. Many states and licensing boards are very clear on this point. "Except in emergencies, it is not appropriate for physicians to write prescriptions for controlled substances for themselves or immediate family members," writes the New Hampshire Board of Medicine.

You are at a high school reunion, and an old friend asks your advice about some numbness and tingling he's been having in his left thigh. How do you proceed?

It's common for acquaintances and friends to ask physicians for medical advice in social settings. In these situations, it's rare for a physician to have the detailed information required to provide specific advice. Many physicians would offer general information and then ask the friend or acquaintance to follow-up with his or her own physician. "Based on what you've told me, I would recommend talking with your physician about..." Some physicians would not feel comfortable offering any advice, and would cite ethical or legal reasons for their inability to do so.

While driving through rural Montana, your friend develops urinary symptoms, and you suspect she has a bladder infection. You believe she would benefit from antibiotics. She recently lost her job, and doesn't have medical insurance. Should you prescribe antibiotics for her?

If medical care can't be easily accessed, it would be reasonable for physicians to treat friends or family, especially if there is an emergent need for treatment.

Case # 17

Mr. N is a 35-year-old patient who is concerned about his weight. As the years have passed, he has put on considerable weight, and now weighs nearly 250 pounds. He has tried a variety of diets and exercise regimens without success. He recently read about a Chinese herbal supplement that has shown amazing results. You are not familiar with the supplement but are concerned about potential side effects. You have had other patients who have developed side effects after taking supplements. In some cases, there have been some worrisome interactions between herbs and prescribed medications. Discuss the issues involved, and how you would handle the situation.

Sample Answer

Losing weight is difficult for so many people. With this patient, it seems that he has tried different diets and exercise programs. I'm sure he's concerned about obesity and its associated health risks. I'm sure that he's also frustrated by his inability to lose weight. I can see why he would explore other options. It seems that he is hopeful that an herbal supplement may help him reach his goal.

First, I would tell the patient that I'm glad he's taking such an active interest in his health, and researching possible treatments. I know that some patients may be reluctant to share their thoughts of taking an herbal supplement with their doctor so I would be very gentle in the way that I discussed this with him. I would ask him how he came to learn about the supplement, and if he knows others who have used it.

I would then take the time to review all of his prior efforts to lose weight. I would patiently listen to his story, and inquire about the factor or factors that he believes prevented him from reaching his goals. If there were some options that we hadn't explored in terms of conventional medical therapy for weight loss, this would seem to me a good time to discuss them.

If he felt strongly about the herbal medication, I would be honest with him and tell him about my lack of experience with the supplement. I would ask him to give me some time to research it. I would remind him that herbs may also have side effects, and we would need to make sure there are no interactions with other medications he takes.

Analysis

Complementary and alternative medicine (CAM) is defined as practices that are outside of mainstream or conventional medicine.

Recent studies have shown that CAM use is common, especially by patients having chronic conditions. Forms of CAM include, but are not limited to, naturopathic medicine, homeopathy, Ayurveda, and traditional Chinese medicine. Perhaps the most common form of CAM is the use of herbal products.

Doctors are encouraged to make decisions based on available research. However, CAM research is very much in its infancy, and there is much we don't know about its efficacy.

It's clear that our patients are turning to CAM, and therefore it's important to engage in dialogue with our patients about this important issue. Doctors should avoid dismissing or ridiculing CAM therapies because it can certainly affect the patient relationship.

Any consideration of therapy must take into account the risk of harm and potential benefits. A CAM therapy that does not appear to be harmful can be harmful if it prevents the patient from utilizing established and effective treatment.

Once I reviewed what we know about the supplement, I would present this information to him and let him know if I think it would be safe to take. If he chose to take it, I would monitor him very carefully for side effects.

Case # 18

You are the head of a committee that has been tasked with developing policy to guide allocation of donated organs for transplant. Discuss the issues you will consider in developing this policy.

Sample Answer

There are many ethical issues related to the allocation of human organs. These issues have raised so many questions. How can organs be allocated fairly? What are the medical criteria that should be used for allocation? Should non-medical criteria be factors in the decision-making? These are all valid questions and we need to have a system in place for allocation because the demand for organs greatly exceeds supply. The system that's chosen should be a just system.

Medical need would be an important part of this system. I would say that those in greatest need would be patients who would die soon without transplantation. It would make sense to give these patients priority on the waiting list over those who are stable.

In terms of allocation criteria, I would favor criteria that are solely medical. However, I do realize that a person's psychosocial issues need to be considered. If someone's social situation would affect the outcome of transplantation, then would it be appropriate to transplant the organ into that individual? For example, if the patient was homeless, then he may not be able to adhere to treatment recommendations. But who's to say that the patient with social issues can't overcome these issues with the right support?

Time spent on the waiting list is also an issue to consider. Many people believe that those who have been waiting longer should receive higher priority if the level of medical urgency was the same.

Analysis

In the United States, the United Network for Organ Sharing (UNOS) suggests allocation criteria. Transplantation centers usually keep their own waitlist based on UNOS criteria.

Scoring systems have been developed to determine severity of illness. In selecting liver recipients, for example, doctors use the MELD system which yields a severity of illness score based on laboratory tests.

Some people maintain that social worth should be considered in organ allocation decisions. Opponents argue that it is difficult to measure social worth. How can anyone objectively assess potential contributions someone may make to society in the future?

Location is another consideration. When an organ becomes available, it may be better for people who live closest to receive priority. This would be especially important if the success of transplantation drops the longer we wait.

In summary, these are the major factors I would use to help me develop a fair system for allocation of organs for transplantation. Because this is such an emotionally charged topic, I would rely on a team of experts to help guide me. I would consult with all stakeholders to understand different perspectives and viewpoints. In the end, we could develop a system based on consensus but I don't believe that we would be able to please everyone. Although we may not be able to please everyone, I would want the system to be transparent so that the public doesn't lose faith in the importance of organ donation.

This is a strong conclusion because the applicant informs the interviewer that he won't make such an important decision on his own. He will consult with leaders in the field, and obtain opinions of all stakeholders. He is not afraid to seek input from others. He also realizes that no matter which system is adopted, there's likely to be criticism. He ends with a key point. If the public doesn't believe the system is fair, they may be less willing to donate organs.

Challenge Questions for Allocation of Organs for Transplantation

What do you think about age as a criterion?

Some argue that it makes more sense to transplant organs in younger individuals. They maintain that an 80-year old organ recipient is very likely to pass away soon even with a transplant. Contrast this with a 25-year old who has many years of life left.

Age as a consideration is taken even further by some who argue that the quality of life is very different for younger and older individuals. They feel that the younger recipient would have many more enjoyable years left. Opponents maintain that quality of life is very subjective, and that you can't know for sure if a younger or older recipient will have better quality of life in the years they have left to live.

What if the patient is at fault for the disease that now requires transplantation?

Alcohol abuse is one example. Some people argue that potential recipients who are fully or partially to blame for their illness should not have priority over others who have suffered for no fault of their own. However, others maintain that there are genetic and environmental predispositions to alcoholism, and therefore it would be unfair to penalize alcoholic patients for something they can't fully control. In clinical practice, transplant teams will often require patients to show proof of abstinence for a period of time. This is not done to hold the patient accountable for his actions but because continued alcohol abuse increases the risk of a poor outcome following transplantation.

What if the patient is not a citizen?

Should citizenship be a criterion for transplant? Some people strongly believe that organ recipients should be citizens. However, we don't restrict noncitizens from donating organs for transplant. Noncitizens also follow the laws of our country, and pay taxes to federal and state governments just like citizens. Noncitizens also are eligible to receive other types of medical care so why should organ transplantation be any different?

References

Abouna G. Ethical issues in organ and tissue transplantation. *Exp Clin Transplant* 2003; 1 (2): 125-38.

Caplan A. Bioethics of organ transplantation. *Cold Spring Harb Perspect Med* 2014; 4 (3).

Case # 19

Alzheimer's disease is an incurable disease of the brain that destroys memory and thinking skills. It is a slow disease that progresses in stages. In its early stage, patients have no symptoms. In its next stage, there are mild symptoms which are often simply attributed to the aging process. Recently, researchers reported promising preliminary results of a blood test developed to detect patients with Alzheimer's disease at a very early point. Discuss the pros and cons of having such a test available.

Sample Answer

This case really resonates with me because I volunteered in a nursing home where many of the patients had Alzheimer's disease. I've seen up close what the disease does to a person, and the effect that it has on the family. I remember reading a bit about the disease, and I was surprised to see how many people have Alzheimer's. A blood test that could detect patients with Alzheimer's disease early would be an exciting development but also one that could cause some problems.

If there was a blood test which would allow early detection, it's possible that treatment could be started earlier. The hope would be that early treatment might slow down the progression of the disease.

Early detection would also allow patients to make important decisions about their future. Patients would be able to make decisions at a time when their neurological function was relatively intact. These decisions would include how they would want to be taken care of once the Alzheimer's disease became much more symptomatic. They could be very specific, and leave no doubt about their choices regarding medical and financial decisions. For example, patients could indicate how aggressive they wanted their medical care to be. They could appoint someone to make medical decisions on their behalf if they weren't able to. They could make arrangements with their family about how they will be taken care of. Will they be in a nursing home? If so, which one?

There's another potential benefit of the test. If patients knew they had Alzheimer's disease early, they might start doing all the

Analysis

The interviewee begins with a personal story of his involvement with Alzheimer's disease patients in the nursing home.

Currently available Alzheimer's medications can help with the management of symptoms but do not offer cure or stop progression of the disease. Over time, these drugs lose effectiveness.

In a study of Alzheimer's disease patients having no advance directives upon initial presentation for cognitive evaluation, only 39% had initiated advanced care planning by 5 years of follow-up.

things that they had delayed. If they knew their time was limited, they could take trips, strengthen bonds, and even clear up any conflicts in their life.

In terms of problems with a test of this sort, I could see how someone might be impacted with an early diagnosis. The patient could become stressed, depressed, or even anxious. It may be hard for the patient to live life with this sense of doom.

An early diagnosis would also affect the patient's relationships with family, friends, and coworkers. Others may begin treating the patient differently, and that might embarrass the patient.

Another problem would have to do with the test itself. How accurate is it? If a person was falsely diagnosed with early Alzheimer's because of the blood test, it would be so devastating. It would essentially destroy someone's life for no reason.

In summary, there are risks and benefits to the use of a test for early detection of Alzheimer's disease. Continued dialogue about this will be necessary to develop policies to guide decision-making.

This interviewee could also have examined the issue from the standpoint of cost benefits associated with early diagnosis. Billions of dollars are spent every year for long-term care of Alzheimer's disease patients. A significant portion of this expense is taken care of by the government through Medicaid and Medicare programs. Early diagnosis and treatment could significantly reduce costs.

References

Garand L, Dew M, Lingler J, DeKosky S. Incidence and predictors of advance care planning among persons with cognitive impairment. *Am J Geriatr Psychiatry* 2011; 19 (8): 712-20.

MULTIPLE MINI INTERVIEW

Case # 20

Your patient returns for check of his blood pressure. For the past year, you have been making adjustments to the patient's blood pressure medication. Although the patient has not developed any problems related to the high blood pressure, you have been worried about the toll the blood pressure is taking on the patient's body. You are specifically concerned that he may develop a heart attack, stroke, or kidney disease. You have prescribed medication to control the blood pressure and reduce the risk of problems related to it. Unfortunately, efforts to control the blood pressure have not been successful. Today, the patient's blood pressure remains high. Before entering the patient's room, the nurse informs you that he hasn't been taking his blood pressure medication. Enter the room and talk to the patient about why he hasn't been taking his blood pressure medication.

MMI SCENARIOS

Sample Answer

Doctor: I see that your blood pressure is still high today. The nurse was telling me that you haven't been able to take your medication. Are you having a problem taking it?

Patient: It's not good to be off the medication. I should be taking it.

Doctor: Is there something that concerns you about the medication?

Patient: I've never been keen about taking medication. I keep hoping that if I exercise and eat right that I won't need to take the medication.

Doctor: So it sounds like you don't like the idea of having to take medication. Are you worried about side effects?

Patient: It's something to think about but it's more the thought of taking medication.

Doctor: Before we discuss this, I thought we could take some time to review some important points about high blood pressure. I'd like to start by asking you a question. We've talked about the importance of controlling blood pressure in the past. Do you know why it's so important?

Patient: You told me about the dangers of blood pressure. I know it can damage my heart or even cause stroke.

Doctor: That's right. High blood pressure can lead to heart attacks, kidney disease, and stroke. Do you know why I've recommended medication to control your blood pressure?

Analysis

Note that the interviewee has broached the topic in a nonjudgmental manner. The encounter is more likely to be productive if the patient does not feel threatened. Open-ended questions are best at first.

Patients who are noncompliant with treatment often feel guilty, self-conscious, defensive, or ashamed. Blaming or accusing the patient may inflame the situation.

To effect change in behavior, it's important to first understand if the patient recognizes the importance of the medical problem, and the health risks if the problem is untreated.

Patient: The medication can control my blood pressure, and that would cut down my risk of running into problems.

Doctor: You're absolutely right. What we have tried so far hasn't been working. I'm concerned about what high blood pressure can do to your health. What do you think?

Use of "we" shows the patient that this is more of a partnership rather than the doctor imposing his viewpoint on the patient.

Patient: I know have to get more serious about this. I don't want to develop any problems.

Doctor: Let's get back to what you said earlier. You were hoping that diet and exercise would help lower your blood pressure.

Patient: That's why I don't always take the medication. I keep hoping that diet and exercise will do the job.

Doctor: What can I do differently to help you with this?

Asking the patient for his thoughts to address the problem builds a stronger partnership.

Patient: I've tried diet and exercise for so long. I think it's time for me to give the medication a real chance.

Case # 20: Key Points

- In a meta-analysis of compliance in common conditions, such as diabetes and high blood pressure, researchers found that only 59% of patients take medication as prescribed most of the time.
- Noncompliance is a major cause of treatment failure, and is not often appreciated by physicians.
- If the MMI asks you to engage in a dialogue with an actor playing the role of a noncompliant patient, remember to be gentle and nonthreatening in your approach. Many noncompliant patients feel guilt, embarrassment, or a sense of failure. These are strong negative emotions, and your ability to show concern for the patient will be the key to a successful encounter.
- Avoid blaming or accusing the patient with such statements as "You're not doing a good job taking your medication." Contrast this with "I'm concerned that if we don't get your blood pressure under control, you could develop some problems with your heart." Statements starting with the word "I" and expressing your concern set the tone for partnership to solve the problem.

Approach to the Noncompliant Patient

Step 1: With any noncompliant patient, be gentle in your approach. To understand its root cause and solve the problem, discuss noncompliance in a nonjudgmental manner. Use open-ended questions to begin the dialogue.

Step 2: Assess the patient's understanding of the medical problem, and risks to health if the problem is not treated.

Step 3: Determine if the patient has any concerns or questions about the recommended treatment.

Step 4: Determine if the patient has been considering or using other treatments.

Step 5: Make noncompliance a shared problem.

Step 6: Ask the patient about strategies that he believes might be effective.

References

Cramer J, Benedict A, Muszbek N, Keskinaslan A, Khan Z. The significance of compliance and persistence in the treatment of diabetes, hypertension and dyslipidaemia: a review. *Int J Clin Pract* 2008; 62 (1): 76–87.

Kleinsinger F. Working with the noncompliant patient. *Perm J* 2010; 14 (1): 54–60.

Case # 21

After returning from Sierra Leone where she had nursed Ebola Virus patients, Kaci Hickox was placed in an isolation tent in New Jersey. At the time, she had no symptoms of infection. Critical over her forced isolation, she was driven to her boyfriend's home in Maine four days later. The Governor of Maine ordered her quarantined but she refused to comply with the order. Medical science has shown that a person infected with the Ebola Virus doesn't become infectious until the onset of symptoms such as fever. Discuss the ethical issues involved.

Sample Answer

What makes the United States great is the freedom to choose how we live our lives. So I can see how a quarantine order would be difficult for people because of its impact on individual freedom.

However, we also have a responsibility to the community and the public. And that's what quarantine asks us to do, protect the health of the public. In this case, the government is asking the nurse to not put others at risk.

In terms of the appropriateness of the quarantine order, I would first look at the risk involved. We have to ask ourselves how likely are we to be harmed and how great will the harm be. In the Ebola Virus crisis, the harm is of great magnitude – serious illness or even death.

Although risk is an important consideration, understanding the science behind the virus and its transmission is crucial. From my understanding, unless people exhibit symptoms, they are not contagious. So if someone is without symptoms, there would be no reason to severely restrict their movements. I believe to quarantine someone when harm is unlikely would be unfair.

What I would consider doing is separating people at risk of acquiring Ebola Virus into different groups. One group could be those exposed but asymptomatic. Another group would be patients who are symptomatic but not yet known to have infection. It's the latter group that I would consider quarantining and testing for the virus.

Analysis

The interviewee begins by discussing the importance of individual freedom. Also presented is the responsibility that people have to protect the community.

In medicine, if possible, we like to make decisions based on the available evidence.

Here the interviewee offers a strategy to divide people into different risk groups.

However, before resorting to quarantine, I would talk with public health officials about less restrictive ways to handle the situation. What about having the person stay at home voluntarily and monitoring themselves for symptoms? If the person notices a rise in temperature, then he or she can seek medical attention and then enter isolation.

The interviewee realizes that quarantine may be needed but looks for less restrictive ways to protect the public while maintaining the person's autonomy. She does not hesitate to seek the help of others.

It's the responsibility of governors to make important decisions on behalf of their constituents. So I can understand their desire to move quickly to protect the public. Their intentions are good but I do believe that decisions have to be made based on science rather than fear.

The interviewee looks at the issue from the perspective of the governor.

In summary, I would not favor mandating an Ebola Virus quarantine for all people traveling to the United States from affected countries. I base this recommendation on the available science. However, I do believe that individuals at risk for infection have a responsibility to the public to not put others in harm's way.

Ethical Issues Related to Ebola Virus

MMI applicants should be familiar with "hot topics" in medical ethics. In 2015, perhaps no other topic received as much attention as the Ebola Virus Disease. Below are some other ethical issues related to the disease that we recommend you read about before your MMI.

- Is it ethically appropriate for healthcare professionals to opt out of care of patients with Ebola Virus Disease?

- Should residents be allowed to participate in the care of suspected or confirmed Ebola Virus Disease patients?

- Should Americans infected with the Ebola Virus be airlifted out of Africa when others are not?

- Should Americans infected with Ebola Virus be given a highly experimental treatment?

- Should Africans infected with Ebola Virus be given a highly experimental treatment?

Chapter 13

MMI And Your Future

As evidence supporting the multiple mini interview process in medical school admissions has accumulated, educators have started to examine the potential role of this interview format in residency admissions. Below we have listed and described some studies and their findings:

- In one study performed at a single family medicine residency program, the MMI was found to be a useful way to assess characteristics and behaviors valued in residents.[1]

- Researchers in Pennsylvania found the MMI process to yield reliable results among internal medicine residency applicants. Surveys of faculty and applicants showed that the format was preferred over the traditional interview.[2]

- Several programs in emergency medicine have adopted the MMI in their residency selection process. A recent article discussed whether the format addressed stakeholder needs.[3]

- At a recent Pediatric Academic Societies Meeting, Dr. Mona Attisha, Program Director of the Pediatric Residency Program at Hurley Medical Center, shared the findings of her research utilizing MMI in the residency selection process. She found that MMI data allowed for more informed rank-order decisions and was more predictive of future performance.[4]

- A study utilizing the MMI in the otolaryngology residency selection process found good reliability. Researchers also noted that the approach was considered acceptable to all major stakeholders.[5]

What does this mean for you? It may be that you will encounter the MMI again when it comes time to apply for residency.

References

[1] Hofmeister M, Lockyer J, Crutcher R. The acceptability of the multiple mini interview for resident selection. *Fam Med* 2008; 40 (10): 734-40.

[2] Fraga J, Oluwasanio A, Wasser T, Donato A, Alweis R. Reliability and acceptability of a five-station multiple mini-interview model for residency program recruitment. *Community Hosp Intern Med Perspect* 2013; 3 (3-4): 10.

[3] Phillips A, Garmel G. Does the multiple mini-interview address stakeholder needs? An applicant's perspective. *Ann Emerg Med* 2014; 64 (3): 316-9.

[4] Hanna-Attisha M, Cederna-Meko C, Campe B. Modified multiple mini interview (3MI): An effective & efficient approach for screening critical milestones during resident selection. Presented at Pediatric Academic Societies Poster Session (Publication 1533-510), Vancouver 2014.

[5] Campagna-Vaillancourt M, Manoukian J, Razack S, Nguyen L. Acceptability and reliability of multiple mini interviews for admission to otolaryngology residency. *Laryngoscope* 2014; 124 (1): 91-6.

Chapter 14

The Preclinical Years Of Medical School

Note: The following chapter is excerpted from the book – Success in Medical School: Insider Advice for the Preclinical Years

The preclinical years of medical school are extremely challenging, and that may be understating the reality. At one medical school, faculty assigned "29,239 pages of reading for the 12 basic science modules that were scheduled during 71 weeks."[1]

As you begin med school, you'll hear a lot of advice.

- "If you thought the MCAT was tough, wait until you see the USMLE."

- "The material it took you a semester to cover in college? You'll get through that in a week in med school."

- "If you want to go down the ROAD, you'd better start planning now, figure out your research, and make your connections early - and you'll have to maximize that first summer off." [ROAD = Radiology, Ophthalmology, Anesthesiology, Dermatology]

There is at least some truth in every one of those statements.

Medical school is extremely challenging, and not just in the ways that you'd assume. The sheer volume of material covered is staggering. And most importantly, unlike in some of your college courses, much of it builds upon prior material. Your study methods therefore have to ensure long-term retention. In Chapter 2 [Preclinical Courses], you'll hear advice from students, faculty, and experts, as well as the results of research, on how to learn such a large volume of material, and how to ensure retention. In one study, researchers found that "in general, study skills are stronger predictors of first-semester total grades than aptitude as measured by the MCAT and undergraduate GPA."[2] The importance of long-term retention of basic science material is emphasized by the United States Medical Licensing Exam. The USMLE Step 1 exam is taken at the end of the preclinical years, and your score on this single exam can influence the course of your career. The exam tests your ability to take the basic science material covered over two years in medical school and apply it to clinical situations. In Chapter 3, you'll learn about the exam itself, as well as the most common mistakes that students make when preparing. You'll learn about resources that can aid your preparation, and you'll learn about the importance of this single score in the residency application process. Chapter 4 provides specifics about the COMLEX Level 1 exam. This exam, taken by osteopathic students, is of similar importance.

While mastering such a large amount of basic science material is extremely challenging, unfortunately that's not enough. Your skills in the hands-on art and science of patient care will be critical. Learning about a disease and its manifestations in the classroom does not ensure that you'll know what to do when faced with a patient in the clinic. It is widely believed that physicians' examination skills have deteriorated over the years. While a number of factors may be responsible, it is believed that clinical skills training may play a role. In fact, if you don't adequately learn certain skills and techniques during your preclinical courses [Introduction to Clinical Medicine or Physical Diagnosis], you may never learn them, not even during clerkships. "Surveys have indicated that less than 16% of attending time may be spent at the patient's side."[3] This has important ramifications for patient care. When researchers observed interns and residents, they noted frequent errors in physical exam technique, including improper use of instruments. In Chapters 5 [Taking a Patient History] and 6 [Physical Examination], you'll learn how to make the most of your history and physical exam education.

The challenges of the preclinical years extend beyond the well-known. Chapters 11 and 12 provide some startling statistics on medical student well-being and issues of professionalism. Physicians are challenged on a daily basis with the stressors of clinical patient care, and the coping mechanisms and buffering strategies you develop now, as a preclinical student, will be vital throughout the course of your career.

Several chapters highlight the significant opportunities available to medical students. Medical schools, organizations, and individual medical students have all been able to impact medical practice or their communities in significant ways, and their accomplishments are inspiring. Chapters on Community Service, Extracurricular Activities, and Research serve as a guide on how to get started, and highlight the numerous opportunities for preclinical students to become involved and thus have the opportunity to make a meaningful impact. Chapters on teaching, awards, and international experiences provide details on further opportunities.

Throughout these challenges, you do have to consider your future. As the residency selection process for certain fields becomes ever more competitive, students who have at least started strategizing early in their education will be at an advantage. Chapter 16 [Choosing a Specialty] reviews the process of strategizing in detail. For the most competitive specialties, great grades and high USMLE scores are not enough. You'll need great letters of recommendation and support from faculty advocates. In Chapter 10 [Mentoring], you'll learn ways in which preclinical students can approach established faculty members and obtain their assistance and guidance. You'll also need additional distinctions. Most applicants to the competitive specialties will have performed research, and many will have publications or presentations to their name. Chapter 7 [Research] reviews the process, demonstrates how students can begin, details what to seek in a research project, and provides specifics on research, publication, and presentation opportunities available to medical students. Some residency programs also seek additional factors of distinction, such as involvement in extracurricular activities, evidence of leadership, and commitment to service. In "Choosing a Specialty," you'll learn how to start the process of exploring a specialty. The chapter also includes specifics about identifying research opportunities, locating specialty-specific mentors, seeking out community service projects within the field, and other specialty-specific opportunities.

Throughout the next 300+ pages, we'll review each of these areas in detail. From grades and exams, to the art of patient care, to strategizing for your career, you'll learn specific, detailed information relevant to the preclinical medical student. These reviews and recommendations are based on the experiences of students, residents, and faculty, as well as a thorough review of the scientific literature in the areas of medical education and patient care. This combination of insider information and evidence-based advice is utilized to help you gain the strongest foundation as you face the challenges of medical school. Your goal is to become the best doctor possible, and that process begins on day one of medical school.

Preclinical courses/grades

At one medical school, faculty assigned "29,239 pages of reading."[1]

The core of this chapter centers on one vital question related to that startling fact. How can a student read and retain such a large volume of information?

In Chapter 2, you'll learn what students, faculty, and experts advise on how to get through the mountain of material a med student is expected to master. The most common mistake that med students seem to make? They assume that studying longer and harder will be enough to succeed.

It's not.

The students who are able to excel in medical school have learned how to effectively strategize and utilize the techniques of active learning, among other study strategies. Reading and highlighting material, even multiple times, won't be enough to ensure the long-term retention that medical school requires.

Upperclassmen at the University of Alabama Birmingham School of Medicine offer the following advice to new students: "The material is rarely difficult; there is just a mountain's worth to cover. A normal medical school exam seems like a cumulative final in the most strenuous science course you took in undergraduate. You simply cannot learn the material overnight or with one quick read-through of the scripts."[4]

Prior to med school, you no doubt heard about the heavy academic workload. The volume of material to be covered is truly enormous, and while students expect this, it doesn't fully sink in until the first week when you receive lecture materials, syllabi, and books. Consider the following comments made by new medical students:

- "I was worried that I wouldn't be able to keep up."

- "What scared me most was the amount of information I was asked to master."

- "It was all so overwhelming. How could I possibly learn it all? After all, I could barely carry it."

While the preclinical curriculum will vary among medical schools, most schools will focus on the same core subjects. In 2006, the International Association of Medical Science Educators convened a group of respected medical educators to answer some key questions about the role and value of the basic sciences in medical education.[5] The educators identified eight sciences - anatomy, physiology, biochemistry, neuroscience, microbiology, immunology, pathology, and pharmacology – as "vital foundations of medical practice." Also deemed critical to a strong foundation was education in behavioral sciences, genetics, epidemiology, molecular biology, and biostatistics.

Given the significant challenges of learning and retaining this much material, what is the best way for students to approach their preclinical courses? In this chapter, you'll learn the differences between top and average performers, and you'll learn about study strategies that have led to success. In one study, researchers found that "in general, study skills are stronger predictors of first-semester total grades than aptitude as measured by the MCAT and undergraduate GPA."[2] You'll learn about common mistakes that students make when approaching the basic sciences, and how to avoid those mistakes. You'll also hear suggestions from students who have successfully navigated these challenges.

USMLE Step 1 Exam

The USMLE Step 1 exam is a critical factor in the residency selection process. While there's a lot that can be said about preparation for this exam, it can be summarized in one sentence: typical study methods don't work for this exam.

To become an allopathic physician with the license to practice in the United States, you must pass the three-part United States Medical Licensing Exam, referred to as the USMLE. Medical students typically take the first part of the USMLE (Step 1 exam) at the end of the second year of medical school. The Step 1 score is also an important criterion used by residency programs in the selection process. In a 2006 survey of over 1,200 residency program directors across 21 medical specialties, the USMLE Step 1 score was found to be the second most important residency selection factor, following only grades in required clerkships.[6]

In competitive specialties such as dermatology, plastic surgery, ophthalmology, otolaryngology, radiology, neurosurgery, orthopedic surgery, and urology, many programs have a cut-off, or threshold, USMLE Step 1 score. Highly sought-after programs in less competitive specialties may also have threshold scores. Applicants who score above the cut-off are considered for interviews. Those below the cut-off may be removed from consideration.

"Many medical students that we have talked to underestimate the amount of clinical material on the USMLE Step 1 examination.... Furthermore, many students also leave the exam feeling somewhat intimidated regarding the clinical slant of how the basic science material is tested." - Drs. Tao Le and Chirag Amin, authors of the popular book *First Aid for the USMLE Step 1*.[7]

The National Board of Medical Examiners (NBME), which administers the exam, states that the USMLE Step 1 exam "assesses whether you can understand and apply important concepts of the sciences to the practice of medicine, with special emphasis on the principles and mechanisms underlying health, disease, and modes of therapy."[8]

While strong factual knowledge is necessary for exam success, most questions seek to determine your ability to apply basic science knowledge to clinical problems, rather than regurgitate isolated facts. In a recent posting at www.usmle.org, the National Board of Medical Examiners announced a further reduction in the number of Step 1 items presented without a clinical vignette.

This focus on clinical applications, rather than rote memorization, makes the USMLE a distinctive and challenging exam for most students. Adding to the challenge is the amount of information that students are expected to master. The content of the exam is drawn from the following disciplines: Anatomy, Physiology, Biochemistry, Pathology, Pharmacology, Microbiology, Behavioral Sciences, and Nutrition/Genetics/Aging. The Step 1 exam, therefore, covers information that requires 2 years of medical school to learn. Most students devote a 6 week block of time to review material and prepare for this exam. Cramming, obviously, won't work.

In Chapter 3, you'll learn the basics of the Step 1 exam. What material does it cover, and what material do you need to review? Does the curriculum offered by your school provide adequate preparation? Most schools adhere to a disciplines-based, organ-based, or problem-based curriculum, or a combination thereof. Researchers have utilized AAMC [Association of American Medical Colleges] data to determine what effects, if any, the curricular approach had on USMLE scores.

What are the mistakes that students make when preparing for the exam? Dr. Judy Schwenker, Kaplan's Curriculum Director, has identified the five most common mistakes students make when preparing for the Step 1 exam.[9] These include passive studying, insufficient practice with questions, memorizing without understanding the material, inappropriate test day strategies, and misreading or misinterpreting questions. In this chapter, we provide suggestions on exam preparation that avoid these common mistakes.

How should you study for an exam of this importance that's so distinct from other exams? Drs. Helen Loeser and Maxine Papadakis, Deans at the UCSF School of Medicine, advise: "Use active learning methods as you integrate your knowledge and apply basic science information to clinical vignettes."[10] Research has shown that active learning leads to better long-term retention of information and easier retrieval of information when needed. In this chapter you'll learn about techniques of active learning, and resources that can aid in your preparation.

COMLEX Level 1 Exam

For osteopathic students, the route to licensure requires passage of the three-level COMLEX. These parts include COMLEX Level 1, COMLEX Level 2 (further subdivided into Level 2 Cognitive Evaluation or CE and Level 2 Performance Evaluation or PE), and COMLEX Level 3. Osteopathic students typically take the COMLEX Level 1 exam near the end of the second year, while both components of the Level 2 exam are taken in the fourth year.

According to the National Board of Osteopathic Medical Examiners (NBOME), which administers the exam, the COMLEX Level 1 exam "emphasizes the scientific concepts and principles necessary for understanding the mechanisms of health, medical problems and disease processes."[11] Information about the content of the exam is available at their website (see Bulletin of Information), and should be reviewed carefully. In contrast to the USMLE, the COMLEX examination incorporates osteopathic principles, including the use of osteopathic manipulative treatment.

Like the USMLE, the COMLEX Level 1 exam is used by programs in the residency selection process. This process can be divided into two phases – screening and ranking. In the screening phase, programs whittle down a large applicant pool into a smaller group. The members of this group will be offered interview invitations. The COMLEX Level 1 score is frequently used in the screening process by allopathic and osteopathic residency programs. In 2010, a survey of several thousand allopathic residency program directors representing multiple specialties was performed by the National Resident Matching Program. The survey found that the Level 1 score was the factor used most commonly in the screening process.[12]

In competitive specialties such as dermatology, plastic surgery, ophthalmology, otolaryngology, radiology, neurosurgery, orthopedic surgery, and urology, many programs have a cut-off or threshold COMLEX Level 1 score. Highly sought-after programs in less competitive specialties may also have threshold scores. Applicants who score above the cut-off are considered for interviews. Those below the cut-off may be removed from consideration.

In this chapter, you'll learn about how the COMLEX Level 1 score is used by residency programs in the selection process. You'll learn about ways to identify your strengths and weaknesses, as well as indicators that you may be at risk for a low COMLEX score. You'll also hear tips to help you prepare for the exam. For example, the NBOME offers students the opportunity to take the Comprehensive Osteopathic Medical Self-Assessment Exam (COMSAE) as a means to assess readiness for the COMLEX Level 1 exam. The format and structure of the Phase 1 COMSAE resembles that of the Level 1 exam. Furthermore, scoring and reporting of the two exams are similar. In a study performed by the NBOME, the organization found that the two scores were highly related. While candidates can take a timed or untimed COMSAE, the data seems to suggest that the timed exam has higher self-assessment value.

While we review the role of the COMLEX in the residency selection process, in this chapter you'll learn that this score, by itself, may not be sufficient for all residency programs. In recent years, an increasing number of osteopathic students have applied to residency programs approved by the Accreditation Council for Graduate Medical Education (ACGME). According to Drs. Cummings and Sefcik, Deans at the Michigan State University College of Osteopathic Medicine, "in 2006, more than two of every three DOs [6,629 of 9,618] in postdoctoral training were in an ACGME program."[13] Since ACGME-accredited programs are less familiar with the COMLEX score, these programs often recommend that osteopathic applicants take the USMLE Step 1 exam. This allows programs to make easier comparisons between MD and DO student applicants.

Taking a Patient History

It's well-known that the transition between learning about medicine in the classroom and actually applying that knowledge in the care of real patients is quite challenging. Studies have confirmed that students have high levels of stress and anxiety as they move from the preclinical to clinical years of medical school.[14]

Clinical skills, including the history and physical exam, are often mentioned as a major struggle in the transition period. One student described her discomfort. "I felt uncomfortable talking to the patient and trying to come up with methodical ways of asking questions and making sure I didn't miss things, not just jumping around all over the place."[15]

Traditionally, preclinical students have had limited contact with patients. In recent years, however, schools have placed new emphasis on clinical skills training in early medical education. Some schools now even introduce students to patients as soon as the first week or month of medical school.

Medical organizations have also recognized the importance of an early emphasis on clinical skills, including communication. In 2004, the Institute of Medicine made the acquisition and development of communication skills a top priority during medical education. That same year, the National Board of Medical Examiners (NBME) began requiring students to take a clinical skills exam (USMLE Step 2 CS) as a means to assess competence in communication. The hope is that through education on effective communication, students will be better versed in how to listen, question, counsel, and motivate patients.

Your efforts to improve communication skills will also impact your clerkship performance. In a survey of clerkship directors, while over 95% felt that students require an intermediate to advanced level of communication skills, approximately 30% felt that new clerkship students aren't sufficiently prepared.[16]

Medical schools evaluate communication skills in different ways. One is through comprehensive clinical skills assessment using standardized patients. Researchers have interviewed faculty members responsible for helping those students who don't perform well in these assessments. Some of the issues have focused on patient histories.[17] "Many low-scoring students focused prematurely, failing to ask open-ended questions or adequately characterize the chief complaint. Respondents also observed students being too focused on the history of present illness, omitting or incompletely exploring the pertinent past medical, social, or family history, particularly as they related to the chief complaint." Some students failed to explore the patient's perspective on the illness. The authors wrote that "these students treated standardized patients as symptoms or diagnoses rather than as people with feelings or concerns."

In Chapter 5, you'll learn how to make the most of your clinical skills education. You'll learn about the deficiencies that have been documented in the physician-patient communication literature with respect to history taking, and how educators have developed benchmarks to guide medical students in their acquisition of important communication skills. As you develop your history taking skills, you'll learn how to use these benchmarks, solicit feedback to assess your progress, and reflect on your own performance in order to improve your skills.

Physical Examination

Although 80% of diagnoses are made based on the history and physical examination, evidence indicates that the physical exam skills of physicians today are inadequate. It is widely believed that physicians' examination skills have deteriorated over the years. While advances in technology, including laboratory testing and radiologic imaging, are partly to blame for this decline, clinical skills training during medical school and residency are also factors. According to Dr. Sal Mangione, Director of the Physical Diagnosis Curriculum at Jefferson Medical College, too little time is spent during medical school learning these skills. "Surveys have indicated that less than 16% of attending time may be spent at the patient's side."[18]

Physical exam skills have important, obvious ramifications for patient care, and the education you receive in this area during medical school is critical. If you don't learn certain skills at this stage of your education, you may never have the opportunity to do so. In one study, researchers observed interns and residents, and noted frequent errors in physical exam technique.[19] Errors included improper manual technique or use of instruments. The authors asserted that these errors resulted from a failure to learn the necessary psychomotor skills during the preclinical years.

In the real world of medicine, these deficiencies in skills have serious consequences. In a study of interns and residents on a general medicine service, at least one serious physical exam error was made for nearly two-thirds of the patients examined. The errors included failure to detect splenomegaly or focal neurological signs, findings that once discovered led to significant changes in diagnosis and treatment.[20]

While clinical courses such as "Introduction to Clinical Medicine" and "Physical Diagnosis" teach these skills, this is one area where students cannot rely on passive learning. In Chapter 6, you'll learn how to make the most of your physical exam education. These skills aren't easy to learn. While a recent study showed that third-year med students felt quite confident about their ability to measure blood pressure, students were significantly less confident in their ability to assess retinal vasculature, detect a thyroid nodule, or measure jugular venous pressure.[21]

You'll also learn the importance of soliciting preceptor feedback. If errors aren't picked up at this stage of your education, they may never be. While you might expect that your future residents or attendings would be able to correct your performance, the literature has shown that students on clerkships often aren't observed while performing physical exams. They are typically assumed to already possess the necessary skills.

The chapter also addresses other facets of physical exams, including the patient's comfort. You'll learn how to approach an often uncomfortable situation in a manner that most reassures the patient. In the article "Learning to Doctor," Conrad aptly describes the concerns of students:[22]

Students tell patients twice their age to get undressed, and then cross conventional barriers of interpersonal space to inspect the intimacies of their bodies. In addition to anxiety about doing it right, students frequently must deal with their own reactions to their patient as well as discomforting feelings of being invasive.

Research

In a presentation to medical students titled "Research in Medical School," Dr. Daniel West discussed reasons why students should consider involvement in research. Dr. West noted that participation in research allows medical students to explore a specialty in more depth, enhance critical thinking and other related skills, assess suitability for a career in academic medicine, and strengthen credentials for residency positions.[23] Medical students recognize these benefits as well. In a survey of students at three medical schools, 83% agreed that participation in research was valuable within their medical education.[24]

In Chapter 7, we'll discuss these benefits in more depth. There are significant benefits to participation in research, and while barriers exist, many medical students are able to overcome these barriers, enhance their own skills and education, and make contributions to the scientific literature.

Research training leads to better critical thinking skills. The ability to critically appraise the literature is essential to the practice of evidence-based medicine. The University of Arizona College of Medicine writes that "as future physicians, being able to critically read a scientific journal along with keeping abreast of new medical innovations is an important facet of practice that can profoundly impact patient outcomes."[25] In a recent article, Mayo researchers wrote about how research benefits medical students.[26] "Studies have shown that students who had conducted research during medical school reported gains in knowledge and skills in appraising the literature, analyzing data, and writing for publication, along with more positive attitudes toward future research." Students report significant benefits from learning the process of research, from conception of an idea to publication and presentation. It is important for all physicians to learn about literature review, hypothesis generation, study methodology, and data analysis.

Research also has known benefits in the residency selection process. Dr. Scott Pretorius, former Radiology Residency Program Director at the University of Pennsylvania, wrote that "in this competitive market for radiology residency slots, medical students with research backgrounds...allow themselves the opportunity to stand out in a field of increasingly highly qualified applicants. As an advisor of medical students, I routinely recommend that students intending to apply for radiology residency seek out a research mentor and undertake some kind of research project."[27] In a survey of University of Tennessee medical students, 63% reported that research experience was beneficial in helping them secure a residency position.[28]

As you're applying for residency positions, it's important to know your competition. Among dermatology applicants, nearly 95% had participated in at least one research project, with over 80% claiming at least one abstract, publication, or presentation.[29] In radiation oncology, among U.S. senior applicants, only 9 of the 152 applicants reported not having a single abstract, publication, or presentation. While it's not a prerequisite for students applying to competitive fields, a student may stand out due to their lack of any research experience in these fields.

While students recognize the benefits of research, many find the barriers to involvement daunting. Difficulty finding a research supervisor can be a significant barrier, with only 44% of students in one study reporting that it was easy to identify one.[24] In this chapter, you'll learn how to identify research opportunities at your institution. We highlight ways to identify the "right" research mentor, as well as what to discuss with potential mentors and how to evaluate potential research projects.

In evaluating research experience during medical school, residency programs will look closely at the level of your involvement. Did you merely collect data? Or were you involved through all phases of the project (design of the project, data collection, analysis of the data, and writing the manuscript)? Programs also assess your productivity. Did your work result in a tangible measure, such as an abstract, manuscript, or presentation at a meeting? For many students involved in research, a publication or presentation resulting from their work would be ideal. While this isn't always possible, in this chapter you'll learn how to approach the issue of publication and learn about journals that are targeted to medical students.

You'll also learn about possibilities for presentation, even if those opportunities aren't initiated by your research mentor. Students may seek out opportunities to present their work at local, regional, national, and international meetings. At Stanford University School of Medicine, 52% of medical students had presented at a national meeting.[30] Symposiums and meetings geared to medical student research presentations include the National Student Research Forum (NSRF), Eastern-Atlantic Student Research Forum (ESRF), and Western Student Medical Research Forum (WSMRF). The NSRF is held at the University of Texas Medical Branch in Galveston, and provides a forum for students to give either poster or oral presentations.[31] Over 30 awards are given at this annual event.

Time has been reported as a major barrier to pursuing research in medical school. Many students become involved in research in the summer between the first and second years of medical school. Opportunities for summer research may also be available for newly admitted students who haven't yet started medical school. At the Mt. Sinai School of Medicine, 54 to 65% of students participated in summer research between 2001 and 2004.[32]

Some students are interested in a more substantial research experience, and in this chapter you'll learn about some of the "year-out" opportunities available to students across the country. The Clinical Research Fellowship for Medical Students, sponsored by the Doris Duke Charitable Foundation, offers one-year fellowships at one of 12 selected institutions in the U.S. The HHMI – NIH (Howard Hughes Medical Institute - National Institutes of Health) Research Scholars Program and NIH Clinical Research Training Program allow participants the opportunity to work on the NIH campus. Research Training Fellowships through the HHMI are also available to students, and support one year of research at a variety of academic institutions. This chapter highlights a number of other opportunities that are available for students interested in more substantial research experience.

Extracurricular Activities

As in college, the learning environment in medical school extends beyond the classroom, and institutions offer valuable opportunities to participate in a variety of extracurricular activities. For example, at the

Case Western Reserve University, there are over 40 medical student organizations.[33]

Involvement in these organizations provides a number of opportunities and benefits, and in Chapter 8 you'll learn more about the opportunities available. One of the most important is the further development of skills that are directly applicable to success as a physician. A few examples of vital skills in the daily life of a physician are teamwork, self-discipline, time management, and leadership, all of which are strengthened outside of the classroom through extracurricular involvement. Involvement in organizations is a way to develop and strengthen bonds with classmates, and since student organizations often have a faculty advisor or sponsor, students have extraordinary opportunities to work closely with faculty members. Such opportunities are usually unavailable to students during the preclinical years.

Some students are awarded recognition for their involvement. Every year, the American Medical Association honors 15 students with AMA Foundation Leadership Awards. These awards recognize students who have demonstrated "strong, nonclinical leadership skills in advocacy, community service, public health, and/or education."[34] Many other organizations recognize student involvement as well. When evaluating a student's contributions, organizations seek evidence of leadership, commitment, and the ability to make meaningful contributions to the goals of an organization. Some students, after reviewing the opportunities available at their school, commit to starting a new organization or founding a new chapter of a national organization. In this chapter, you'll learn what questions to ask, and what resources are available, as you review your opportunities.

Involvement may also help students reach their professional goals. Extracurricular activities "might provide evidence for non-cognitive attributes that predict success," writes Dr. Andrew Lee, Chairman of the Department of Ophthalmology at The Methodist Hospital.[35] "Leadership skills demonstrated by being an officer in extracurricular activities or being an Eagle Scout, or a leader or founder of a new organization or club are all looked upon favorably. The second goal is to look for evidence of non-cognitive attributes that might make a superior ophthalmologist (conflict resolution, team work, leadership ability, communication skills, performance under stress, maturity, seriousness of purpose, prior scholarly activity). Finally, programs are looking to graduate (and thus select) residents who will make the program proud."

In fact, extracurricular activities do serve as a significant nonacademic factor in the residency selection process. In a recent NRMP survey of 1,840 program directors representing the nineteen largest medical specialties, 59% of respondents cited volunteer/extracurricular experiences as a factor in selecting applicants to interview.[36]

Evidence suggests that meaningful contributions in extracurricular activities, particularly leadership, may serve as a predictor of residency performance. In one study of emergency medicine residency program directors, having a "distinctive factor" such as being a championship athlete or medical school officer, was one of three factors most predictive of residency performance.[37] In a study to determine predictors of otolaryngology resident success using data available at the time of interview, candidates having an exceptional trait such as leadership experience were found to be rated higher as residents.[38]

Community Service

In researching community service opportunities for medical students, we found ourselves amazed and inspired by the accomplishments of medical schools, medical school organizations, and individual medical students. In Chapter 9, you'll hear about the significant contributions made by students. You'll learn about opportunities for participation in community service, the impact your participation can have on the health of the community, and how your involvement can help you grow personally and professionally.

According to Dr. Aaron McGuffin, Senior Associate Dean for Medical Education at Marshall University School of Medicine, "there has been 2,700 hours of community service donated from the medical school students in the past 12 months. That is a lot of time in addition to doing their medical school work."[39] In 2008, the AAMC found that a significant percentage of medical school applicants had been involved in community service.[40] Sixty-three percent of the applicants reported nonmedical volunteer experience, while medical volunteer experience was reported by 77% of applicants. "They have a real sense of service, commitment, and discovery that I know we all want in a future doctor at our bedside," said Dr. Darrell Kirch, the AAMC President.[41]

While the provision of community service has been a major area of emphasis at U.S. medical schools for years, educators have recently stressed the importance of fostering education in community service among medical students. In 1998, Seifer defined service learning as "a structured learning experience that combines community service with preparation and reflection."[42] The Liaison Committee on Medical Education (LCME), which is responsible for the accreditation of medical schools, recommends that schools should not only provide students with sufficient opportunities "to participate in service-learning activities," but also "encourage and support student participation."[43]

Many schools provide such opportunities for service learning. In 2001, the Morehouse School of Medicine established the Center for Community Health and Service - Learning to engage students and other healthcare professionals in community service and service learning. Partnering with other organizations in the Atlanta area, the center aims to address the health disparities affecting underserved populations. At the University of New Mexico School of Medicine, community service is a key priority.[44] Educators have gone beyond just encouragement by freeing students in the afternoons during the first year for service engagement.

At other schools, student organizations have been able to make significant contributions to their communities. The AAMC's Medicine in the Community Grant Program (formerly known as Caring for Community) offers grant awards to medical students who wish to initiate, develop, and run a community service project.[45] According to the AAMC, "Medicine in the Community will help students to translate great ideas into meaningful service by contributing needed start-up and supplemental funds." Past recipients of the grant include the Medical College of Wisconsin Hmong Health Education Program. HHEP is an effort to improve health education and healthcare services for Wisconsin's Hmong population through educational workshops, outreach programs, support groups, and public service announcements. Another past recipient is the University of New Mexico School of Medicine Community Vision Project. Through the use of mobile eye clinics, basic vision care services are provided to American Indian and Hispanic populations.

For students wishing to make significant contributions to their communities, a number of organizations provide grants and assistance. In this chapter, you'll learn about grants and resources available to students who wish to initiate their own service project, as well as hear about other successful projects. For example, the Medical Student Section of the AMA (AMA-MSS) has created a list and description of projects that AMA-MSS chapters across the country have developed and implemented.[46] Since the 1970s, *Project Bank: The Encyclopedia of Public Health and Community Projects*, a tool offered by the AMA Alliance, has served as a useful compendium of community service projects conducted by state and county Alliances.[47]

Student-run health clinics have been initiated at many medical schools, and such involvement can have a significant impact on the personal and professional growth of medical students. At the University of California Davis, 85% of medical students volunteer in student clinics during their tenure in medical school.[48] "Students are often changed in unexpected, profound, and lasting ways after experiencing firsthand healthcare delivery to the poor, underserved, and marginalized," explains Dr. Ed Farrell, a physician volunteer at the Stout Street Clinic, which is run by students attending the University of Colorado School of Medicine.[49]

Not all schools have initiated such clinics. For motivated students, a number of resources are available for those wishing to establish a student-run health clinic. In an article published in JAMA, Cohen wrote "Eight Steps for Starting a Student-Run Clinic."[50] Another useful resource, "25 Steps to Starting a Student-Run Clinic," is available at the Society of Student-Run Free Clinics website.[51]

Community service provides known benefits to students as well. Research has shown that volunteering increases positive feelings, improves mental health, reduces the risk of depression, and lowers stress levels.[52-54] Participation may also improve communication skills, a vital skill in medicine. Community service is also a significant nonacademic factor in the residency selection process. Once accepted for an interview, the depth and breadth of your involvement in community service may help you stand out in a sea of academically qualified applicants.

Mentoring

The further we've progressed in our own careers, the more it becomes apparent how many individuals have helped us along the way. To achieve professional success in almost any field requires help. This may not be initially obvious to medical students, who are used to studying hard and achieving high grades on their own. Reaching medical school though, definitely required help. Professors who provided help outside of the classroom, researchers who offered the opportunity to participate in their project, advisors who provided letters of recommendation: the list goes on.

Succeeding in medical school, and succeeding in the residency match itself, requires even more assistance. At this next stage of your career, informed guidance and advice becomes even more important. For more competitive specialties or programs, you'll also require additional qualifications, which may mean approaching faculty members for research opportunities, in addition to the critically important letters of recommendation.

The definition of a mentor is one who "takes a special interest in helping another person develop into a successful professional."[55] Information, advice, and guidance from a knowledgeable faculty member is invaluable, and has the potential to impact your career in significant ways.

Sometimes the hardest part of initiating an effective relationship is just knowing how to get started. You'll be approaching respected, accomplished, busy individuals, and it can be difficult to know how to approach faculty members without appearing intrusive or presumptuous. For most students, asking for help from individuals in a position of authority can be intimidating. As a preclinical student, you also may have had limited experience in dealing with faculty on an individual level, and knowing what's acceptable can be hard to determine. Therefore, we provide advice from faculty experienced in this area. Certain approaches would be considered acceptable and non-intrusive by most faculty.

Some medical schools have formal mentoring programs. If such a program doesn't exist at your school, then you'll need confidence and possibly persistence to initiate a relationship. In one study, 28% of students met their mentors during inpatient clerkships, 19% through research activities, and 9% during outpatient clerkships.[56]

Local, regional, and state medical societies may have established mentoring programs. For example, the Santa Clara County Medical Association has a Mentor Program for Stanford medical students.[57] National organizations are committed to mentoring future doctors also. The Society of Academic Emergency Medicine (SAEM) has a medical student virtual advisor program open to students at all institutions.[58] Through this program, students can query experienced individuals about a variety of issues, including the EM residency application process. Dr. Joshua Grossman reminds students that mentors don't have to be in close proximity to you. "Your mentor does not need to be someone involved with your residency program that you see on a daily basis. By sharing your experience with someone removed from the situation you may be able to gain a different and beneficial perspective.[59]

While many of us have worked with assigned advisors during our education, a mentoring relationship is unique, and can be hard to delineate. In Chapter 10, you'll hear from mentors and organizations about the best way to develop such a relationship, and specifics on expectations and etiquette. The Association of Women Surgeons writes "A mentor is a unique individual to you: neither friend, nor colleague, but something of a combination of these and more. Because the relationship differs from those you have with others in your department, you may feel more relaxed and less constrained by professional protocol. This is acceptable to a point, but make certain that you respect the relationship."[60]

What do students talk about with a mentor? Issues may include those related to specialty choice, career satisfaction, wellness, work/life balance, residency selection process, research, interpersonal skills, professionalism, ethics, and courses. Once they have a firm idea of career choice, many students schedule meetings to discuss match strategy, seeking advice on steps they can take at their level to establish their credentials and strengthen their applications.

It can be intimidating and challenging to seek advice from qualified, well-informed faculty members. Is it worth seeking a mentor? While mentors can prove helpful throughout medical school, they can provide invaluable guidance during the process of preparing for the residency match. In researching our companion book, *The Successful Match: 200 Rules to Succeed in the Residency Match*, we asked applicants what they found most difficult about the residency application process. A number of applicants commented on the same issue. "There's so much conflicting information out there. How do you know what to believe? Who should you listen to?" Applicants with mentors have a decided advantage. Students benefit greatly when the wisdom, experience, and perspective of a knowledgeable faculty member are used to help them. Having a mentor to guide you through the complex residency application process is recognized by students as an important factor in boosting the strength of their application.

Well-being

In the past, issues of medical student well-being weren't a priority. Today, though, medical educators recognize that the intense pressures of medical school can have serious consequences for a medical student's physical health and emotional well-being. Research has demonstrated that these aren't just soft issues; they have real ramifications for patient care as well. In a recent study of pediatric residents, 20% of participants met criteria for depression, and these residents made over six times as many medication errors as their non-depressed colleagues.[61]

It's clear that medical school can be intensely stressful. In a survey of medical students, Wolf asked students to rate medical school stressors on a scale of 1 (not stressful) to 7 (extremely stressful).[62] The top four stressors, out of 16 ranked, were examinations, amount of classwork, financial responsibilities, and lack of time for recreation and entertainment. In a survey of medical students at 16 U.S. schools, 60% of first-year students reported either "moderate" or "a lot" of stress in the last two weeks.[63] This stress can lead to physician burnout, a condition which is characterized by emotional depletion from one's work, depersonalization, and the perception that one's work is inconsequential. In a survey of medical students in Minnesota, 45% had burnout.[64]

We chose to emphasize issues of medical student well-being within this chapter for several reasons. One was to highlight the impact of med school stressors on a student's health and well-being. Evidence indicates that this impact can be significant, and it is common for medical students to be affected. Even more importantly, in this chapter you'll learn how to buffer this stress. You'll learn about effective coping strategies identified by researchers. There is significant evidence that sleep, exercise, and the maintenance of strong social connections can provide strong buffers against the stressors of med school. Many students let these activities go first, though, in their efforts to focus on coursework and exams. However, studies indicate that these strategies, and others, should actually be priorities at times of intense stress. In a cross-sectional study of medical students, approximately 77% suffered some degree of anxiety.[65] Anxiety symptoms were considerably less common in students exercising at least 30 minutes three times a week. Another study revealed that "strong social ties was the factor most positively related to better health and life satisfaction" among a group of first-year medical students.[66]

It's important to develop effective coping strategies during the preclinical years, as the clinical care of patients only adds to stress. Dr. Liselotte Dyrbye, a faculty member at the Mayo Clinic, has performed extensive research in this area. She states that medical students need to have "the skills necessary to assess personal distress, determine its effects on their care of patients, recognize when they need assistance, and develop strategies to promote their own well-being. These skills are essential to maintain perspective, professionalism, and resilience through the course of a career…"[64]

In this chapter, you'll learn more about coping strategies. One effective strategy is problem-focused coping, in which efforts are made to solve or manage the problem causing the distress. Emotion-focused coping is another effective strategy, among many others. As a new med student, it's helpful to learn about how you cope with issues. In 1997, Charles Carver, a professor at the University of Miami, developed the brief COPE questionnaire, which can be used as a tool to help determine the coping strategies that you tend to use.[67] If your total scores are higher in the coping strategy categories of self-distraction, denial, substance abuse, or self-blame, you'll need to learn how to develop and use healthier and more effective coping skills. Dr. Julie Gentile, Director of Medical Student Mental Health Services at the Boonshoft School of Medicine at Wright State University, states that medical school "is a critical period in which to develop and utilize functional and effective coping strategies"[68]

Professionalism

What is professionalism, and why does it matter?

Consider the following observation made by a student:

Two doctors were down the hall from each other, and there were people around. One said to the other, "Did you hear about Mr. X?" And the other doctor said no, and he made a face like a dead face...sticking his tongue out, crossing his eyes, and tilting his head to the side. If anybody had noticed they wouldn't have been too happy with it.[69]

Students must be prepared to deal with issues of professionalism in their peers, in members of the healthcare team, and even in their teachers. Researchers found that exposure to unprofessional behavior began early in the medical education process and increased in each successive year. In Year 1 of medical school, 66% of students had "heard derogatory comments not in patient's presence" and 35% had "observed unethical conduct by residents or attending physicians."[70]

Why else does professionalism matter?

The vast majority of the students we meet have core values and a strong sense of personal integrity. Many therefore assume that issues of professionalism, while they may impact others around them, don't have any relevance to their own behavior. This is due to the common assumption that our core values regarding unethical behavior are stable over time. Studies of medical students contradict this assumption.

In one study, medical students were given a list of 11 unprofessional behaviors, and asked "Is the following behavior unprofessional for a medical student?"[71] Students were surveyed before matriculation and again six months into their first year of medical school. Researchers found that behaviors originally considered unprofessional rapidly became more acceptable. Medical students were also presented with four different scenarios, and asked "Must one do the following to be professional?" For the scenario "Report Cheating to a Professor or Administrator," 69% of students originally answered "yes." Six months into medical school, only 41% answered "yes."

There are therefore two core reasons to focus on this field. If you're a medical student, you are likely to witness lapses in professionalism in patient care, and you need to be prepared to deal with those lapses and protect your patients. You also need to define and protect your own core values and personal integrity.

What is professionalism? The foundation of the medical profession rests upon the trust that patients place in their physicians. Professionalism focuses on this foundation of trust. Although it's been defined in various ways, the core values and elements agreed upon include honesty, integrity, compassion, empathy, ability to communicate effectively with patients, and respect for others. Professionalism is a hot topic in undergraduate medical education. A number of medical education organizations, including the American Board of Internal Medicine, the Association of American Medical Colleges, and the National Board of Medical Examiners, have established professionalism as a required competency across the spectrum of medical education. Medical schools, in turn, have made it a point to educate preclinical students.

Many students, when hearing about a curriculum on professionalism, have similar reactions. "I already hold these values. Why should any of this concern me?" The studies that we describe in this chapter provide a definitive answer to that question. Most students are surprised to learn that the stresses and challenges of medical school can affect attitude, behavior, and conduct. However, this conclusion is clearly supported by a number of studies.

Even though medical students may actually harm patients when they act unethically, such actions persist. In a survey of students at a single medical school, 13 to 24% admitted to cheating during the clinical years of medical school.[72] Examples included "recording tasks not performed" and "lying about having ordered tests." In another study, students were asked whether they had heard of or witnessed unethical behaviors on the part of their student colleagues.[73] In response, 21% had personal knowledge of students "reporting a pelvic examination as 'normal' during rounds when it had been inadvertently omitted from the physical examination."

As students, you are likely to witness lapses in professional behavior, and may witness outright unethical behavior and fraud. These issues affect every level of our profession, and therefore you have to be prepared. You must guard against lapses in your own behavior, and be prepared to deal with lapses in colleagues or supervisors. As physicians, our goal is to treat and protect the patient, and this can be challenging in the real world of clinical medicine.

In a survey, third-year students at the University of Texas Medical Branch at Galveston were asked to evaluate their physicians' professionalism.[74] Although this review of nearly 3,000 evaluation forms revealed significant praise for positive faculty role modeling, negative comments were not infrequent. The majority dealt with "issues of language use, inappropriate use of humor, disrespectful treatment of patients or colleagues, and apparent disinterest in teaching."

Although we think of physicians as highly compassionate and ethical individuals, ethical lapses can extend to the highest levels of our profession. In a stunning case of scientific fraud, Dr. Scott Reuben, a highly regarded anesthesiologist whose research has significantly impacted how physicians treat surgical patients for pain, was found to have fabricated results in over 20 published studies.[75] In some cases, he is alleged to have even invented patients.

Choosing a Specialty

For many students, having just arrived at med school and facing voluminous amounts of material to be learned and retained, the focus will be on just making it through. Why, then, have we devoted a large chapter to the topic of choosing and exploring a specialty?

Those medical students who are able to plan and strategize for the residency match have a decided advantage. For the most competitive specialties, great grades and high USMLE scores are not enough. You'll need great letters of recommendation and support from faculty advocates. You'll also need additional distinctions. Most applicants to the competitive specialties will have performed research, and many will have publications or presentations to their name. Some programs look for additional factors of distinction, such as involvement in extracurricular activities, evidence of leadership, and commitment to service.

We present this information not to scare you, but to prepare you. These are the realities of the residency match today, and students who are prepared for these realities have a definite advantage. Your preparation doesn't need to be an overwhelming experience, either. It can start with the basics, such as exploring different specialties by shadowing faculty or speaking to residents. You may choose to take an aptitude test to help guide you in your exploration of specialties. Many students maximize their free summer after first year by participating in research. Those who are knowledgeable can obtain research grants from organizations to fund their research. This has tangible benefits. It results in research experience, an awarded research grant, and the opportunity to develop a relationship with a research mentor who may be able to support your application down the road.

In this chapter, you'll learn more about how to approach the process of choosing a specialty. You'll learn how to approach your target department, and how to cultivate opportunities. You'll gain from the insider knowledge presented in this section, as the chapter outlines, for each and every specialty, detailed specifics about medical student opportunities. These include mentorship programs, research grants targeted to medical students, and information about national meetings.

Why is it important to at least start thinking about your specialty choice now? While many med students wait until the clinical years to assess fit, this approach can be problematic. At most schools, students are required to rotate through the major or core specialties (internal medicine, general surgery, pediatrics, psychiatry, family medicine, obstetrics & gynecology) before pursuing clerkships in other fields. After completing these core rotations during the third year, students aren't left with much time. Most have two to three months of elective time to explore other specialties before they need to decide, since residency applications are typically submitted in September of the fourth year. For example, in a survey of med schools, it was found that anesthesiology is an elective rotation in 66% of schools.[76] For most students, this means that unless you attend a school with a flexible clerkship curriculum, you won't be able to rotate through the specialty until the beginning of your fourth year.

This can have a decided impact on a student's career. In one study of medical students, 26.2% were unsure of their specialty choice at matriculation.[77] Surprisingly, a similar proportion remained undecided at graduation. According to Gwen Garrison, Director of Student and Applicant Services at the AAMC, 30% of residents "either switch from their intended specialty after a transitional or preliminary year or switch outright during their specialty residency."[78] Dr. George Blackall, Director of Student Development at Penn State University College of Medicine, offers some reasons why residents switch. "Residents primarily switch because they a) realize their initial choice is not as interesting as another specialty, or b) desire a different lifestyle, level of flexibility, or income."[78]

In this chapter, you'll learn how to start the process of exploring a specialty. During the preclinical years, one way to assess fit for specialties is by completing personality-type inventories. The premise of this approach is that people are most satisfied professionally when there is a good match between their specialty choice and their values, skills, and interests. Commonly used assessment methods include the AAMC Careers in Medicine program and the Glaxo Wellcome Pathway Evaluation Program. The AAMC Careers in Medicine (CiM) is a structured program designed to help students gain a better understanding of their personality, values, skills, and interests. The program also allows for exploration of different specialties. The AAMC writes that "as you work through the CiM program, you'll gain the tools to make an informed decision, based on guided self-reflection and the information you'll gather about many career options available to you."[79] Another resource is the Medical Specialty Aptitude Test, an online test developed by the University of Virginia School of Medicine.[80] It is based on content and material from the book, How to Choose a Medical Specialty, by Anita Taylor. The website indicates that "you will be asked to rate your tendencies compared to the tendencies of physicians in each specialty. The higher your score for a given specialty, the more similar you are to the physicians in that specialty."

What is the most important factor in choosing a specialty? In a recent survey of graduating medical students, approximately 97% reported that fit with personality, skills, and interests was moderately or strongly influential in choosing which specialty to pursue as a career.[81] No other factor was given as much importance.

For many students, work/life balance also plays an important role. In the 2010 AAMC Medical School Graduation Questionnaire, over 11,000 graduating students were asked, "How influential was work/life balance in helping you choose your specialty?"[81] Over 70% of respondents reported work/life balance as being either moderately or strongly influential in their decision-making process. In 1989, Schwartz introduced the term controllable lifestyle to refer to "specialties that offer regular and predictable hours."[82] These specialties are often characterized by fewer hours spent at work and less frequent on-call duties, allowing for greater personal time and flexibility to pursue other activities. Specialties that are generally felt to offer a controllable lifestyle include anesthesiology, dermatology, neurology, ophthalmology, otolaryngology, pathology, psychiatry, and radiology.

Research has shown that efforts to explore specialties during the preclinical years can increase the certainty of specialty choice.[83] In this chapter, you'll learn about multiple avenues to learn more about specialties during the preclinical years. Examples include:

- Identify and work with a mentor
- Volunteer for clinical experiences (e.g., shadowing)
- Perform specialty-specific research
- Meet and speak with as many physicians as you can in your specialties of interest
- Attend local and national specialty organization meetings
- Join specialty interest groups (e.g., Internal Medicine Interest Group, Emergency Medicine Interest Group)

For each of these avenues, we've included specifics on how to proceed. Medical students value mentoring relationships, but identifying and working with a faculty member can be difficult. According to Dr. Gus Garmel, Co-Program Director of the Stanford-Kaiser Emergency Medicine Residency Program, finding a mentor is not easy.[84] "How students find faculty mentors is challenging, because their exposure to a broad selection of emergency medicine faculty may be limited early in their training." We've provided suggestions on how to proceed for each of the specialties. For example, the American College of Physicians (ACP) has created a Mentoring Database. To access the database, which includes program directors, clerkship directors, chairs of medicine, practicing internists, and residents, you must be a member. Mentors are available to answer "specific questions about scheduling your summer preceptorships, getting through the match, and preparing for clerkships and residency interviews…"[85]

We've also included further information about identifying research opportunities. For many of the most competitive specialties, such as dermatology and radiation oncology, your competition will almost all have performed research. Therefore, if you're considering dermatology as a career, you may wish to participate in research between the first and second years of medical school. Research experience has significant educational benefits. Beyond those benefits, research allows a student the chance to develop a relationship with their research supervisor.

In this chapter, you'll gain from the insider knowledge presented for each and every specialty, with detailed, specific information about medical student opportunities.

Chapter excerpted from the book - Success in Medical School: Insider Advice for the Preclinical Years

References

[1] Klatt E, Klatt C. How much is too much reading for medical students? Assigned reading and reading rates at one medical school. *Acad Med* 2011; 86(9): 1079-83.
[2] West C, Sadoski M. Do study strategies predict academic performance in medical school? *Med Educ* 2011; 45(7): 696-703.
[3] Collins G, Cassie J, Daggett C. The role of the attending physician in clinical training. *J Med Educ* 1978; 53: 429-31.
[4] University of Alabama Birmingham School of Medicine. Advice from MS-2 Students. Available at: http://main.uab.edu/uasom/2/show.asp?durki=111766. Accessed October 22, 2011.
[5] Finnerty E, Chauvin S, Bonaminio G, Andrews M, Carroll R, Pangaro L. Flexner revisited: the role and value of the basic sciences in medical education. *Acad Med* 2010; 85 (2): 349-55.
[6] Green M, Jones P, Thomas J. Selection criteria for residency: results of a national program directors survey. *Acad Med* 2009; 84(3): 362-7.
[7] Medscape. The USMLE: Ten Questions. Available at: http://www.medscape.com/viewarticle/403686. Accessed October 19, 2011.
[8] NBME. Available at: http://www.nbme.org. Accessed October 29, 2011.
[9] University of Utah School of Medicine. Preparing for Step 1. Available at: medicine.utah.edu/learningresources/usmle/step1.htm. Accessed October 19, 2011.
[10] University of California San Francisco School of Medicine. Rx for Success on STEP 1 of The Boards. Available at: http://medschool.ucsf.edu/medstudents/documents/step1success.pdf. Accessed October 19, 2011.
[11] NBOME. Available at: http://www.nbome.org. Accessed November 4, 2011.
[12] NRMP. Available at: http://www.nrmp.org. Accessed September 12, 2011.
[13] Cummings M, Sefcik D. The impact of osteopathic physicians' participation in ACGME-accredited postdoctoral programs, 1985-2006. *Acad Med* 2009; 84(6): 733-6.
[14] Moss F, McManus I. The anxieties of new clinical students. *Med Educ* 1992; 26: 17-20.
[15] O'Brien B, Cooke M, Irby D. Perceptions and attributions of third-year student struggles in clerkships: do students and clerkship directors agree? *Acad Med* 2007; 82(10): 970-978.
[16] Windish D, Paulman P, Goroll A, Bass E. Do clerkship directors think medical students are prepared for the clerkship years? *Acad Med* 2004; 79(1): 56-61.
[17] Hauer K, Teherani A, Kerr K, O'Sullivan P, Irby, D. Student performance problems in medical school clinical skills assessments. *Acad Med* 2007; 82(10): S69-S72.
[18] ACP Internist. Good diagnostic skills should begin at the bedside. Available at: http://www.acpinternist.org/archives/2001/02/diagnostics.htm. Accessed February 1, 2012.
[19] Wiener S, Nathanson M. Physical examination: frequently observed errors. *JAMA* 1976; 236(7): 852-5.

[20] Wray N, Friedland J. Detection and correction of house staff error in physical diagnosis. *JAMA* 1983; 249: 1035-7.
[21] Wu E, Fagan M, Reinert S, Diaz J. Self-confidence in and perceived utility of the physical examination: a comparison of medical students, residents, and faculty internists. *J Gen Intern Med* 2007; 22(12): 1725-30.
[22] Conrad P. Learning to doctor: reflections on recent accounts of the medical school years. *Journal of Health and Social Behavior* 1988; 29(4): 323-32.
[23] University of California Davis School of Medicine. Available at: http://mdscholars.ucdavis.edu/Research%20in%20Medical%20School.ppt. Accessed February 9, 2012.
[24] Siemens D, Punnen S, Wong J, Kanji N. A survey on the attitudes towards research in medical school. *BMC Med Educ* 2010; 22: 10: 4.
[25] University of Arizona Medical Student Research Program. Available at: http://www.msrp.medicine.arizona.edu/dist_guidrat.htm. Accessed February 9, 2012.
[26] Dyrbye L, Davidson L, Cook D. Publications and presentations resulting from required research by students at Mayo Medical School, 1976-2003. *Acad Med* 2008; 83(6): 604-10.
[27] Pretorius E. Medical student research: a residency director's perspective. *Acad Radiol* 2002; 9(7): 808-9.
[28] Solomon S, Tom S, Pichert J, Wasserman D, Powers A. Impact of medical student research in the development of physician scientists. *J Investig Med* 2002; 51(3): 149-56.
[29] National Resident Match Program Charting Outcomes in the Match. www.nrmp.org. Accessed August 1, 2010.
[30] Jacobs C, Cross P. The value of medical student research: the experience at Stanford University School of Medicine. *Med Educ* 1995; 29(5): 342-6.
[31] National Student Research Forum. Available at: http://www.utmb.edu/nsrf/. Accessed February 9, 2012.
[32] Zier K, Friedman E, Smith L. Supportive programs increase medical students' research interest and productivity. *J Investig Med* 2006; 54(4): 201-7.
[33] Case Western Reserve University School of Medicine. Available at: http://casemed.case.edu/. Accessed February 12, 2012.
[34] American Medical Association. Available at: http://www.ama-assn.org/ama/pub/about-ama/ama-foundation/our-programs/public-health/excellence-medicine-awards.page. Accessed February 12, 2012.
[35] The Successful Match: Getting into Ophthalmology. Available at: http://studentdoctor.net/2009/08/the-successful-match-interview-with-dr-andrew-lee-ophthalmology/. Accessed February 12, 2012.
[36] NRMP 2010 Program Director Survey. Available at: http://www.nrmp.org/data/index.html. Accessed February 12, 2012.
[37] Hayden S, Hayden M, Garnst A. What characteristics of applicants to emergency medicine residency programs predict future success as an emergency medicine resident. *Acad Emerg Med* 2005; 12(3): 206-10.
[38] Daly K, Levine S, Adams G. Predictors for resident success in otolaryngology. *J Am Coll Surg* 2006; 202 (4): 649-54.

[39] Joan C. Edwards School of Medicine at Marshall University. Available at: http://www.marshallparthenon.com/news/med-students-earning-cash-for-community-service-1.1936252. Accessed September 12, 2011.
[40] Association of American Medical Colleges. Available at: http://www.aamc.org/newsroom/pressrel/2008/enrollmentdata2008.pdf. Accessed July 23, 2011.
[41] American Academy of Family Physicians. Available at: http://www.aafp.org/online/en/home/publications/news/news-now/resident-student-focus/20081119med-school-enroll.html. Accessed February 12, 2012.
[42] Seifer SD. Service-learning: community-campus partnerships for health professions education. *Acad Med* 1998; 73(3): 273-7.
[43] Liaison Committee on Medical Education (LCME) Available at: http://www.lcme.org/standard.htm#servicelearning. Accessed February 12, 2012.
[44] University of New Mexico School of Medicine. Available at: http://hsc.unm.edu/som/. Accessed February 22, 2012.
[45] AAMC Medicine in the Community Grant Program. Available at: http://www.aamc.org/about/awards/cfc/start.htm. Accessed February 12, 2012.
[46] American Medical Association Medical Student Section. Available at: http://www.ama-assn.org. Accessed February 12, 2012.
[47] AMA Alliance Project Bank. Available at: http://www.amaalliance.org/site/epage/40331_625.htm. Accessed February 12, 2012.
[48] University of California Davis School of Medicine. Available at: http://www-med.ucdavis.edu/. Accessed September 12, 2011.
[49] American Medical Association Virtual Mentor. Available at: http://virtualmentor.ama-assn.org/2005/07/medu1-0507.html. Accessed February 12, 2012.
[50] Cohen J. Eight Steps for starting a student-run clinic. *JAMA* 1995; 273: 434-5.
[51] Society of Student-Run Free Clinics. Available at: http://www.studentrunfreeclinics.org/index.php?option=com_content&view=article&id=65&Itemid=144. Accessed February 12, 2012.
[52] Thoits P, Hewitt L. Volunteer work and well-being. *Journal of Health and Social Behavior* 2001; 42(2): 115-31.
[53] Van Willigen M. Differential benefits of volunteering across the life course. *The Journals of Gerontology Series B: Psychological Sciences and Social Sciences* 2000; 55B(5): S308-S318.
[54] Rietschlin J. Voluntary association membership and psychological distress. *J Health Soc Behav* 1998; 39; 348-55.
[55] Adviser, teacher, role model, friend. Available at: http://stills.nap.edu/readingroom/books/mentor. Accessed March 13, 2008. Washington, DC: National Academy Press; 1997.
[56] Aagaard E, Hauer K. A cross-sectional descriptive study of mentoring relationships formed by medical students. *J Gen Intern Med* 2003; 18: 298-302.
[57] Santa Clara County Medical Association Mentor Program for Stanford medical students. Available at: http://med.stanford.edu/mentors/. Accessed February 9, 2012.

[58] Society of Academic Emergency Medicine (SAEM). Available at: http://www.saem.org/e-advising-faqs-students. Accessed February 9, 2012.

[59] American College of Physicians. Finding the right mentor for you. Available at: http://www.acponline.org/medical_students/impact/archives/2010/11/feature/. Accessed February 9, 2012.

[60] Association of Women Surgeons. Available at: https://www.womensurgeons.org/CDR/Mentorship.asp. Accessed February 9, 2012.

[61] Fahrenkopf A, Sectish T, Barger L, Sharek P, Lewin D, Chiang V, Edwards S, Wiedermann B, Landrigan C. Rates of medication errors among depressed and burnt out residents: prospective cohort study. *BMJ* 2008; 336(7642): 488-91.

[62] Wolf T, Faucett J, Randall H, Balson P. Graduating medical students' ratings of stresses, pleasures, and coping strategies. *J Med Educ* 1988; 63(8): 636-42.

[63] Compton M, Carrera J, Frank E. Stress and depressive symptoms/dysphoria among US medical students: results from a large, nationally representative survey. *J Nerv Ment Dis* 2008; 196(12): 891-7.

[64] Dyrbye L, Thomas M, Huntington J, Lawson K, Novotny P, Sloan J, Shanafelt T. Personal life events and medical student burnout: a multicenter study. *Acad Med* 2006; 81 (4): 374-84.

[65] Hussein E, Gabr A, Mohamed A, Hameed A. Physical exercise and anxiety among medical students at Ain Shams University. Presented at the 13th Annual International Ain Shams Medical Students' Congress, Feb 14-16, 2005.

[66] Parkerson G, Broadhead W, Tse C. The health status and life satisfaction of first-year medical students. *Acad Med* 1990; 65(9): 586-8.

[67] Carver C. You want to measure coping but your protocol's too long: consider the brief COPE. *International Journal of Behavioral Medicine* 1997; 4: 92-100.

[68] Gentile J, Roman B. Medical student mental health services; psychiatrists treating medical students. *Psychiatry* 2009; 6(5): 38-45.

[69] Baernstein A, Oelschlager A, Chang T, Wenrich M. Learning professionalism: perspectives of preclinical medical students. *Acad Med* 2009; 84(5): 574-81.

[70] Satterwhite W, Satterwhite R, Enarson C. Medical students' perceptions of unethical conduct at one medical school. *Acad Med* 1998; 73(5): 529-531.

[71] Humphrey H, Smith K, Reddy S, Scott D, Madara J, Arora V. Promoting an environment of professionalism: The University of Chicago "Roadmap." *Acad Med* 2007; 82(11): 1098-1107.

[72] Dans P. Self-reported cheating by students at one medical school. *Acad Med* 1996; 71 (1, suppl): S70-72.

[73] Anderson R, Obenshain S. Cheating by students: findings, reflections, and remedies. *Acad Med* 1994; 69(5): 323-332.

[74] Szauter K, Turner H. Using students' perceptions of internal medicine teachers' professionalism. *Acad Med* 2001; 76(5): 575-6.

[75] Kowalczyk L. Doctor accused of faking studies. *The Boston Globe*; March 11, 2009.

[76] Lin S, Strom S, Canales C, Rodriguez A, Kain Z. The impact of the anesthesiology clerkship structure on medical students matched to anesthesiology. Abstract presented at the 2010 Annual Meeting of the American Society Anesthesiologists. A1106.
[77] Kassebaum D, Szenas P. Medical students' career indecision and specialty rejection: roads not taken. *Acad Med* 1995; 70(10): 937-43.
[78] Association of American Medical Colleges. Available at: http://www.aamc.org/students/cim/august10choices.pdf. Accessed November 21, 2011.
[79] Association of American Medical Colleges (AAMC). Available at: http //www.aamc.org/students/cim/about.htm. Accessed September 23, 2011.
[80] University of Virginia School of Medicine Medical Specialty Aptitude Test. Available at: http://www.med-ed.virginia.edu/specialties. Accessed January 24, 2012.
[81] 2010 AAMC Medical School Graduation Questionnaire. Available at: http://www.aamc.org. Accessed August 13, 2011.
[82] Dorsay E, Jarjoura D, Rutecki G. Influence of controllable lifestyle on recent trends in specialty choice by US medical students. *JAMA* 2003; 290(9): 1173-8.
[83] Weinstein P, Gipple C. Some determinants of career choice in the second year of medical school. *J Med Educ* 1975; 50(2): 194-8.
[84] Garmel G. Mentoring medical students in academic emergency medicine. *Acad Emerg Med* 2004; 11(12): 1351-7.
[85] ACP Mentoring Database. Available at: http://www.acponline.org/residents+fellows/mentors/. Accessed January 25, 2012.

Chapter 15

Medical School Scholarships & Awards

Note: The following chapter is excerpted from the book – Medical School Scholarships, Grants, & Awards: Insider Advice on How to Win Scholarships

According to the Association of American Medical Colleges (AAMC), the median four-year cost to attend medical school for the class of 2014 was over $218,000 and $286,000 for public and private schools, respectively.[1] The following table shows how the median cost of attendance has changed over time.

Change in 4-Year Median Cost to Attend Medical School (AAMC Data)[1-2]		
Year	Public	Private
2000	$100,215	$161,760
2008	$159,396	$225,215
2014	$218,898	$286,806

Although the average annual cost to attend medical school has risen at a rate that has outpaced inflation, this has not prevented a record number of students from applying to medical school. In 2013, there were over 48,000 applicants to U.S. medical schools, breaking the mark set in 1996.

Medical schools have been graduating more students than ever, the result of a nationwide effort to meet the needs of an anticipated physician manpower shortage. As these students fulfill their professional dreams of becoming physicians, they leave medical school with considerable debt. AAMC research indicates that the median education debt for the class of 2013 was $175,000.[1]

Fortunately, there are hundreds of scholarships available to medical students to help offset the cost of medical school education. Although there are few "full-ride" scholarships, there are many awards that can significantly lessen the burden. "Every $1,000 in scholarship support reduces a student's potential indebtedness by more than $8,400," writes the Wake Forest School of Medicine.[3]

Although financial relief is a major reason to pursue scholarships, the benefits of receiving such awards and honors extend well beyond money. Does winning a medical student award or scholarship make a difference in the

MEDICAL SCHOOL SCHOLARSHIPS & AWARDS

residency match? It certainly does with multiple research studies demonstrating that awards provide a competitive edge.

Election to the Alpha Omega Alpha Honor Medical Society (AOA) is perhaps the most well studied award as it relates to residency admission. Eligibility is limited to only allopathic medical students, and members are selected based on academic achievement, leadership, professionalism, and commitment to service by school chapters. According to the AOA Constitution, no more than 1/6 of the graduating class can be elected into the school's chapter. In 2012, the National Resident Matching Program, the organization that administers the Match, surveyed 1,960 residency programs representing 21 specialties about the importance of various residency selection criteria.[4] Overall, membership in AOA was cited by 51% as a factor in selecting applicants to interview. Membership in AOA was also an important factor in the ranking of applicants. Overall, it received a mean rating of 3.4 on a scale of 1 (not at all important) to 5 (very important). Data for the individual specialties is presented in the table on the following page.

Percentage Of Residency Programs Citing AOA As A Factor In Selecting Applicants To Interview By Specialty[4]	
Specialty	**% of Programs**
Anesthesiology	69%
Dermatology	57%
Emergency Medicine	57%
Family Medicine	24%
General Surgery	60%
Internal Medicine	51%
Neurosurgery	76%
Obstetrics & Gynecology	47%
Orthopaedic Surgery	68%
Otolaryngology	76%
Pathology	40%
Pediatrics	55%
Physical Medicine & Rehabilitation	26%
Plastic Surgery	75%
Psychiatry	38%
Radiation Oncology	61%
Radiology	66%

Although osteopathic students are not eligible for AOA induction, both allopathic and osteopathic students may be elected into the Gold Humanism Honor Society (GHHS). Started in 2002 by the Arnold P. Gold Foundation, GHHS honors medical students for "demonstrated excellence in clinical care, leadership, compassion and dedication to service."[5] In a study conducted to determine if GHHS membership influences residency selection, the authors wrote that "membership in GHHS may set candidates apart from their peers and allow PDs to distinguish objectively the candidates who demonstrate compassionate medical care."[6] In the 2012 NRMP Program Director Survey, 23% reported using Gold Society Membership as a factor in selecting applicants to interview.[4]

AOA and GHHS are not the only awards or honors viewed favorably by residency programs. In a survey of over 1,200 residency program directors in 21 specialties, Dr. Marianne Green, Associate Dean of Medical Education at the Northwestern University Feinberg School of Medicine, determined the relative importance of various residency selection criteria.[7] Dr. Green found that medical school awards (non-AOA) were tenth in importance among a group of 14 residency selection criteria. Although not as important as USMLE Step 1 scores, clerkship grades, and letters of recommendation, awards were ranked higher than such factors as preclinical grades, research while in medical school, and published medical school research.

Benefits of winning medical school awards and scholarships include the following:

- Awards can provide a significant boost to the strength of your residency application, and distinguish you from your peers. Awards and scholarships can easily be placed in the residency application, MSPE (Dean's Letter), letters of recommendation, and CV. We have found that interviewers often ask about awards during residency interviews.

Did you know...

In 2013, Justin Berk, a medical student at Texas Tech University School of Medicine, received the American Medical Association Foundation National Leadership Award. "For Justin, it's obviously a huge accolade and something that will follow him for the rest of his medical career," said Dr. Tedd Mitchell, President of Texas Tech Health Sciences Center, in an interview with *The Daily Toreador*. "As he's applying for residency programs, it will stand out."[8]

Did you know...

Alexander Gallan, a medical student at the Boston University School of Medicine, was the recipient of the 2012 American Society of Clinical Pathology Academic Excellence Award. "The award was a common topic during my residency interviews. I believe it helped my residency application immeasurably by providing justification for all the hard work I have done."[9]

- Competitive specialties and residency programs value students who have been recognized with awards. There is belief among educators that you will make similar contributions as a trainee.

> **Did you know...**
>
> When Casey DeDeugd, a medical student at the University of Central Florida, won the Medical Student Achievement Award from the Ruth Jackson Orthopaedic Society, she enhanced her visibility in the field. "Your accomplishments thus far are very impressive!" wrote Dr. Gloria Gogola, Chair of the Society's Scientific Committee. "We look forward...to welcoming you to our field of orthopaedic surgery."[10]

> **Did you know...**
>
> In 2008, Brian Caldwell, a medical student at the University of Arkansas for Medical Sciences, was the winner of the Dr. Constantin Cope Medical Student Research Award from the Society of Interventional Radiology. "Brian carried the whole project with very little help and really did a nice job," said Dr. William Culp, Professor of Radiology and Surgery. "I am so pleased that he won the national SIR award, because his participation in the conference introduced him to national leaders in interventional radiology and will help jumpstart his career."[11]

- You gain visibility in your school, and bring recognition to the institution.

> **Did you know...**
>
> When Ramy El-Diwany, an M.D./Ph.D. student at Johns Hopkins University, won the 2014 Excellence in Public Health Award from the U.S. Public Health Service (USPHS) Physician Professional Advisory Committee, his institution was also lauded. "This award is a testament to the education provided by the Johns Hopkins University School of Medicine and to the high caliber of its students," wrote USPHS Lt. Cmdr. Kimberly Smith. "We hope that this award will encourage other Johns Hopkins faculty and students to continue their strong work in public health."[12]

> **Did you know…**
>
> After Rahul Vanjani received the AMA Foundation Leadership Award, Dr. Scott Schroth, Senior Associate Dean of Academic Affairs at George Washington University, took pride in his student's accomplishment. "Rahul's commitment to the community and leadership of service efforts are unparalleled. He exemplifies the sort of creativity and dedication that we look for in medical students at GW, and we are extraordinarily proud of him as a winner of the AMA Foundation's 2011 Leadership Award."[13]

- Recipients have found that awards have made them more attractive for other awards and scholarships. Awards follow you throughout your career, and can make you more competitive for future opportunities, programs, and employment.

- You further your professional reputation and enhance your credibility in the areas that form the basis for the award.

- Winning an award or scholarship can give you the confidence to pursue other goals.

- Applying for an award requires the support of advocates who become reference letter writers. Strengthening these relationships over time allows faculty members to write strong letters of recommendation for residency.

> **Did you know…**
>
> In applying for awards, you often have to submit reference letters. Over time, your letter writers become even stronger advocates with a vested interest in furthering your career. After David Leverenz won the Southwestern Medical Foundation Ho Din Award, his mentor had this to say. "Dr. Leverenz has done exceptionally well in medical school, performed research, worked, volunteered, and completed multiple mission trips," said Dr. David Balis, his faculty mentor at UT Southwestern Medical Center. "But what strikes me most about David is his caring, sincere, compassionate personality." Dr. Leverenz is now a resident at Vanderbilt University.[14]

> **Did you know…**
>
> Winning a scholarship may also affect the way in which you view your specialty choice. "This scholarship has allowed me the freedom to broaden my thoughts about what field I want to pursue," said Mike Bosworth, a medical student at Tulane University. "My focus is more on how I can help patients versus what I can make."[15]

It is clear that there are compelling reasons to pursue medical school scholarships, awards, and grants. In this book, we'll show you how to maximize your chances of winning these awards. Although our book includes an extensive list of scholarships and awards, we've also placed considerable emphasis on strategy. Some examples of what you'll find in our book include:

- Although we encourage you to apply for the most competitive scholarships and awards, we also show you how to identify awards that are easier to win. There is considerably less competition for these awards, and we'll show you how you can significantly enhance your chances of winning.

- Since letters of recommendation are a critical component of most scholarship applications, how can you work closely with your letter writers to have the best possible letters written?

- The personal essay is an opportunity for you to stand out from the rest of the applicant field. What's the best approach to take with the essay? What makes an essay particularly compelling to the scholarship committee? How can you avoid common errors?

- Scholarship programs may ask you to submit a CV or enter information from your CV directly into the application. Content and appearance are important factors in the way your CV will be assessed, and we'll show you how to create one with maximum impact.

Our recommendations are based on data from a full spectrum of sources. Whenever possible, we present evidence obtained from scientific study and published in the academic medical literature. We also take an insider's look at the entire process based on our experiences. For years, we've helped applicants match successfully into competitive specialties and residency programs. We've worked with medical students at all levels, and we always try to identify scholarship and award programs that will bolster their credentials. In the process of helping students win scholarships and awards, we've gained insight into the factors that lead to success. There's much that can be learned from your predecessors, and we've included the profiles of past scholarship winners. Reading about their stories will help guide your strategy and application.

Although it's been a joy for us to help medical students win scholarships and awards, we know that the process is difficult. Although success is never guaranteed, our advice and perspectives provide the specific, concrete recommendations that will maximize your chances of being an award recipient.

A Medical Student Scholarship Winner Speaks...

"The scholarship will greatly ease the trouble and distraction of growing debt so that I can focus on my studies, my family and my community. It is a generous gift, and I am reminded that it is an investment in my future. I know that it is my role in the future to give back to my community as a physician."[16]

Chapter excerpted from the book – Medical School Scholarships, Grants, & Awards: Insider Advice on How to Win Scholarships

An excerpt from the best-selling book:

Medical School Interview: Winning Strategies from Admissions Faculty

By Dr. Samir P. Desai
and Dr. Rajani Katta

Chapter 1

Introduction

Why do you want to be a doctor? Why did you choose to apply to our medical school?

Many interviewers will ask variations of these basic, standard questions. And many applicants will have prepared answers for these. Many applicants, though, will get it wrong.

We've interviewed hundreds of applicants. Some we've grilled and some we've coached. And from these hundreds of applicants, we've learned one thing: almost every single one could have been better.

Write down your own answers to these questions, and then take a look at our approach.

Why our school?

You may be asked a number of variations of this same question:

- What qualities are you looking for in a school?
- Describe your ideal medical school.
- What interests you most about our school?
- Tell me what you know about our school.
- Why do you want to be a student here?
- What two or three things are important to you in a medical school?

While the question asks about the school, the best answers highlight the applicant. You need to make a strong case that YOU are the perfect fit for this exact school. Few applicants are able to do that well.

Here are examples of the typical responses that we've heard over the years:

"Well, I've lived here for three years so I know that I would want to live here. One of the things I like is the diversity and clinical opportunities you offer. I know I would see all kinds of different patient populations. The school has a good reputation which I know would help me get into a good residency program. The atmosphere is excellent, students help each other, and this is a place which will challenge me but not bring out the worst in me."

"I'm really looking for two things. First, a program that really integrates the clinical with the basic sciences. My impression is that [your school] does a good job with that. The second thing is the breadth of opportunities here. All the research that's going on. I can't imagine that it would be difficult to find many people I would be interested in working with."

"It seems like the school will help you reach your goals. You also have a lot of hospitals you can work at. Also, I'm interested in the International Health Track."

"I'll get a great education here. There are so many research opportunities. And students really seem to love the school. Also, the faculty is very involved with the students. Also having all the affiliated hospitals that you have here."

"The shorter basic science period really appeals to me. So does the way the basic science is structured, for example the way anatomy is spread over a number of semesters. I really like the medical center and Houston. The center is top notch."

What do all of these responses have in common? They're all underwhelming. While there a number of reasons for this, the main one is that all of these applicants end up sounding pretty generic. The responses are fine and nobody's sending up any red flags, but at the same time you'd be hard pressed to remember any of these applicants.

Why is that? First, most of these responses are too brief. Second, most of these responses lack specific details about the school, and all of them lack specific details about the applicant. Third, there's very little here that would convince the interviewer that this specific applicant would be a perfect fit with the school. And finally, there's nothing memorable in any of these responses. In other words, just about any applicant could have given the same response.

The biggest fail here is that every single applicant lost out on a valuable opportunity to impress the interviewer.

To see how a student could answer this question in a more compelling manner, let's meet Elena, an undergraduate student in Arkansas.

Elena's story

Elena grew up in a medically underserved area with a significant Latino population. There were relatively few primary care physicians in her community, and even fewer specialists. Several of Elena's relatives passed away of cancer, and Elena developed an early interest in oncology. After finishing medical school, Elena hopes to pursue residency training in internal medicine followed by fellowship training in oncology. She plans to return to her hometown to practice oncology, and would be one of only two oncologists serving a four-county area. In college, Elena worked with Dr. Garcia, a dermatology faculty member at a local medical school, to develop an instructional module to help primary care physicians differentiate benign from cancerous skin lesions. The main goal was to provide a resource for primary care physicians practicing in parts of the state lacking access to dermatologists. Elena was also involved in organizing and implementing skin cancer screenings in these underserved areas.

Elena's answer

"I first heard about your school from my faculty mentor, Dr. Garcia. Your school has an excellent reputation, and she spoke very highly of the education you offer. You're also well known for quality of teaching and diversity of patients, which I value. I also would love to live in Dallas, and have family in the Fort Worth area."

Analyzing Elena's answer

Be as specific as possible to confirm that your selection of their school was based on some thought and effort. Too often, applicants give a general answer. If you could give the exact same answer at another school, then your answer isn't good enough. If you examine Elena's response, you'll see that her answer, for the most part, was short on specifics. A better response is shown below.

Begin by researching the school thoroughly. What makes this school unique? What aspects of the school or its curriculum do you find particularly compelling? This information allows you to tailor your responses. In simple terms, if the school highly values research, and you have an interest or experience in that area, then you need to discuss it.

If a faculty member recommended the program, then by all means say so, as Elena did. Schools like to know that they're well regarded. Speaking with someone who has firsthand knowledge of the school also demonstrates that you've taken the time and initiative to learn as much as you can about the school. It demonstrates the seriousness of your interest.

There are also certain responses that you need to avoid at all costs. Avoid answers that confirm a disconnect between what you're seeking and what the school offers. Never put down another school. Lastly, while the geographic location of the school may be a major factor in your interest, avoid offering location as the only or initial reason for applying to the school.

A better answer

"I first learned about your school through my faculty mentor. Dr. Garcia is a graduate of your school and she's always spoken highly of the training she received. I would love to be a medical student at your school for a number of reasons. In shadowing physicians, I've learned that it's important to go to a school that places an emphasis on clinical skills. Your school has a reputation for being a leader in clinical skills development. The early patient contact, frequent observation of skills followed by regular feedback, and simulation lab are particularly appealing to me. It's also important to me that I develop a strong foundation for the practice of high quality care with patient safety in mind. That's why I'm really excited about your unique patient safety curriculum. And finally, I know that your school has a track for the underserved, and I could really see myself thriving in this track. In college, some of my most rewarding experiences occurred when I was involved in organizing and implementing health fairs for rural communities. Receiving education in caring for an underserved population would be fantastic because I would like to make this an important part of my future career in medicine. I grew up in a medically underserved area, and would like to return to my hometown as an internist and oncologist. On a personal note, I do have family in the Forth Worth area, and training in Dallas would allow me to spend time with family."

In the following pages, you'll learn how to create this type of response.

A response that is very memorable. A response that confirms that you have the qualities that this medical school seeks. The type of response that confirms to the interviewer that you are the perfect fit for their medical school. The type of response that so impresses the interviewer that they become your advocate in committee meetings.

In the next 200+ pages, we'll review, in depth, the medical school interview. You'll learn how critical the interview is in the admissions process. The Association of American Medical Colleges (AAMC) evaluated the importance of 12 variables on admissions decisions. Of these, the MCAT score was rated sixth. Cumulative science and math GPA was rated third.

The most important factor in admissions decisions was, in fact, the interview.

You'll learn why the interview is so important to admissions officers. It's widely recognized that the best physicians have more than just great scores and grades. The most effective physicians display a number of non-academic attributes. These traits are difficult to evaluate, and admissions officers rely on the interview to help assess these traits. In Chapter 3 we present the results of a survey of admissions officers that focuses on traits that are valued in future physicians. Over 20 traits are ranked, including such items as motivation for a medical career, empathy, personal maturity, service orientation, and leadership.

Research has also identified qualities that may hurt your chances for admission. Some of these qualities can be surprisingly easy to display in the high-pressure setting of an interview. It's easy to predict that schools don't seek out blunt or uninhibited applicants, but even traits such as self-critical or apologizing can hurt your chances.

You'll learn how to research the medical school, and how to determine the type of student that the school seeks. With an analysis of your own strengths and skills, you can begin to tailor your responses. Chapter 9 reviews the typical interview questions, and provides examples of other students' thoughtful, tailored, and memorable responses.

In the past, students could focus just on these types of standard interview questions. Why do you want to be a doctor? Why are you interested in our school? What are your strengths? While some schools still utilize the standard format of one interviewer speaking to one applicant for 30 minutes, many schools are adopting other formats.

Are you prepared for the MMI? This format has been utilized by such diverse medical schools as Stanford, Oregon Health Sciences University, Virginia Tech, UC Davis, and University of Cincinnati, among others. In the multiple mini-interview, the applicant moves from one station to another over a two-hour period. At each station, he or she is asked to respond to a question, a short structured scenario, or even a task. In Chapter 5, you'll learn more about the MMI, as well as the behavioral interview, the panel interview, and the group interview, among others.

In the following chapters, we review, in detail, other important aspects of the interview. You'll learn how to maximize your interview preparation, and what to expect on the typical interview day. We review the common pitfalls that we've seen multiple applicants make, over and over again, every interview season. You'll even learn about the best thank you notes, how to handle an offer of acceptance, and what to do if you're on the waitlist.

The recommendations in this book are based on multiple sources. Throughout the book, you'll see quotes from many different admissions officers. There's also been a substantial body of research on the topic of predicting which applicants will make the best physicians. We've included the results of these research studies, which have shaped and guided our recommendations. Lastly, the recommendations are based on extensive discussions with admissions faculty as well as applicants. Dr. Desai has served on the admissions committee at Baylor College of Medicine for over 10 years. He also provides interview preparation services for applicants to other medical schools, and both he and Dr. Katta have advised many applicants as they prepare for the residency match. The Successful Match is the best-selling title in the field of residency match preparation. In this book, we've applied the same combination of evidence-based advice and insider knowledge.

From personal experience, we've seen what works in an interview, and we've seen where students have failed. In the next 200+

pages, you'll learn how to apply these lessons to your own application. It's taken years of intense work for you to reach this point, and receiving an invitation to interview is a strong vote of confidence from the medical school. In the following pages, you'll learn how to make the most of this opportunity in order to reach your goal: medical school.

Excerpted from the book – Medical School Interview: Winning Strategies from Admissions Faculty

Take a Break from Your Interview Prep with our Humorous but Poignant Tale of one Student's Journey from Medical Student to Attending Physician in a County Hospital

An excerpt from the book:

Hopes and Fears, Dreams and Tears: A County Memoir

By Dr. Niraj Mehta

"Dr. Niraj Mehta's medical memoir is at once honest and thought provoking. He has a great sense of humor: the book will keep you laughing even as it helps you understand the difficult and stressful challenges faced by medical students and interns, and also the exhilaration of being able to save lives. The book teaches us several important lessons about compassion as well. A great read!"

- Chitra Banerjee Divakaruni, Author of *Palace of Illusions* and *Oleander Girl*

1

Internal Medicine

We're so smart, we speak in riddles.

July 1, 1991. The day every medical student yearns for was finally here. We were starting our clinical years, the rotations that would ultimately help us choose a career pathway. This was true of most medical students, anyway—except that lame student who knew in kindergarten that he or she would grow up to be a left maxillary sinus specialist of thirty-two-year old Caucasian women whose last name began with the letter *B* (and perhaps ended with a *t*). Now there would be no more Krebs Cycle to memorize! No more looking for *ora serrata* on your cadaver! Yes, the best years of our medical school were about to begin.

I was nervous and excited to begin at the local county hospital, Lyndon B. Johnson (LBJ) in Houston, Texas. Unlike the third-year students starting similar rotations in today's medical schools, I had no orientation. I was told to report to 3C where the "team will explain the rest." So I jumped into my blue Nissan 200SX convertible, an upgrade from the scooter I'd had during the first two years of medical school, and took US-59 North to The County.

I'd lived in Houston since 1979, but had never been to this part of the city for reasons that would soon become obvious to me. As I approached LBJ, I realized that I was no longer in middle-class Houston, such as Alief on the southwest side, where I was raised. Instead, I was in the middle of mom and pop shops, small grocery stores, and what appeared to be fast food heaven. Only years later would I realize that the so-called McDonald's heaven was leading my patients at LBJ to a faster hell.

I saw more motorized scooters and wheelchairs than I could count and wondered if I was at Wal-Mart. Although every gate leading to the hospital parking lot was open, it seemed that every space was full. I would learn later that unless you arrived by 8:00 a.m. (something I would do consistently for the next seven years, even if I was running two hours late), there would be no parking spaces—you would be left to do laps in your own Indy 500, competing for the space that would hopefully vacate at the exact right time. After doing my own AJ Foyt routine for thirty minutes, I hopped out of the car and approached the seemingly harmless building with my short white coat—long coats were worn by doctors, and I wasn't one quite yet—and an overnight bag.

I was assigned to Team B, who happened to be on call that day. What luck! On the first day of my third year of medical school, I'm on an internal medicine service team that was on call! I didn't know anything yet, though. What would I do?!

I asked directions for 3C, and was told to take the elevators up and ask again. "Oh, by the way, only one of the elevators is working, so you might want to take the stairs, but I'm not sure which doors are open on which floors."

Where was I? Afraid that I might get lost if I used the stairs, I waited impatiently for the elevators, which patiently arrived fifteen minutes later. When I finally reached the third floor, I fumbled my way to 3C, wondering why Team B rounded on C. As if to feed my dry sense of humor, I almost collapsed—internally, of course, since I didn't want to be admitted to a county hospital after fainting—from laughter as the resident stated that B would usually meet on A, but not to confuse 3A with 4A because post-call we would start on 3C. Was he making this up just to mess with my mind?

We received our so-called formal introductions at this time. I quickly assigned a nickname to each member of the group, a skill that has served me well even to this day. The lead resident was from India and had a mustache that matched the one made famous by my favorite Indian movie actor. *Did I really say that? After all the years of torturing my parents by criticizing Indian movies, had I entered a parallel universe? Should I have taken the parallel hallway to the left instead of the right?* I naturally named him "Stache." One intern had a nose bigger than mine, which was no small feat, so I named him "Senior" since I was now officially "Junior" (thank God). This would create confusion because I would at times spit out "Senior," and Stache would turn around instead.

I wasn't sure what to do with the other intern until he began to speak. He had a very thick accent and was from Vietnam. I decided to call him "Morning" after *Good Morning Vietnam*. This moniker led to even more confusion because, at times, I would say "Morning," not always under my breath, at 11:00 p.m.

Finally, we were introduced to our attending physician, often called just "attending." The first thing I noticed was his age. I called him "Harvard," having been told that he graduated from "the med school beast in the east" in 1938. Now that I was standing in front of Harvard, I wondered if my friend meant 1838. This is when Harvard spoke to us for the first time. *Are you kidding? Was this guy a plantation owner? Was Lincoln still the President when he graduated?* I later learned that Harvard was from Charleston, South Carolina and had been a big shot at a medical school in "Carolinaahh" before coming to Houston. I would realize only much later the importance of what I learned during the introductions that day; there is no substitute in medicine for the power of humor and observations.

My first month at The County on an internal medicine service would be my first step on a journey I didn't know I was embarking on at the time. Since this was July, I learned later that the interns only one day earlier had been students, and that by extension (no pun intended in spite of the length of the worm under his nose) that Stache had been an intern. At least two things were working in my favor. Harvard had clearly been an attending for a long time, and more importantly, I wasn't the patient. I was told to leave my things in the call room and report to the EC. This was my first introduction to initials and abbreviations that I would continue to learn on the fly. The only things that weren't abbreviated in the chart, and especially during senior/junior conversations, were curse words. Or did "SOB" in the chart mean something else?

I came to the emergency room (ER=Emergency Room, EC=Emergency Center, both being one and the same) where I was assigned my first patient who—surprise, surprise—didn't speak a word of English. Morning told me that before things became even busier, I needed to see this patient with melena.

"What?" I asked.

"He has a GI bleed," responded Morning.

"Huh?" I continued with a look of confusion.

"He has a goddamned ulcer!"

Oh, sort of like the one I'll probably have by the end of this rotation! I said to myself.

"What do you want me to do?" I continued out loud.

"Well, he's Vietnamese, and I'm too busy to translate for you, so just go and tilt him."

I was too proud—or perhaps too terrified—to ask for help. I had no idea what "tilt" meant, at least not in the context that Morning meant. So, I approached the patient, who had a tube in his nose draining material that looked like ground coffee, and shook his hand. This was when the comedy of errors began. I started to shift the patient on his bed from side to side, in essence tilting him like I had been asked. I immediately felt as if a laugh track had been turned on for a live taping of *Happy Days*. The entire ER staff, which had been tense only two minutes earlier from what appeared to be a *M.A.S.H.* unit of endless patients, was on the floor, laughing uncontrollably after witnessing my ridiculous act.

Thirty days and counting, I said to myself as Morning, between bouts of humorous tears, showed me how "tilt" meant orthostatic hypotension, and how to correctly assess the patient for this important sign. I was crushed, but I'd made my first therapeutic intervention without realizing it.

When Morning translated what had just transpired to the patient, the seventy-plus-year-old-man with one tube, two IVs, and three concerned family members at his bedside, burst into laughter. It was my first honors grade as an MD-to-be, and like most other such rewards on this journey, it was only with time that I was able to appreciate its true meaning.

After a sleepless night of continued mishaps, I saw my first patient (Mr. Tilt) at 7:00 a.m. two hours before rounds with Harvard. The patient was now on 3C, but something was clearly wrong. He tried to communicate with me, but I couldn't make out what he was trying to say. Alarm bells in my mind were starting to match the butterflies in my stomach. I asked Senior for help. He was frantically preparing for rounds and in no uncertain terms told me, "Go away—it couldn't be that important." I ran to Morning for assistance and was told, "He can't speak English, nothing is wrong." I tried to tell him that the patient doesn't speak English, but now I wasn't sure if he couldn't speak at all because he was gesturing. There were no family members present, and I didn't know what else to do. Stache was nowhere to be found because, as the interns told me, "He's getting his ass kicked in morning report and whatever you do, don't page him."

Frustrated, I gave up until rounds. I presented the story to Harvard, leaving out, of course, the details of the tilt episode, and noticed that Harvard was smiling. I told him that something had changed that morning but I didn't know what it was. Harvard kept smiling. I told him that the patient had been talking yesterday and now I wasn't sure if he couldn't talk or didn't want to talk.

Harvard kept smiling and asked, "What else?"

Without trying to be funny, I stated, "The end."

At this point, Harvard turned crimson red and lifted the patient's right arm. To my surprise, the arm fell back onto the bed.

"My God, Niraj, this man has had a goddamn stroke involving his speech-dominant left hemisphere, and all you can say is 'THE END!'"

Since crap rolls downhill and I was at the bottom, I chose not to tell Harvard that I had run this by Senior and Morning, both of whom had dismissed my concerns and told me not to disturb Stache. I thought I would be perceived as a team player for falling on the proverbial sword, but I was wrong. I received the blame for not presenting information to the team in a manner that would have alerted them to the disaster. I learned another lesson that day. No matter what, the lowest rank receives the blame and the higher-ups are not held accountable. I would hope to change that someday.

You would think that the story of Mr. Tilt would end there, but it didn't. Usually when the proverbial you-know-what hits the fan as it did that morning, it's only the beginning. Why? We live in a society where someone must pay for the bad things that happen, and anger from family members can lead to litigation. As it turned out, one of the family members was a doctor who lived in another city. *What was the father of an MD doing at a county hospital?* I still haven't found a clear answer to that, even today, because I haven't seen another family member of an MD since that day at The County.

So what came next? Yes, you guessed it: a lawsuit. And yes, the family sued everyone who remotely had contact with the patient, including the medical student—me—who had nothing to do with the outcome. Once the lawyers found out who did and didn't have money, I was dropped from the lawsuit. I still remember the sick feeling I experienced when I was handed the subpoena, and I'm sure that my heart was probably visible in my mouth. I wrote to the best of my ability about my role—or lack thereof—in the care of the patient. I haven't been sued since that day, but as Tears for Fears suggested "Memories fade, but the scar still lingers." The litigation process is fraught with emotions for both physicians and patients. In the end, there are no winners, just losers with lost or broken lives that will never be the same.

I continued to excel at my deficiencies throughout the month, but at least I was consistent, for I knew nothing. I missed a Grade V tricuspid regurgitation murmur that Harvard claimed he could hear while driving home from work. Morning told me to read about the antibiotic vancomycin "pig and trough" and was upset the next day when I told him I could find nothing on the topic. I'd forgotten about his accent—I was supposed to look up "peak and trough" as it applied to the dosing of vancomycin. Senior continued to scold me about my lack of knowledge in neurology—the field he'd chosen, of course. I was called a "smart ass" (*but you just said I know nothing!*) when I reminded him that my knowledge was lacking in all fields of medicine equally, not just neurology.

With all my shortcomings, what was I good at? I didn't know then how important it was, but I spent as much time as I could with my patients. I would watch TV with them. I would follow stroke patients, including Mr. Tilt, with the therapist and even take them outside the hospital for a walk and a conversation, if they spoke English. I didn't understand why an eighty-four-year-old guy with lung cancer and end-stage emphysema couldn't smoke, so I would take him outside to smoke a cigarette. I would drive the team crazy by reminding them that another family member wanted to talk about their loved one. These requests inevitably came at the end of a long day because most family members worked and could only visit at night.

I would feed patients breakfast if they needed help. And most importantly, I couldn't understand death, and the twin lakes on my face would routinely flood over when a patient would die. Without realizing it, I was learning how to take care of people, not just their diseases. *Hopes, fears, dreams, and tears...*

I never received a Harvard education, and maybe that's why I never understood Harvard, the attending. Was I alone? There was a generation gap—or in this case, maybe a century gap—but Harvard spoke in riddles and analogies that I just didn't understand. From the chuckles I heard from other team members, I knew I wasn't the only one. One day, Stache asked if 40 milliequivalents of potassium chloride infusion administered intravenously (IV) over four hours was reasonable to correct a potassium value of 2.5 in a patient admitted the night before. Harvard responded with, "Am I my mother's keeper?"

Harvard's notes were just as ambiguous. An eighty-two-year-old patient was admitted with a heart attack and Harvard's note stated, "This man's children don't love him. Life is just not fair!" We were going over Killip classification (a system used to risk stratify heart attack patients) with Senior, and meanwhile Harvard was worried about love! Years later, I realized that Harvard's language had meaning, but back then, we were only hearing, not listening. Harvard wasn't his mother's keeper because part of residency was a learning curve of making mistakes—hopefully not catastrophic ones. What else could be more important at age eighty-two, after having lived a full life, than the love of your dear ones, especially after a heart attack? I chuckle now thinking of how history repeats itself, because my students now wonder why I speak in riddles. In time, they'll understand.

Finally, the last day of the rotation arrived, and it was time for me to receive my grade for the month. I had been dreading this day for some time. I was great at getting "informal honors" from patients, but the actual grade was a different story. Harvard sat me down in his office and started with yet another analogy. "Niraj, a few of you medical students need to be taken out to the parking lot and shot!*"*

Excerpted from the book – Hopes and Fears, Dreams and Tears: A County Memoir

An excerpt from the best-selling book:
Success on the Wards:
250 Rules for Clerkship Success

By Dr. Samir P. Desai
and Dr. Rajani Katta

Chapter 1

Introduction

Rule # 1 **You came to medical school to be a great doctor. That process begins now.**

Why did you become a doctor? There may be a number of reasons, but the most important one is the same across the board: to take care of patients. You will read startling amounts of information during medical school, and your training will include many procedures and new techniques, but all of it is in the service of patient care. You are here to make each and every individual patient better.

That process starts now.

It is an amazing privilege to take care of patients. You can read about a disease all that you want, but to be able to speak to and examine a patient with that disease is an unsurpassed learning experience. It is an incredible responsibility as well. You will be asking patients the most intimate and intrusive types of questions. You will be asking patients to offer their arm for a needle, to disrobe for an exam, to let you literally poke and prod at their body. In return, you are responsible for protecting them from harm, and for healing them.

Starting as a medical student, and progressing to a respected physician, is a long, difficult, and intense process. It takes years of education, and years of training. The privileges granted to physicians are remarkable. In return, you have a great responsibility. Your education is in the service of patient care. You have a responsibility to make the most of that education.

What does it take to be a great doctor? There is an impressive body of research devoted to medical student education, and to the factors and interventions that ensure good doctors. Medical educators work hard to ensure that students master these different facets of the practice of medicine.

Why are clerkships so important to the process of producing great doctors?

The areas emphasized in clerkships are those that are integral to becoming a great physician.

Patient care requires the daily use of many skills. On a daily basis, a physician may need to:

- Obtain an accurate medication history.
- Detect a heart murmur.
- Create a differential diagnosis for the patient with abdominal pain.
- Interpret an elevated alkaline phosphatase.
- Formulate a management plan for the patient with a myocardial infarction.
- Communicate that plan through oral discussions and written documentation.
- Utilize the talents of an entire health care team to maximize patient care.
- Manifest their concern for the patient in every interaction.

Clerkships teach students how to accomplish these difficult, vital skills.

If you don't learn certain skills in medical school, you may never learn them.

Clinical clerkships provide the foundation of successful patient care. They represent a critical time in your education. If you want to become proficient in exam skills, you have to learn now. These aren't skills you can learn from reading a textbook. You need to evaluate patients with these findings, and you need to have a teacher that can demonstrate these findings. You need to be able to ask questions freely in order to learn all the finer points of physical exam skills. This isn't something you can easily do as a resident, and certainly not as a board-certified physician. If you don't know how to assess jugular venous distention by the end of medical school, you may never learn.
    While you would assume that medical school teaches you everything you need to know to function well as a resident, that isn't true for all students, particularly those who take a passive approach to learning or those who focus their education on textbook learning. You need to maximize your learning experiences and teaching opportunities on the wards. Passive learning has real consequences.

In one eye-opening study, internal medicine residents were tested on cardiac auscultatory skills. They listened to 12 prerecorded cardiac events. American residents demonstrated poor proficiency, with mean identification rates of only 22%.[1] In another study of resident skills, ECG proficiency was measured. Surprisingly, 58% of residents wrongly diagnosed complete heart block, and only 22% were certain of their diagnosis of ventricular tachycardia.[2] In a study of radiologic proficiency, participants included mainly residents, with some students. In x-rays representing emergency situations, pneumothorax was misdiagnosed by 91% of participants overall, while a misplaced central venous catheter was missed by 74%.[3]

Skills in patient examination, interpretation of tests, synthesis of information, and medical decision-making are honed through years of practice. Clerkships are only the first step, but provide an invaluable education, with supervisors there to demonstrate, to model, and to teach skills. The best medical students regard clerkships as a unique and invaluable learning experience, difficult to replicate in residency or later through seminars and conferences.

If you don't learn it now, you may have problems as a resident.

Medical school is the time to learn and develop your clinical skills. It's also the time to develop and hone the learned attributes and attitudes that predict success as a physician. In a study of residents with problematic behavior, investigators sought to determine if there were prognostic indicators in their medical school evaluations.[4] The short answer is yes.

Students whose evaluations indicated that they were timid, had problems in organization, displayed little curiosity, and had difficulty applying knowledge clinically, among other types, were more likely to become problem residents. The authors "found a rather robust multilevel correlation between residents who have problems, major or minor, during or after residency, and negative statements, even subtle ones, in the dean's letter." The predictive statements noted in the dean's letter included:

Very nervous, timid initially/ Displayed little curiosity/ Had difficulty applying knowledge clinically/ He came across as confrontational/ Maybe somewhat overconfident for his level of training/ Lack of enthusiasm and problems in organization/
Needs to read more on her own/ Lots of effort, uneven outcome

Difficulties during clerkships may predict difficulties as a physician, including disciplinary actions by the State Medical Board.

Clerkships are the foundation of successful patient care. During clerkships, medical students also develop and hone the attributes and attitudes that are required of successful physicians. These are referred to collectively as medical professionalism. "The specific attributes that have long been understood to animate professionalism include altruism, respect, honesty, integrity, dutifulness, honour, excellence and accountability."[5] –Dr. Jordan Cohen, President Emeritus, Association of American Medical Colleges

If you don't hone these traits during medical school, you may have problems as a physician. Unprofessional behavior in medical school is a possible predictor of future disciplinary action. A particularly notable study was performed by Dr. Maxine Papadakis, associate dean for student affairs at the UCSF School of Medicine. She and her team examined the medical school records of 235 graduates of three medical schools. Each of these physicians had been disciplined by one of 40 state medical boards over a 13-year period. The disciplined physicians were three times more likely than a control group to have negative comments about their professionalism documented in their medical school record.[6]

Another study sought to identify the domains of unprofessional behavior in medical school that were associated with disciplinary action by a state medical board.[7] Three domains of unprofessional behavior were significantly associated with future disciplinary action: poor reliability and responsibility, poor initiative and motivation, and lack of self-improvement and adaptability.

Your core clerkship grades may either limit or expand your future career options.

The skills and traits reflected in core clerkship grades are considered so important to future success as a resident that residency programs use these grades as a major criteria in the selection process. Program directors are decision-makers in the residency selection process. In a survey of over 1,200 residency program directors across 21 medical specialties, grades in required clerkships were ranked as the # 1 factor used in the selection process.[8]

Studies across multiple specialties have supported the predictive nature of clerkship grades. In one study, researchers sought to determine which residency selection criteria had the strongest correlation with performance as an orthopedic surgery resident. The authors concluded that the "number of honors grades on clinical rotations was the strongest predictor of performance."[9] In a study of physical medicine and rehabilitation residents, "clinical residency performance was predicted by clerkship grade honors."[10] In one study of internal medicine residents, performance as a resident was significantly associated with the internal medicine clerkship grade.[11]

In the next 400 plus pages, we review each of the areas that students need to master in clerkships. The book contains a great deal of in-depth content across a range of areas vital to medical student success. It's also arranged to ensure ease of use. The first sections serve as straightforward how-to guides for each of the core clerkships. If you're starting your Pediatrics clerkship, and aren't sure how to write the daily patient progress note, Chapter 4 walks you through that process. If you're starting the Ob/Gyn clerkship, and don't know how to write a delivery note, Chapter 6 provides a template and sample note that details exactly what you'll need to include. The latter chapters provide more wide-ranging content. If you'll be presenting in rounds for the first time, you can turn to the chapter on oral case presentations and review the features you'll need to include. If you are committed to fully protecting your patients from the hazards of hospitalization, Chapter 8 Patients includes several tables that outline the steps that medical students can take, even at their level, to protect their patients. Chapter 22 reviews the impact of collaborative care on patient outcomes, and provides recommendations that students can implement.

The recommendations presented here are based on discussions with numerous faculty members, residents, and students, as well as our own experiences. We've also focused our efforts on evidence-based advice. This evidence-based advice is based on our review of the substantial medical literature in the area of medical student education. The book includes over 400 references from the relevant literature.

Over the next 400 plus pages, you'll learn how to maximize your education during core clerkships, as well as your performance. Your success on the wards will become the foundation of outstanding patient care.

Patients

We begin this chapter with one of the most famous quotes in the history of medicine. "First, do no harm." From ancient times onwards, medical practice has posed dangers to patients. In modern times, those dangers are shockingly common. Medical error is thought to be the <u>third</u>

leading case of death in the US.[12] Those errors include the unbelievable: one report described an average of 27 cases in one year, per New York hospital, of invasive procedures performed on the wrong patient.[13] Some of those dangers have become so commonplace that we consider them routine. When a patient develops a hospital-related infection, we document it as a nosocomial infection and treat the infection without questioning why it occurred. However, many of those infections are preventable, and should never have occurred at all. In this chapter, we document a number of specific measures that medical students can implement to protect their patients, from the use of standardized abbreviations to ensuring that patients receive venous thromboembolism prophylaxis when indicated. We outline how medical students can identify the hazards of hospitalization, thus ensuring that you can act to mitigate those hazards. We review nosocomial infections, and how you may be a culprit through your hands, your clothing, and even your stethoscope.

We also review the type of skills that ensure that patients feel comfortable with your care. The best medical care necessitates that patients trust their physicians and have confidence in both their abilities and the fact that the physician cares about the patient, not just the illness. In this chapter, our focus is on the patient, and how medical students can improve the care provided to patients. We outline steps that students can take, even at their level, to protect their patients from physical harm. We emphasize the different ways in which medical students can enhance patient care, patient education, and patient counseling. On a daily basis, you have the opportunity and the power to enhance the care provided to your patients.

Internal Medicine Clerkship

The field of internal medicine (IM) has a broad impact on all fields of medicine. "Learning about internal medicine – the specialty providing comprehensive care to adults – in the third year of medical school is an important experience, regardless of what specialty the medical student ultimately pursues," says Dr. Patrick Alguire, the Director of Education and Career Development at the American College of Physicians.[14] Through this clerkship, you will hone your skills in history and physical examination, diagnostic test interpretation, medical decision-making, and management of core medical conditions. These skills are important ones for all physicians, even if you ultimately decide to enter radiology, pathology, emergency medicine, or another field. Overall, internal medicine does stand as the most frequently chosen specialty in the residency match. In 2010, over 3,000 allopathic and osteopathic medical students matched into an internal medicine residency program.

Your IM clerkship grade can impact your career. It's a factor in the residency selection process for all specialties, not just internal medicine. In a survey of over 1,200 residency program directors across 21 medical specialties, grades in required clerkships were ranked as the # 1 factor used in the selection process.[8] "Do well in your clerkship," writes the Department of Medicine at the University of Washington. "Yes, this is obvious – and easier said than done – but it's also important. Most residency programs look closely at the third-year clerkship grade when selecting applicants."[15]

Many medical students find this clerkship formidable. A lack of knowledge isn't the main factor. The main factor is a lack of preparation for your many responsibilities. How do I evaluate a newly admitted patient? What do I need to include in a daily progress note? What information do I need to include in a comprehensive write-up? How do I present newly admitted patients to the attending physician?

In this chapter, templates and outlines are included for each of these important responsibilities. You'll also find a number of tips and suggestions on how to maximize your learning and performance during this rotation. You'll find detailed information that will help you effectively pre-round, succeed during work rounds, deliver polished oral case presentations, create well-written daily progress notes, and generate comprehensive write-ups.

For students interested in a career in internal medicine, this chapter also details how to strengthen your application. You'll learn how to identify potential mentors and obtain strong letters of recommendation. You'll learn about recommended electives and sub-internships, as well as specifics that detail how to maximize the impact of your application.

Surgery Clerkship

The surgery clerkship provides significant exposure to common surgical problems, and allows you to evaluate the specialty as a potential career choice. Although the bulk of your education will take place on the general surgery service, most rotations provide the opportunity to explore several surgical subspecialties. A surgical clerkship education is very valuable, whether or not you choose to practice in a surgical field. Primary care physicians must be familiar with the evaluation and management of patients in the pre-operative and post-operative settings. An understanding of core surgical principles is important across many fields, including ones such as anesthesiology, dermatology, and emergency medicine. From a personal standpoint, you or a family member is likely to undergo surgery in your lifetime, and you'll find that an understanding of the pre-operative, operative, and post-operative stages will be valuable.

Regardless of your chosen career, your surgery clerkship grade will be a factor used in the residency selection process, due to an emphasis on core clerkship grades in the residency selection process. In a survey of over 1,200 residency program directors across 21 medical specialties, grades in required clerkships were ranked as the # 1 factor used in the selection process.[8] The University of Colorado Department of Surgery writes that "most surgery programs look very favorably on an 'Honors' grade in your MS3 surgery clerkship rotation and may factor in the grades you received in your Medicine and Ob/Gyn rotations."[16] It's not easy to honor the clerkship. In a survey of medical schools across the country, Takayama found that only 27% of students achieve the highest grade in the surgery clerkship.[17]

Many students approach the surgery clerkship with considerable anxiety. In one study, students were most concerned about fatigue, long hours, workload, insufficient sleep, lack of time to study, mental abuse (getting yelled at or relentless pimping), and poor performance.[18] Unfamiliarity with the operating room environment was also concerning.

In the Surgery Clerkship chapter, we provide tips for operating room success, a checklist for thorough pre-rounding, a step-by-step guide to presenting patients, and time-saving templates for the pre-op, post-op, and op notes. This information will maximize your education as well as your performance.

In 2010, approximately 2,500 allopathic and osteopathic medical students matched into general surgery or related surgical specialty, such as ophthalmology, orthopedic surgery, otolaryngology, plastic surgery, or urology. This chapter includes recommendations for those students interested in pursuing general surgery as a career. When should you do a sub-internship? Should you do an away elective? What are considered negatives in a residency application? These questions, and others, are answered.

Excerpted from the book *Success on the Wards: 250 Rules for Clerkship Success*.

Read more of the first chapter at www.TheSuccessfulMatch.com.

An excerpt from the best-selling book:
The Successful Match:
200 Rules to Succeed in the Residency Match

By Dr. Rajani Katta
and Dr. Samir P. Desai

The Application

What does it take to match successfully? What does it take to match into the specialty and program of your choice?

In the 2007 Match, over 40% of all U.S. senior applicants failed to match at the program of their choice. In competitive fields such as dermatology and plastic surgery, over 37% of U.S. senior applicants failed to match at all.

Percentage of U.S. senior applicants who failed to match in 2007	
Specialty	% of U.S. seniors failing to match
Dermatology	38.8%
Plastic surgery	37.5%
Urology	31.3%*
Ophthalmology	30.7%*
Neurological surgery	28.3%*
Orthopedic surgery	19.7%
Otolaryngology	18.4%
Radiation oncology	18.4%
Radiology	9.2%
*All applicants (U.S. seniors + other applicants) From www.nrmp.org, www.sfmatch.org, www.auanet.org.	

The numbers are significantly worse for osteopathic and international medical graduates:

- 28.4% of the 1,900 osteopathic students and graduates who participated in the 2008 Match failed to match at all.
- 55% of the 10,300 international medical graduates who participated in the 2008 Match failed to match at all.

> **Did you know…**
>
> Applicants who fail to match may participate in the Scramble. During the Scramble, applicants try to secure a first-year residency position in a program that failed to fill during the Match. In 2008, over 12,000 applicants scrambled for one of only 1,300 positions.

What does it actually take to match successfully? The issue is a hotly debated one, and surveys of students, reviews of student discussion forums, and discussions with academic faculty all find sharp divisions on the topic. In the following 400 plus pages, we answer the question of what it takes to match successfully. We also provide specific evidence-based advice to maximize your chances of a successful match.

Our recommendations are based on data from the full spectrum of sources. We present evidence obtained from scientific study and published in the academic medical literature. The results of these studies can provide a powerful impetus for specific actions. We present anecdotal data and advice that has been published in the literature and obtained from online sources. We also provide an insider's look at the entire process of residency selection based on our experiences, the experiences of our colleagues in the world of academic medicine, and the experiences of students and residents with whom we have worked.

Who actually chooses the residents? We review the data on the decision-makers. What do these decision-makers care about? We review the data on the criteria that matter to them. How can you convince them that you would be the right resident for their program? We provide concrete, practical recommendations based on this data. At every step of the process, our recommendations are meant to maximize the impact of your application.

In Chapter 2, starting on page 21, we present specialty-specific data. Given the high failure to match rates for certain specialties, is there any literature available to applicants to guide them through the residency application process? For each specialty, we present the results of those studies. For example, in radiology, a 2006 survey of residency program directors obtained data from 77 directors on the criteria that programs use to select their residents (Otero). Which criteria did these directors rank as most important in deciding whom to interview? Which selection factors were most important in determining an applicant's place on the program's rank order list? What were the mean USMLE step 1 scores among matched and unmatched U.S. seniors? What percentage of U.S. seniors who matched were members of the Alpha Omega Alpha Honor Medical Society (AOA)? This powerful evidence-based information is data that you must have to develop an application strategy that maximizes your chances of a successful match.

We review each component of the application in comprehensive detail in the following chapters. Each single component of your application can be created, modified, or influenced in order to significantly strengthen your overall candidacy. We devote the next 400 plus pages to showing you, in detail, exactly how to do so.

LETTERS OF RECOMMENDATION

Letters of recommendation are a critical component of the residency application. Since you won't be directly writing these letters, it may seem as if you have no control over their content. In reality, you wield more influence than you realize. In our chapter on letters of recommendation, we detail the steps that you can take in order to have the best possible letters written on your behalf. These steps include choosing the correct letter writers and asking in the correct manner. We also discuss the type of information to provide, and the manner in which to provide it, in order to highlight those qualities that you hope your letter writer will emphasize.

The purpose of these letters is to emphasize that you have the professional qualifications needed to excel. The letters should also demonstrate that you have the personal qualities to succeed as a resident and, later, as a practicing physician. Since these letters are written by those who know you and the quality of your work, they offer programs a personalized view. In contrast to your transcript and USMLE scores, they supply programs with qualitative, rather than quantitative, information about your cognitive and non-cognitive characteristics.

What do the faculty members reviewing applications look for in a letter of recommendation? The first item noted is the writer of the letter. In a survey of program directors in four specialties (internal medicine, pediatrics, family medicine, and surgery), it was learned that a candidate's likelihood of being considered was enhanced if there was a connection or relationship between the writer and residency program director (Villanueva). "In cases where there was both a connection between the faculty members and in-depth knowledge of the student (i.e., personal knowledge), the likelihood was that the student's application would be noted." In a survey of 109 program directors of orthopedic surgery residency programs, 54% of directors agreed that the most important aspect of a letter was that it was written by someone that they knew (Bernstein).

In another study, the academic rank of the writer was found to be an important factor influencing the reviewer's ranking of the letter (Greenburg). 48% of the reviewers rated it as important. A survey of physical medicine and rehabilitation (PM&R) program directors asked respondents to rate the importance of letters of recommendation in selecting residents (DeLisa). The study showed that the "most important letters of recommendation were from a PM&R faculty member in the respondent's department, followed by the dean's letter, and the PM&R chairman's letter." Next in importance were letters from a PM&R faculty member in a department other than the respondents', followed by a clinical faculty member in another specialty. The University of Texas-Houston Medical School Career Counseling Catalog gives this advice: "letters of recommendation from private physicians or part-time faculty, and letters from residents are generally discounted."

For internal medical graduates (IMGs), this issue becomes even more important. A survey of 102 directors of internal medicine residency programs sought to determine the most important predictors of performance for IMGs (Gayed). When rating the importance of 22 selection criteria, the lowest rated criterion was letters of recommendation from a foreign country, with 93% of program directors feeling that such letters were useless.

What else do the faculty members reviewing applications look for in a letter of recommendation? They seek evidence of an applicant's strengths and skills. Most applicants assume that their letter writers know what to say and what information to provide in a letter to substantiate their recommendation. However, that's a dangerous assumption. In an analysis of 116 recommendation letters received by the radiology residency program at the University of Iowa Hospitals & Clinics (O'Halloran), reviewers noted that:

- 10% of letters were missing information about an applicant's cognitive knowledge
- 35% of letters had no information about an applicant's clinical judgment
- 3% of letters did not discuss an applicant's work habits
- 17% of letters did not comment on the applicant's motivation
- 32% of letters were lacking information about interpersonal communication skills

In another review of recommendation letters sent during the 1999 application season to the Department of Surgery at Southern Illinois University, writers infrequently commented on psychomotor skills such as "easily performed minor procedures at the bedside," "good eye-hand coordination in the OR," "could suture well," and so on (Fortune).

Our chapter on letters of recommendation, starting on page 159, reviews strategies to locate those letter writers who will be most helpful to your candidacy. We review how to identify these writers and how to approach them. Most importantly, we discuss the type of evidence you can provide to the writer and the professional manner in which to provide it. Your letter writers want to write the best letter possible, and you can do much more than you realize to make this a reality.

Excerpted from the book *The Successful Match: 200 Rules to Succeed in the Residency Match*.

Read more of the first chapter at www.TheSuccessfulMatch.com.

Medical School Interview: Winning Strategies from Admissions Faculty

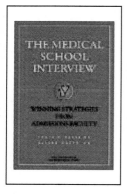

By Samir Desai and Rajani Katta

ISBN # 9781937978013

The medical school interview is the most important factor in the admissions process. Our detailed advice, based on evidence from research in the field and the perspectives of admissions faculty, will provide you with the insiders' perspective.

How can you best prepare for the traditional interview, group interview, panel interview, and behavioral interview? What qualities would make applicants less likely to be admitted? What personal qualities are most valued by admissions faculty? What can students do to achieve maximum success during the interview?

This book shows medical school applicants how to develop the optimal strategy for interview success.

"…this is an extremely thorough handbook, covering the questions applicants are likely to be asked and the appropriate and inappropriate answers…likely to be found indispensable by readers embarking on the arduous process of applying to medical school."

- Kirkus Reviews

Hopes and Fears, Dreams and Tears: A County Memoir

By Niraj Mehta, MD

ISBN # 9781937978037

Every destination has a journey and every journey has a story.

Hopes and Fears, Dreams and Tears: A County Memoir traces the story of a young medical student full of idealism as he starts his training. Yet lacking in knowledge, he embarks on a confusing journey full of Hopes and Fears, Dreams and Tears at a County Hospital similar to one that most doctors in United States train at today.

Using humor to deal with triumphs and tragedies, both personal as well as those involving his patients, the young doctor in training finally achieves wisdom decades later as a full-time medical educator teaching at the same County Hospital. Having come full circle, he finally realizes that perhaps all he ever needed to know to be a successful healer he already knew as a naive young medical student.

"Dr. Niraj Mehta's medical memoir is at once honest and thought provoking. He has a great sense of humor: the book will keep you laughing even as it helps you understand the difficult and stressful challenges faced by medical students and interns, and also the exhilaration of being able to save lives. The book teaches us several important lessons about compassion as well. A great read!"

- Chitra Banerjee Divakaruni, Author of *Palace of Illusions* and *Oleander Girl*

"Hopes & Fears, Dreams & Tears is an exceptional look into Niraj's Mehta's long career at LBJ Hospital in Houston, Texas, from his days as a medical student to his very last day as an attending physician. Mehta's recollections - unrelentingly honest, critical, touching and hilarious - provide a unique glimpse into day-to-day life as a physician providing safety-net care in the U.S., and how patients and physicians are both permanently changed by their time at the 'County'."

-Nathan Moore, MD, Co-Author, *The Health Care Handbook*

Success in Medical School: Insider Advice for the Preclinical Years

By Samir P. Desai and Rajani Katta

ISBN # 9781937978006

According to the AAMC, the United States will have a shortage of 90,000 physicians by 2020. In the mid-1990s, the AAMC urged medical schools to expand enrollment. Class sizes have increased, and new schools have opened their doors. Unfortunately, rising enrollment in medical schools has not led to a corresponding increase in the number of residency positions.

As a result, medical students are finding it increasingly difficult to match with the specialty and program of their choice. "Competition is tightening," said Mona Signer, Executive Director of the National Resident Matching Program. "The growth in applicants is more than the increase in positions."

Now more than ever, preclinical students need to be well informed so that they can maximize their chances of success. The decisions you make early in medical school can have a significant impact on your future specialty options.

To build a strong foundation for your future physician career, and to match into your chosen field, you must maximize your preclinical education. In *Success in Medical School*, you'll learn specific strategies for success during these important years of medical school.

"Overall, I recommend this book...The book has so much information about everything that there has to be a part of the book that will satisfy your interests."

- Medical School Success website

Medical School Scholarships, Grants & Awards: Insider Advice On How To Win Scholarships

By Samir P. Desai and Anand Trivedi

ISBN # 9781937978044

Named a high-value resource by the AAMC Group on Student Affairs

Residency match expert Dr. Samir Desai has helped students win medical school scholarships, grants, and awards, and now shares his perspectives in this new resource.

Over 1,000 awards are featured along with profiles of winners, proven strategies for success, and crucial tips. Learn how to craft a powerful scholarship application, write compelling essays, secure strong letters of recommendation, and stand out from the competition. Discover the best scholarships for you with awards for research, leadership, writing, global health, service, extracurricular activities, ethnicity, and gender.

Winning can:

- Significantly reduce your debt.
- Provide a major boost to your residency application, and set you apart from your peers. Awards can be placed in the application, MSPE, letters of recommendation, and CV.
- Elevate your profile with competitive specialties and residency programs.
- Raise your stature in medical school.
- Make you more attractive for other awards and scholarships.
- Further your professional reputation and enhance your credibility in the areas that form the basis for the award.
- Solidify the support of faculty who become reference letter writers. Strengthening these relationships over time allows faculty members to write strong letters of recommendation for residency.

Clinician's Guide to Laboratory Medicine: Pocket

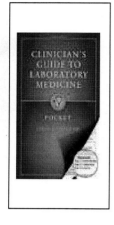

By Samir P. Desai

ISBN # 9780972556187

In this book, you will find practical approaches to lab test interpretation. It includes differential diagnoses, step-by-step approaches, and algorithms, all designed to answer your lab test questions in a flash. See why so many consider it a "must-have" book.

"In our Medicine Clerkship, the Clinician's Guide to Laboratory Medicine has quickly become one of the two most popular paperback books. Our students have praised the algorithms, tables, and ease of pursuit of clinical problems through better understanding of the utilization of tests appropriate to the problem at hand."

- Greg Magarian, MD, Director, 3rd Year Internal Medicine Clerkship, Oregon Health & Science University

"It provides an excellent practical approach to abnormal labs."

- Northwestern University Feinberg School of Medicine Internal Medicine Clerkship website.

Success on the Wards: 250 Rules for Clerkship Success

By Samir P. Desai and Rajani Katta

ISBN # 9780972556194

This is an absolute must-read for students entering clinical rotations.

The authors of *The Successful Match: 200 Rules to Succeed in the Residency Match* bring their same combination of practical recommendations and evidence-based advice to clerkships.

The book begins as a how-to guide with clerkship-specific templates, along with sample notes and guides, for every aspect of clerkships. The book reviews proven strategies for success in patient care, write-ups, rounds, and other vital areas.

Grades in required rotations are the most important academic criteria used to select residents, and this critical year can determine career choices. This book shows students what they can do now to position themselves for match success. An invaluable resource for medical students - no student should be without it.

"*Success on the Wards: 250 Rules for Clerkship Success* is an excellent reference for any 3rd year medical student and some is probably great reading for advanced students and even residents and interns…Given the heavy importance of being successful on the wards as a student for future residency, it's really easy to recommend this book."

- Review by Medfools.com

"*Success on the Wards* is easily the best book I have read on how to succeed in clerkship. It is comprehensive, thorough and jam-packed with valuable information. Dr. Desai and Dr. Katta provide an all encompassing look into what clerkship is really like."

- Review by Medaholic.com

The Successful Match 2017: Rules to Succeed in the Residency Match

By Rajani Katta, MD and Samir P. Desai, MD

ISBN # 9781937978075

Named a high-value resource by the AAMC Group on Student Affairs

What does it take to match into the specialty and program of your choice?

The key to a successful match hinges on the development of the right strategy. This book will show you how to develop the optimal strategy for success.

Who actually chooses the residents? We review the data on the decision-makers. What do these decision-makers care about? We review the data on the criteria that matter most to them. How can you convince them that you would be the right resident for their program? We provide concrete, practical recommendations based on their criteria.

At every step of the process, our recommendations are meant to maximize the impact of your application. This book is an invaluable resource to help you gain that extra edge.

"Drs. Rajani Katta and Samir P. Desai provide the medical student reader with detailed preparation for the matching process. The rules and accompanying tips make the book user-friendly. The format is especially appealing to those pressed for time or looking for a single key element for a particular process."

- Review in the American Medical Student Association journal, *The New Physician*

The Resident's Guide to the Fellowship Match

By Samir P. Desai

ISBN # 9781937978020

What does it take to match into the subspecialty and fellowship program of your choice?

Our detailed advice, based on evidence from research in the field and the perspectives of fellowship program directors, will provide you with the insiders' perspective.

What are criteria most important to decision-makers? What can you do to have the best possible letters of recommendation written on your behalf? How can you develop a powerful and compelling personal statement? How can you overcome the obstacles of residency to publish research? What can you do to achieve maximum success during the interview?

This book shows fellowship applicants how to develop the optimal strategy for success - an invaluable resource to help applicants gain that extra edge.

"The Resident's Guide to The Fellowship Match is a great book...It helps you prepare for the fellowship application starting on the first day of residency. I personally learned a lot from it...The book is very systematic and covers everything you need to ace your fellowship interviews. I would strongly recommend this book..."

- Huda Khaleel (Amazon Review)

The Successful Match website

Our website, TheSuccessfulMatch.com, provides students with a better understanding of the medical school admissions and residency selection processes. You'll find:

- Articles about the medical school interview
- Resources to help you succeed in the preclinical years and clerkships
- Information to position yourself for residency match success

Consulting services

We also offer expert one-on-one consulting services to premedical and medical students. For premedical students, mock interview services are available with Dr. Samir Desai. Dr. Desai has years of experience interviewing applicants, and will offer you a detailed strategy for success tailored to your medical school of interest. We have the knowledge, expertise, and insight to help you achieve your goals. If you are interested in our consultation services, please visit us at www.TheSuccessfulMatch.com. The website provides further details, including pricing and specific services.

MD2B Titles

Medical School Interview: Winning Strategies from Admissions Faculty

Multiple Mini Interview: Winning Strategies from Admissions Faculty

Hopes and Fears, Dreams and Tears: A County Memoir

Medical School Scholarships, Grants, & Awards: Insider Advice on How to Win Scholarships

Success in Medical School: Insider Advice for the Preclinical Years

Success on the Wards: 250 Rules for Clerkship Success

The Successful Match 2017: Rules to Succeed in the Residency Match

Clinician's Guide to Laboratory Medicine: Pocket

Available at TheSuccessfulMatch.com

Bulk Sales

MD2B is able to provide discounts on any of our titles when purchased in bulk. The discount rate depends on the quantity ordered. For more information, please contact us at info@md2b.net or (713) 927-6830.